Student Successes

With

Thinking Maps®

Edited by David Hyerle
with Larry Alper and Sarah Curtis

Student Successes

With

Thinking Maps®

School-Based Research,

Results, and Models

for Achievement

Using Visual Tools

Foreword by Pat Wolfe

CORWIN PRESS
A Sage Publications Company
Thousand Oaks, California

For information:

Corwin Press
A Sage Publications Company
2455 Teller Road
Thousand Oaks, California 91320
www.corwinpress.com

Sage Publications Ltd.
1 Oliver's Yard
55 City Road
London EC1Y 1SP
United Kingdom

Sage Publications India Pvt. Ltd.
B-42, Panchsheel Enclave
Post Box 4109
New Delhi 110 017 India

Printed in the United States of America

The term "Thinking Maps" and the term "Thinking Maps" with the graphic forms of the eight Maps have registered trademarks. No use of the term "Thinking Maps" with or without the graphic forms of the eight Maps may be used in any way without the permission of Innovative Sciences, Inc. For use of Thinking Maps® in the classroom, inquiries regarding Thinking Maps® and training can be made to Innovative Learning Group, 1-800-243-9169, www.thinkingmaps.com.

Library of Congress Cataloging-in-Publication Data

Student successes with thinking maps®: school-based research, results, and models for achievement using visual tools / David Hyerle, editor ; with Sarah Curtis and Larry Alper, coeditors.
    p. cm.
Includes bibliographical references and index.
ISBN 1-4129-0473-0 (cloth) — ISBN 1-4129-0474-9 (pbk.)
  1. Visual learning—United States. 2. Learning—Psychology. 3. Thought and thinking. I. Hyerle, David. II. Curtis, Sarah. III. Alper, Larry.
LB1067.5.S78 2004
371.33′5—dc22

                                                   2004005725

This book is printed on acid-free paper.

       05 06 07 08 10 9 8 7 6 5 4 3

Acquisitions Editor:	Jean Ward
Production Editor:	Julia Parnell
Copy Editor:	Ruth Saavedra
Typesetter:	C&M Digitals (P) Ltd.
Proofreader:	Teresa Herlinger
Indexer:	Kay Dusheck
Cover Designer:	Anthony Paular
Graphic Designer	Lisa Miller

Contents

List of Figures

Foreword

The brain remembers what it has seen because humans are intrinsically visual beings. The eyes contain almost 70% of the body's sensory receptors and send millions of signals every second along optic nerves to the visual processing centers of the brain. It is not surprising that the visual components of a memory are so robust. And it is not surprising that when teachers use visuals in the classroom to represent concepts, their students retain them longer.

Visuals are not only powerful retention aids but also serve to increase understanding. Imagine trying to comprehend governmental structure or the operation of an internal combustion engine without an accompanying diagram. The ability to transform thoughts into images is often viewed as a test of true understanding.

Many studies have demonstrated the facilitating effect of visual representations on learning and memory. Bull and Wittrock (1973) reported a study examining sixth graders' understanding and recall of vocabulary words using two different strategies. One group memorized the dictionary definitions of the words, while a second group illustrated the meaning of the words. The second group's understanding and retention of the words was much higher. Another study, concerned with learning Spanish vocabulary words, taught students to use an imagery process that linked the sound of the word to an image of a concrete noun in English. The students' retention of the words increased from 28% to 88% (Atkinson & Raugh, 1975).

The Thinking Maps® program takes full advantage of the natural proclivity of the brain to think visually. The authors describe Thinking Maps as a language of visual tools grounded in the thinking process, a most neurally apt description. Neuroscientists tell us that the brain organizes information in networks and maps. What better way to teach students to think about ideas and organize and express their ideas than to use the very same method that the brain uses.

This book provides an invaluable way to help our students truly understand and retain the concepts behind the facts, and to do this in an exciting and motivating way.

Pat Wolfe
Author, *Building the Reading Brain*

Foreword

All students and staff members should have high-quality learning on a daily basis. *Student Successes With Thinking Maps®* examines a series of vignettes that breathe life into this statement, presents a powerful argument for using this tool at every level, and illustrates how students have systematically and deliberately taken charge of their own learning via the transformational power of Thinking Maps. Following a presentation of the "what, why, and how" of Thinking Maps, the reader is treated to a panoramic view of schools that have successfully used this unique tool kit to bridge the gap from research to practice. All are worthy models to examine—and follow—as schools focus on continuous growth for all through individual and school improvement. The book is a must read!

Marti Richardson,
President, National Staff Development Council

An Appreciation

Deepest thanks go the authors who have contributed to this work over the years and to the teachers, administrators and students who continue to inspire us as they use Thinking Maps. We also thank those students quoted in this book who offered their applications with Thinking Maps and profound, magical insights such as these:

"The maps are like a brain . . ."

"Thinking Maps are the paper of my mind . . ."

"While I am reading, my mind adds to my Thinking Maps all by itself, and suddenly I know more than I knew!"

About the Editors

David Hyerle, Ed.D. is an independent researcher, author, and consultant focused on literacy, thinking-process instruction, and whole-school change. He is the developer of the Thinking Maps language and is presently Co-director of Designs for Thinking, a consulting and research group based in New England.

Sarah Curtis, M.Ed., currently works as a researcher and a consultant for Designs for Thinking, providing in-depth training for Thinking Maps, *Write . . . from the Beginning,* and Training-of-Trainer for both approaches. She is passionate about enhancing student and teacher performance by supporting educational discourse through teacher reflection.

Larry Alper, MS, a former elementary school principal, is the Director of Projects for Designs for Thinking, an educational consulting group focused on research, literacy, and whole-school improvement.

For contacting the editors or contributors:
David Hyerle, Ed.D.
www.designsforthinking.com

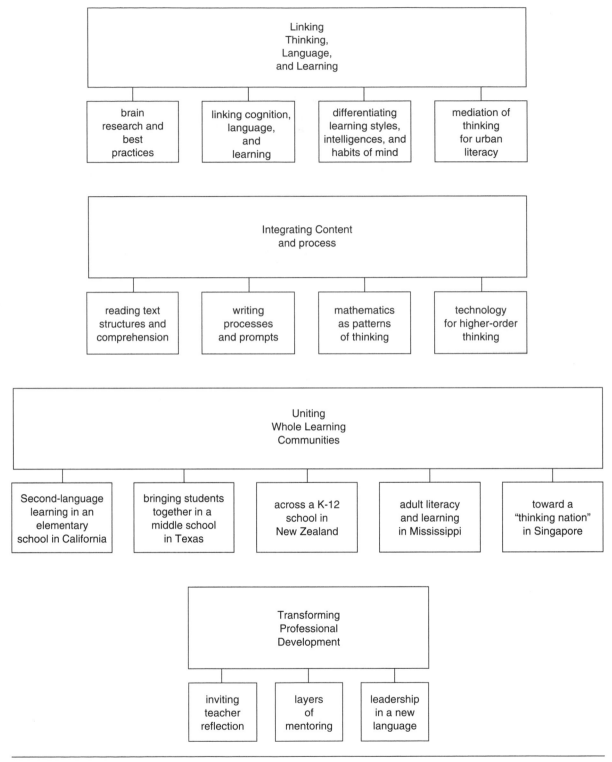

Figure 0.1 Flow of Book

1

Thinking Maps® as a Transformational Language for Learning

David Hyerle, Ed.D.

Topics to be discussed:

- introducing a common visual language for learning
- describing five essential characteristics of Thinking Maps using a Bubble Map
- overviewing the book using a Tree Map for revealing themes of transformational learning using Thinking Maps

Much like a momentary respite before jumping back into an exciting journey, this book represents a resting place for present research, results, and models of practice from over 15 years of bringing Thinking Maps into schools. The authors of the chapters before you bring forth insights grounded in practical examples and experiences from their travels. Together, their work creates a compelling display of what can happen when Thinking Maps are used as a language for learning by students across different cultures and languages, for deepening instruction by teachers in classrooms, and for raising the quality of professional development and change processes within whole schools.

This is because as a language of visual tools grounded in thinking processes, Thinking Maps ultimately unite a school faculty around a well-documented need in classrooms and a central organizing principle for twenty-first century education: *equity of access to—and explicit teaching of—higher-order thinking tools for every child and every adult on the journey of lifelong learning.*

Thinking maps are eight fundamental thinking skills defined and animated by maps, and introduced as *a common visual language* for thinking and learning across whole learning communities (Figure 1.1). From the beginning, the focus of the work using Thinking Maps has been on *all* teachers immediately training *all* of their students across their *whole* school to become fluent with the tools. Over the years, approximately 4000 whole school faculties have implemented the maps, thus representing a great multiplier effect as large numbers of students from kindergarten to college have become fluent in Thinking Maps. From first introductions to complex applications over time, students, teachers, and administrators move from novice to expert use in these tools, using maps independently, in cooperative groups, and as participants in schools for visually sharing ideas and for creating final products.

Common Visual Language: Thinking Maps®   **Thinking Maps**®

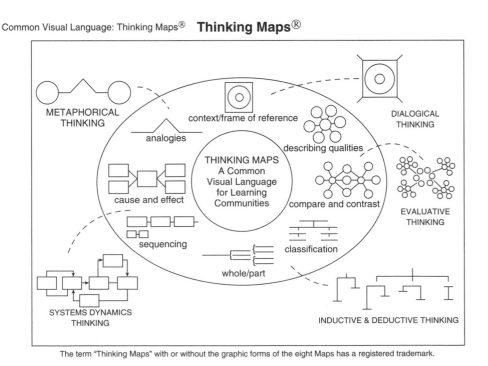

The term "Thinking Maps" with or without the graphic forms of the eight Maps has a registered trademark.

Figure 1.1   Introducing the Thinking Maps Model

From the authors of these chapters, you will learn about schoolwide changes in teachers' perspectives and student performance in an inner-city elementary school in Long Beach, California, where 85% of the students entering classrooms speak Spanish as their first language; special education students in a middle school in North Carolina making performance leaps of over three years' growth in mathematics; girls from a single-sex, independent, K–12 school in New Zealand rising over four years to the top of that nation's educational ladder; and entering junior-college students in Mississippi significantly shifting reading comprehension scores, while those in the nursing program dramatically outperform their peers of previous years.

THE BIG PICTURE

The purpose of this introductory chapter is to give you a big-picture overview of how the wide-ranging stories across the 16 chapters weave together to create a unified theme of Thinking Maps as a transformational language for learning. It also offers readers who are not familiar with Thinking Maps a brief history and theoretical background for the work, definitions of the tools, and a wider description of how the tools support teaching, learning, and leadership in schools. Upon first glance, some educators perceive the maps as just an interesting set of graphics, rather than as a cohesive, theoretically grounded language. One author, the principal of the inner-city elementary school mentioned above, even begins her chapter with this experience: When she first introduced her staff to the idea of implementing the maps across their school, they looked at the maps and said, "But we already do that!" By the end of the school year and into the second year the school had transformed itself into a learning community where students were making performance leaps well beyond teachers' expectations.

Together, the authors share wide-ranging outcomes including *significant* quantitative performance shifts by students and qualitative changes in instruction from schools within cityscapes and sprawling new suburban neighborhoods to rural landscapes and into multiple countries. The chapters come together under four major sections, as shown in the table of contents Flow Map (Figure 0.1), and descriptions below:

Section 1 integrates research on best practices, brain research, and a range of other models such as habits of mind, multiple intelligences, and learning styles with practical examples of how Thinking Maps mediate students' thinking, learning, and metacognitive behaviors. The background offered in the first section lays the foundation for showing how Thinking Maps are used for content-specific learning in Section 2. Applications in the areas of reading comprehension, writing processes, mathematics, and technology offer a view of how thinking skills may be taught directly to students for independent transfer across the disciplines, while directly meeting state standards. This focus on content learning leads into

Section 3, which shows how Thinking Maps work across whole schools for improving teaching and learning, from descriptions of elementary, middle, and K–12 schools that have implemented the tools for multiple years, to research from a junior college revealing significant results, to direct training of students in Singapore. The fourth and final section broadens the focus to look at Thinking Maps as tools that simultaneously support student as well as organizational learning. Thinking Maps facilitate the transformation of professional development within schools by "inviting explicit thinking" by teachers, in the mentoring processes with beginning teachers, and by uniting whole school faculties around a common visual language for "constructivist conversations."

From a big-picture point of view, the successes that shine through the research and results discussed in this book reveal the development of rich content knowledge and, more important, reflections on the continuous cognitive development of every learner—student, teacher, and administrator—in a school. Many educators, as described in this book, brought Thinking Maps into their schools because they believed that there would be an impact on teacher instruction and student performance. They were proven right. Yet many of these teachers and administrators did not foresee that Thinking Maps would also transform the culture of learning across the whole school.

A BRIEF INTRODUCTION TO THINKING MAPS AS A LANGUAGE

Every one of the authors of this book has contributed in different ways over the years to the continuing evolution of Thinking Maps. The themes that emerge here go way beyond the first musings I had back in the spring of 1986. I remember a moment of clarity immediately followed by a humbling awareness. I was eagerly generating ideas for a workbook I was writing, meant for middle school students from underachieving schools. The focus was on the direct facilitation of their thinking skills abilities. I thought I knew what I was doing—and then *I realized what I didn't know.* Two core questions jumped from my mind, the first more theoretical, the second more practical:

What are fundamental thinking skills?

How do we support all learners to transfer these skills across disciplines?

These questions came directly from my frames of reference: I had been teaching in inner-city classrooms in Oakland, California, while studying the continuing underachievement in inner-city schools within low socioeconomic communities (serving mostly African American children). I was also becoming increasingly more aware of the implications of the (still existing) inequalities of access to quality education and the systemic achievement gap. I was looking at the past research on cognition, cognitive styles, and mediation of thinking and learning, while trying to make sense of the array of new theories and practices of thinking skills instruction. During this time, the proponents of the nascent constructivist paradigm were challenging the strict behavioralist mindset. As these many frames of reference converged in my mind, another insight arose, first hurriedly scrawled across a paper napkin. My response was not a grand theory or model, nor a program of developmental lessons with a complex instrument for assessing thinking. It was a language called Thinking Maps.

Calling Thinking Maps a *language* was a clear expression of how these eight visual tools, each surrounded by a visual frame of reference, work in unison, enabling all learners to communicate what and how they are thinking. Through this language, we have found that all learners convey, negotiate, and evolve meanings with others, and within themselves, through visual patterns of thinking.

As human beings, we thrive, creatively and analytically, largely because of our innate capacities for communicating through languages: alphabets, numerical systems, scientific symbols, musical notation, software programs, international sign language, and braille. Yet all of these languages have a foundation of fundamental cognitive structures such as sequencing, categorizing, comparing, etc. Thinking Maps is really a meta-language for learning—an interrelated set of thinking patterns—for communicating and synthesizing our thinking from across these other languages. Because of the universality of the cognitive skills upon which this language is based, and the visual-spatial, nonlinguistic form of the tools, the maps are used fluidly across content areas and cultures as shown in this book.

Thinking Maps, as a language, are eight cognitive skills, each represented and activated by "graphic primitives" as displayed in static form in Figure 1.2 and expanded through our individual and cultural frames of reference. These graphic primitives are used together, linked together, and visually scaffolded to create other products of learning such as a piece of writing. Learners and teachers alike transfer and adapt the maps to shape and re-form otherwise static content knowledge and enter interdisciplinary problem-solving, knowing they have tools to organize their thinking. Ultimately, as the maps expand and integrate with words, numbers, and other symbols on a page, colorfully across a white board, or on computer screens, learners face the boundless nature of their own thinking.

Thinking Maps as Visual Tools for Constructing Knowledge

On a global level, Thinking Maps also may be defined as a synthesis of three types of visual tools that educators and business people have used for generations: mind mapping–brainstorming webs, graphic organizers,

Graphic Primitives and Definitions

primitives	Thinking Maps and the Frame	expanded maps
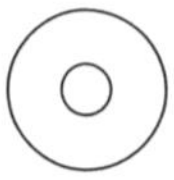	The Circle Map is used for seeking context. This tool enables students to generate relevant information about a topic as represented in the center of the circle. This map is often used for brainstorming.	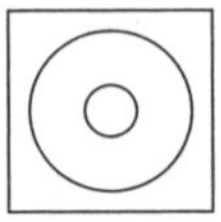
	The Bubble Map is designed for the process of describing attributes. This map is used to identify character traits (language arts), cultural traits (social studies), properties (sciences), or attributes (mathematics).	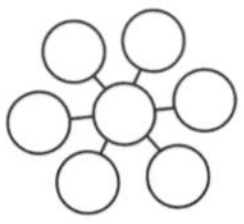
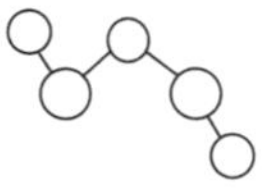	The Double Bubble Map is used for comparing and contrasting two things, such as characters in a story, two historical figures, or two social systems. It is also used for prioritizing which information is most important within a comparison.	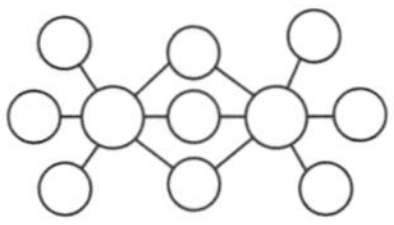
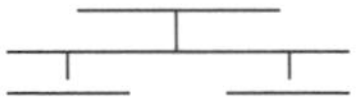	The Tree Map enables students to do both inductive and deductive classification. Students learn to create general concepts, (main) ideas, or category headings at the top of the tree, and supporting ideas and specific details in the branches below.	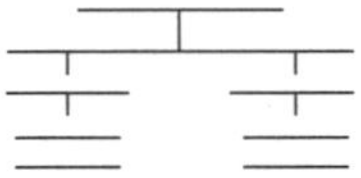
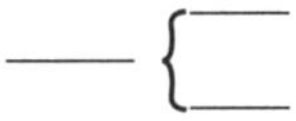	The Brace Map is used for identifying the part-whole, physical relationships of an object. By representing whole-part and part-subpart relationships, this map supports students' spatial reasoning and for understanding how to determine physical boundaries.	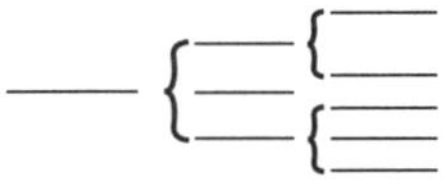
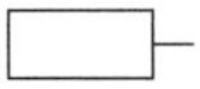	The Flow Map is based on the use of flowcharts. It is used by students for showing sequences, order, timelines, cycles, actions, steps, and directions. This map also focuses students on seeing the relationships between stages and substages of events.	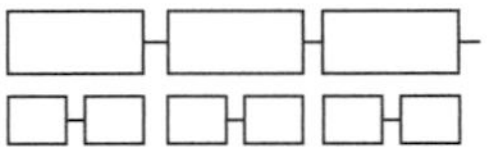
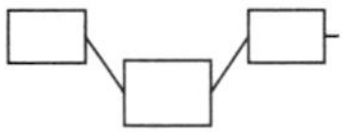	The Multi-Flow Map is a tool for seeking causes of events and the effects. The map expands when showing historical causes and for predicting future events and outcomes. In its most complex form, it expands to show the interrelationships of feedback effects in a dynamic system.	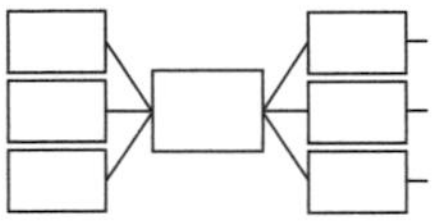
	The Bridge Map provides a visual pathway for creating and interpreting analogies. Beyond the use of this map for solving analogies on standardized tests, this map is used for developing analogical reasoning and metaphorical concepts for deeper content learning.	

The Frame

The "metacognitive" Frame is not one of the eight Thinking Maps. It may be drawn around any of the maps at any time as a "meta-tool" for identifying and sharing one's frame of reference for the information found within one of the Thinking Maps. These frames include personal histories, culture, belief systems, and influences such as peer groups and the media.

Figure 1.2   Thinking Maps Graphics and Primitives

and thinking-process tools such as concept mapping. During my later research on Thinking Maps, I became intrigued by different types of visual tools, finally writing two comprehensive books on the theory, practice, and degree of effectiveness of these tools (Hyerle, 1996, 2000). I discovered through research, my own teaching, and experiences that each of these types of visual tools offered useful ways of visually accessing knowledge.

I also found that each kind of visual tool also had some weaknesses that could not be overlooked. Early mind-mapping techniques that surfaced in the early 1970s facilitate open-minded thinking yet lack the consistent structure and deeper levels of complexity required for today's classrooms. The now familiar "graphic organizers," which surfaced in the 1980s, help students organize large amount of information and scaffold thinking but fail when they become static, blackline masters focused on isolated content tasks selected by the teacher, rather than initiated by the learner. These tools are task-specific organizers because they usually focus on a specific content task and are often confined to the task at hand rather than easily transferable across disciplines.

A third kind of visual tool, "thinking-process" maps, is based on facilitating well-defined thinking processes. Two of these forms, concept mapping and systems diagramming, richly convey complex interdependencies in concepts and systems, respectively. Embedded in the strengths of these two models are also limitations: These models are each dependent on one form of visually structuring knowledge, hierarchical forms for concept mapping and feedback loops for systems diagrams. This leads to an underrepresentation of other thinking processes. In addition, in practice, the translation of these complex models is often daunting to students and teachers alike.

The combined practical, theoretical, and critical attributes of these different types of visual tools have informed the continuing evolution of Thinking Maps into a twenty-first-century language for learning, synthesizing many of the best qualities of these other types of visual tools: an evolution from the generative quality of brainstorming webs, the organizing structure of graphic organizers, and the deep cognitive processing found in concept maps.

FIVE QUALITIES OF THINKING MAPS

The key characteristics of different types of visual tools led to Thinking Maps becoming a language of cognitive patterns that is analogous to the key or legend of symbols that you will find on *any* map. The graphic symbols are the simple visual starting points for generating complex maps for cognitive networks that link together content using a range of thinking processes. Each of the eight maps is theoretically grounded in a fundamental cognitive process or thinking skill. Awareness of five critical attributes of Thinking Maps (Figure 1.3), and a close look at just one of the eight maps (the Flow Map), will clarify how all the maps work, and how they work together.

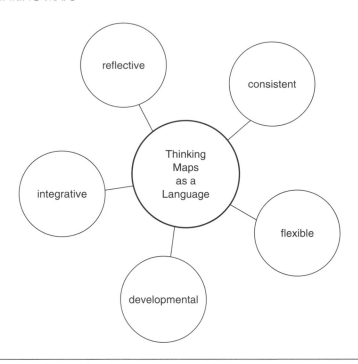

Figure 1.3   Qualities of Thinking Maps Bubble Map

Consistent. The symbol grounding each map has a unique, but consistent, form that visually reflects the cognitive skill being defined. For example, the process of sequencing is represented by the Flow Map starting with one box and one arrow. This is the graphic primitive upon which the map is used to show linear concepts. Thus a Flow Map might show just the three boxes, with key information written inside, showing the beginning, middle, and end of a story.

Flexible. The cognitive skill and the graphic primitive for each map lead to a flexibility in form and to the infinite number of ways the map can grow and be configured. So a Flow Map of a story may start at the beginning but grow in complexity to show many stages and substages of the story. This map could be drawn rising from the bottom left to top right of the page, reflecting the rising action of a story.

Developmental. Because of the consistent graphic primitives and flexible use, any learner (of any age) may begin with a blank sheet of paper and expand the map to show his or her thinking. A Flow Map can be a few boxes long or evolve over time to fill a whole page. The learner—and the content of the learning—determines the complexity of the map. Every learner, from early childhood on, can use the Flow Map to show what he or she knows about a story and thus produce a different configuration of the content.

Integrative. There are two key dimensions of integration: thinking processes and content knowledge. First, all of the maps may be used and integrated together. Using the example of a story, a learner could use the Flow Map to show the plot, a Double Bubble Map to show a comparison of characters, and then a Tree Map to identify the main ideas and supporting details. Multiple Thinking Maps are used for solving multistep problems, for comprehending overlapping reading text structures, and for use during phases of the writing process. Second, the maps are used deeply within and across content areas. For example, the Flow Map is used for plot analysis in reading comprehension, order of operations in math, historical timelines in social studies, and studying recurring natural cycles in science.

Reflective. As a language, the maps unveil what and how one is thinking in patterns. Not only can the learner look down and reflect upon the pattern of content, but the teacher also reflects on and informally assesses the content learning and thinking processes of the learner. In addition, at any time and with every map, learners may draw a rectangular frame around a map. This represents one's frame of reference, or metacognitive frame. For example, a high school student may have sketched out a Flow Map and identified a half dozen turning points in the flow of a novel. By drawing the frame around the map, the student can jot down what influenced this analysis and the references in the text. The framing tool goes beyond merely referencing *what* one knows, to ask the learners *how* they know the information within each map.

These five characteristics are exemplified by the work of Bob Fardy, a science curriculum coordinator in the Concord, Massachusetts, schools. Below, Bob discusses how he used multiple maps and the frame during an action research design to help second grade students in learning about how to understand different types of rocks and how to develop a rubric for further scientific discoveries. He reveals how these consistent and flexible visual tools are integrated together in classrooms through practice that is developmentally appropriate and reflective.

Developing a Rock Rubric using Multiple Thinking Maps

(by Bob Fardy)

At the beginning of a "rocks and minerals" unit, I introduced second-grade students to three Thinking Maps: the Circle, Bubble, and Double Bubble Maps. In our school district, classroom teachers often use the K-W-L strategy (Ogle, 1988) when their students begin a new topic or unit of study. The strategy is an effective way for students, at the beginning of the unit or lesson, to identify what they already know (K) and what they want (W) to know about a topic, and to identify what they have learned (L) at the conclusion. As both teachers and students were familiar with this approach, I introduced the students to the Circle Map and asked them to share what they already knew about rocks.

The Circle Map (Figure 1.4) proved to be an effective brainstorming tool for the students. I recorded and displayed the students' responses between the concentric circles of the map. This tool helped me to carefully avoid any kind of linear listing, clustering, or linking of their responses that might imply or infer some kind of hierarchical ordering of their ideas and/or making connections between and among their comments. In this way, the Circle Map served as a classroom mirror, reflecting the fluency and flexibility of students' thinking, ideas, and information at that moment in time. As the students continued to brainstorm what they knew about rocks, I began to see the Circle Map as more than a mirror that reflected the students' responses. The map was also serving as a window, providing a means to access and assess the students' thinking. I could identify their prior knowledge and surface some possible misconceptions and alternative conceptual frameworks. Indeed, the Circle Map was emerging as an effective tool for both assessment and brainstorming.

For me, the distinguishing feature of the eight Thinking Maps, as compared with more traditional visual tools, is the "Frame" of reference which, as a metacognitive device, added another dimension to the lesson. As the students and I reviewed the Circle Map, we acknowledged the fact that "we already knew many things about rocks." Transferring our attention to the Frame, I asked the students, "How did you learn what you already know ?" In responding to this question, the students were reflecting on their own learning and at the same time were informing me as to the diversity of learning experiences that had been their avenues for acquiring knowledge and constructing meaning. The students identified their "ways of knowing and learning" in the outside frame.

Having surfaced and assessed the students' prior knowledge, I distributed rock samples (granite) to each student and introduced the Bubble Map. With the aid of hand lenses, the students examined the samples of granite using multi-sensory observations, and, using the Bubble Map, recorded their descriptions of the properties of granite. After a few minutes, the students shared their map (Figure 1.5).

Most important, as they shared their maps, the second graders identified the discrete types of properties that they had been observing: color, texture, shape, patterns, luster, minerals in the rock (composition), size, smell. We defined the generated list of rock properties as "Our Rock Rubric." The students subsequently referred to the "Rock Rubric" as they began to observe more rock samples (gneiss) and recorded their observations using a new Bubble Map and Frame.

Having shared their Bubble Maps about granite with their classmates and by using the rock rubric as a guide, the students made and recorded even more observations about the gneiss samples. As the students increased the number of observations, they began to expand their map, adding more "bubbles" of properties as needed. Now the students were beginning to take greater ownership of the visual tool, using and adapting it to meet their needs. For the students, the Bubble Map was not a static "fill-in-the-bubbles worksheet." Instead it became a dynamic, versatile,

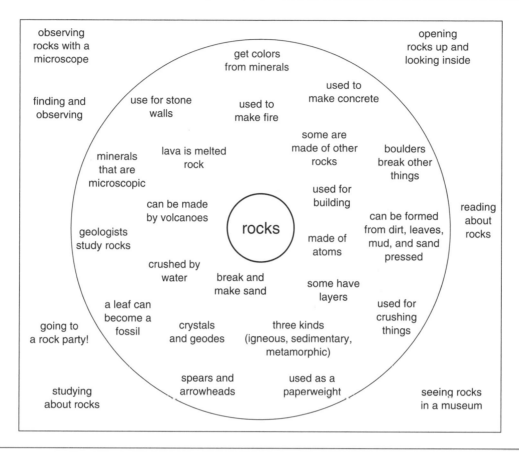

Figure 1.4 "What Do You Know About Rocks?" Circle Map

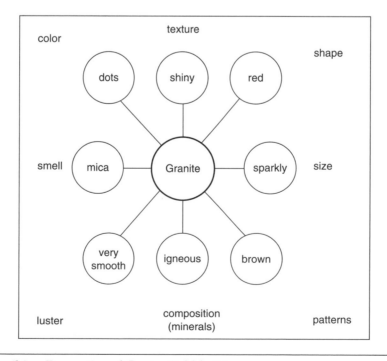

Figure 1.5 Describing Properties of Gneiss Bubble Map

open-ended graphic with a certain "elasticity" that could be stretched in tandem with their thinking.

In the concluding moments of this lesson, I asked the students, "How are granite and gneiss alike and different?" Each student literally had both samples in hand in order to compare and contrast these two types of rocks, but in order to facilitate our discussion, the students also had two Bubble Maps which could be merged into a third Thinking Map, a Double Bubble Map (Figure 1.6).

In the area of science, students are constantly comparing and contrasting objects, organisms, phenomena, events, and ideas within and about the natural world. It has been my experience that we as teachers often use Venn diagrams as "the" graphic organizer for compare–contrast. However I have observed that often certain graphic organizers—such as Venn diagrams—can be problematic. Children, particularly young children, as concrete learners can at times become focused on the seemingly fixed format and nature of the graphic. For example, if the Venn diagram is drawn with a relatively narrow area of intersection, does that imply that there is a limited commonality between the objects that are being compared? If I had asked the students to compare granite and gneiss by constructing and using a Venn diagram, how would they determine to what extent to overlap the circles?

The Double Bubble Map clearly was a more "user-friendly" tool for the students to manipulate as they compared granite with gneiss, developing naturally from the separate Bubble Maps they had created and more in keeping with a constructivist approach to learning. Following this first lesson with rocks and minerals, the students had additional opportunities to observe and describe the properties of ten other types of rocks including conglomerate, sandstone, pumice, obsidian, slate, shale, limestone, marble, basalt and granite schist. These additional rock explorations set the stage for the second lesson (a week later), when the students sorted and classified the twelve kinds of rocks according to their own classification systems. I then introduced the Tree Map that supported students with another key scientific process, categorization, or the creation of taxonomies.

As I reflect on my efforts at using these four visual tools, I find that the insights gained and discoveries made about the relationship between visual tools and teaching, learning, and assessment to be both rewarding and challenging.

As this practical experience shows, Bob and his students were able to fluidly move *with* their thinking and to the conceptual outcomes of this discovery process through the use of multiple Thinking Maps. The kind of scientific thinking and discovery required was not a linear process: The students needed to flexibly pattern information in order to construct understandings. They could evolve ideas from brainstorming to the

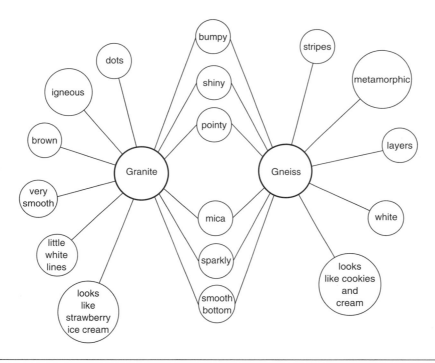

Figure 1.6 Comparing and Contrasting Gneiss and Granite Double Bubble Map

development of a rubric and finally on to the creation of a taxonomic Tree Map. During this process, the class also used the Frame to reflect on the content and experiential background that influenced their perceptions.

This experience in a second-grade classroom—an exemplar of the five qualities of Thinking Maps—may be a guide to reading this book, as all of the authors describe how the consistent, flexible, developmental, integrative, and reflective dimensions of this language draw learning deeper while creating a common form for collaborative problem solving and discovery across content areas.

Thinking Maps as a Transformational Language for Learning

As you review the five qualities of Thinking Maps in the Bubble Map, the Circle Map showing the language in Figure 1.1, and the Flow Map of the contents of this book, you can see the character and sequence of this book. As you read the book, no doubt you will begin to create in your mind an evolving picture of the association of ideas, applications, and results with some of the same findings revealed in Bob Fardy's action research detailed above. With each chapter you read, this picture may shift as you interpret the findings. This certainly happened with me as I read, reread, and began editing these chapters. The themes, large and small, began to emerge in my mind, and I could not keep track of all of the information and concepts, finally leading me to create a Tree Map as one expression of the complex, overlapping discoveries made by the authors (Figure 1.7).

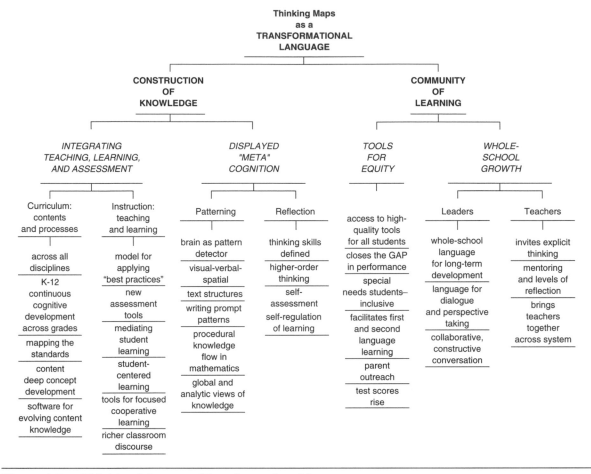

Figure 1.7   Thinking Maps as a Transformational Language

On a blank piece of paper, starting at the bottom of the page, I began associating details that kept growing in clusters, like leaves on a tree, from across chapters. These informal groupings drew me inductively up to the lower branches, revealing seven basic categories near the middle of the page. I finally reached to a new layer of limbs: four generalizations that for me most clearly represented a more expansive view. This structure enabled me to think about and summarize what I interpreted as key concepts: integrating teaching, learning, and assessment; displayed metacognition; tools for equity; and whole-school growth.

Integrating teaching, learning, and assessment. One of the greatest concerns in schools today is how teachers can bring together curriculum and instruction in a way that is meaningful for student learning, while focusing on content standards and assessments. Almost every author in this book addresses this issue in some way, investigating how Thinking Maps become an integration point for these areas, especially across the most crucial areas of performance: reading and writing across disciplines, and mathematics (Chapters, 7, 8, and 9 respectively). For example, in Chapter 8, Jane Buckner shows how the maps support the development of writing processes across disciplines and all grade levels, from emergent writers to high school levels, by providing clear "structures for organization." She emphasizes the need for teachers to model the integrated use of the maps across writing prompts and links this work to specific state assessments.

Displayed metacognition. This term was coined by Dr. Art Costa as a description of the power of visual tools, because these tools display before the learner a range of cognitive patterns of thinking, thus enabling richer reflections. This phrase also captures a central point made by many authors: When using Thinking Maps, students, teachers, and administrators become self-reflective, looking into their own thinking, and become self-regulated learners. These patterns, as Chris Yeager discusses in Chapter 2, are extensions of how the brain works. The brain actively binds data together through neural patterns and networks information, pruning as needed, chunking information, grasping bits of linked information in working memory, and then holding onto them in long-term memory. Chris also dovetails Robert Marzano's research on best practices with brain research using a description of a fifth-grade social studies class. Bonnie Singer follows in the next chapter by telling the "Story of David," a boy with severe learning disabilities who, through the use of these tools over two years, was transformed from being a student with low performance to a self-regulated learner.

Tools for equity. While the idea of facilitating cognitive and metacognitive development has been central to the past 50 years of educational psychology and neuroscience, often the promise of thinking skills instruction remained elusive and inaccessible to those in the greatest need. Another theme that arises from this book is an understanding that the maps directly support teachers in mediating students' thinking. In Chapter 5, Yvette Jackson discusses how the maps become tools for mediating thinking and literacy development, especially when supporting children of color who are struggling to learn in underachieving, inner-city schools. As Yvette points out, these children are often merely remediated through repetitive cycles of content learning but not deeply mediated through their thinking abilities.

Ultimately, the issue here is about equal access to high-quality tools for thinking and instruction that support *all* students' thinking abilities, across languages and cultures at the highest level. This call for equity is answered throughout the book, most clearly in the stories by Stefanie Holzman in Chapter 10 from a school in California and by Marjann Ball in Chapter 13 from a junior college in Mississippi. Both of these chapters present research and results showing significant gains for closing the achievement gap.

Whole-school growth. The field of education is now faced with the complex problem of teaching to the "whole child" while also attempting to transform "whole schools." We are moving away from seeing students as individual learners in straight rows of desks to a model of learning based on a circle of learning. Many schools are directly teaching to the social and

72727272727272 727272727272727

27272727272727272

emotional needs of all children, understanding that these are not just pathways to learning content, but are important in and of themselves. This involves consciously integrating conflict resolution and cooperative and social-emotional learning into the classroom context.

A similar shift is now occurring in the area of organizational change across whole schools as educators are becoming aware of how learning and leadership are intimately connected. An undercurrent of every chapter in this book is the depth of self-learning attained by students, teachers, and administrators *in the context of working across whole schools.* In Chapters 10–12, we are offered detailed histories of how three very different schools across the K–12 spectrum implemented Thinking Maps as a language in their whole schools, clearly demonstrating how learning, teaching, and leadership are united through these common tools. In the last three chapters, the authors focus on how educators learn to work together by visually surfacing perceptions and ideas through their interactions with each other. So often the conversations that happen in meetings in schools become procedural rather than reflective, sometimes combative rather than constructive. Larry Alper closes his chapter and this book by offering the term *constructivist conversations* as an expression of how Thinking Maps become a new language for deepening conversations so that people come together through the maps, facing their own and each other's thinking, "opening the space" for problem-solving and transforming the quality of thinking and learning across the whole school.

The four central ideas discussed above joined together for me as two major themes: "construction of knowledge" as a framework for learning and "communities of learning" expressing the communal quality of the educational experience. I finally reached the top of the tree, discovering the overarching view from which I could see and make sense of the details within the whole of the book *Thinking Maps as a Transformational Language for Learning.* The authors show us that Thinking Maps are a transformative language for learning for personal growth, for collaborative work across complex and increasingly "virtual" technological organizations and societies, and as common pathways for communicating across diverse languages and cultures. As you may see in the written and graphic forms throughout this book, these maps have simple starting points and spread organically as a seed maturing to full growth, providing for the creation of infinitely complex patterns of knowledge for every child, drawing out our multiple frames of reference and mirroring the richly textured landscape of our lives.

SECTION 1

Linking Thinking, Language, and Learning

Linking Brain Research to Best Practices

Chris Yeager, M.Ed.

TRANSLATING THEORY INTO PRACTICE

Topics to be discussed:

- linking Marzano's research on instructional strategies to Thinking Maps®
- showing fundamental brain processes and implications for Thinking Map successes using a Flow Map
- integrating best practices, thinking-process instruction, and brain research

A principal once showed me a *Far Side* cartoon that illustrates one of the major problems we have with staff development and change processes in our profession. The panel shows a woman who has jumped from a burning building only to bounce off of the firefighters' trampoline and into the burning building next door. Under increasing pressure to perform at ever higher levels and with a historic mandate to educate every child, our profession is often guilty of jumping from one new idea to the next, from the frying pan into the fire.

Our greatest challenge and opportunity is to engage deeply with ideas, to examine and conduct research in order to develop a strong foundation for effective teaching and learning. As educators, we must learn to intelligently investigate new ideas toward a new science of education, employing a high level of professional inquiry and curiosity. Jumping from one fire to another simply isn't good enough to meet the complex demands of educating students today. We must focus on instructional strategies that are grounded in quantitative and qualitative research.

One such current of research worthy of our pursuit has been about how the brain learns and, more important, linking its application to the best practices drawn from research on teaching and learning. Knowing more about how the brain works—how it processes information, reacts to emotion, is influenced by the environment—has profound implications for how we teach and how we participate in discussions about effective instruction. As educators, we need to study this new information and work to translate it into our classroom practices, but therein lies one of the problems with brain research. Many teachers, while fascinated by the information, have a hard time wrapping their arms around the research and carrying it into their classrooms. Therefore it would be beneficial for classroom teachers to couple this theoretical research about the brain with the educational research about practice.

One of the most effective applications of these two bodies of research has been the development and use of Thinking Maps, a visual thinking language for patterning, analyzing, and transforming information into knowledge.

BEST PRACTICES IN THE CLASSROOM CONTEXT

Researchers at the Mid-continent Research for Educational Learning, led by Dr. Robert Marzano, have identified nine essentials strategies that have been shown to improve student achievement, as shown in Figure 2.1. This chapter will look at translating what we know about best practices and the brain by examining teaching and learning from the educational research framework and the brain research lens. Through the use of Thinking Maps, teachers have found a practical and effective application of brain research and Marzano's nine classroom strategies.

To best understand how both these research findings can immediately, effectively, and practically translate to teaching and learning, let's explore a classroom in which the use of Thinking Maps supports and connects both the essential nine strategies and information processing in the brain. This classroom experience occurred years ago in Jackson, Mississippi (Hyerle, 1996), and now the Jackson Public Schools are implementing Thinking Maps in all elementary and secondary schools.

1. Identifying similarities and differences

2. Summarizing and note taking

3. Reinforcing effort

4. Homework and practice

5. Nonlinguistic representations

6. Cooperative learning

7. Setting objectives and providing feedback

8. Generating and testing hypotheses

9. Cues, questions, and advance organizers

Figure 2.1   Marzano's Nine Categories of Instructional Strategies

Peek into Norm Schuman's sixth-grade social studies classroom in Jackson, Mississippi, and see groups of students huddled over books, working together, busily and intently sketching a picture of information, drawing to the surface essential knowledge that was once bound by text. All groups use a common visual tool—a hierarchical structure reflected by a Tree Map—to collect, analyze, and synthesize the text into a clearly defined picture of a tribe as shown in Figure 2.2. Each group will also share this mental picture in an oral presentation, using the map as a visual guide on the overhead projector. The six cooperative learning groups have each been asked to read a passage from well-worn texts on a different Native American tribe in order to identify critical information about each Native American group: customs and celebrations, habitats, foods, gender roles and relationships among members, and spiritual beliefs. Norm emphasizes finding details about each of these topics, along with the fact that he will create the final test questions from the information each group presents. He methodically moves around the room and looks down at the developing Tree Maps, guiding here, scanning there, nodding quietly in agreement at another table. The groups redraft these maps several times during two periods of instruction until only the most essential ideas have been distilled and organized from the text.

The following day, oral presentations begin. As each group member speaks about a key point of interest from one area on the map, their peers are busy at their seats, listening, sketching out the map, and making notes and comparisons to their own work.

Days after the presentations are over, Norm gives the students a test including questions based on text information they presented and questions that require them to have linked information from several of the Tree Maps. He also asks questions that involve the use of other thinking skills defined by the maps, such as the Double Bubble Map for comparing tribes, the Flow Map for showing the development of a culture, or the Multi-Flow Map for explaining the causes and effects of outside interventions. Students are ready for such questions because these tools have become a common way of communicating.

When asked about this process and, especially, about the level of his questions (answered by students who have come into his classroom as supposed underachievers from low socioeconomic neighborhoods), Norm responds, "I could never have asked these questions of my previous students, most of whom came into my class several years behind in grade-level reading. I hadn't given them the tools to make inferences like this. They didn't have the organizational abilities to work with so much information."

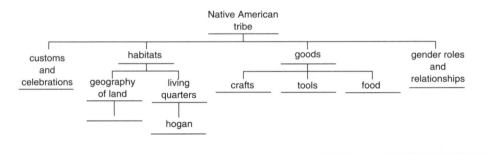

Figure 2.2   Native American Assignment Tree Map

As you can see, Norm and his students apply and *unite* Marzano's effective strategies into fluid practice. From the beginning of the assignment, through the presentations, and ending with the formal assessments, Norm and his students utilized Thinking Maps as tools to support processing, sharing, understanding, refining, presenting, and questioning information in order to transform information into knowledge. The clear categories of the Tree Map and the other thinking processes embedded in the visual tools provided clear objectives, feedback, and a set of cues, questions, and advanced organizers to direct and scaffold as students read for information. Cooperatively, using Thinking Maps as cues and questions, Norm's students were able to identify key similarities and differences and to synthesize chunks of information into meaningful learning during their note taking. During the presentations and assessments, the Thinking Maps continually provided the cues and questions to expand the learning, encouraging students to generate and test their hypotheses as they listened and linked one tribe to the next. This Native American unit takes the list of nine essential classroom strategies, which could be interpreted as isolated practices, and instead, explicitly and richly weaves them together into a multilayered, coherent learning experience.

As we now switch from a strategy-based framework to a brain-based lens, keep in mind how these students' Thinking Map applications and experiences connect to the stages of paying attention, meaning making, and long-term memory through the stages of information processing.

THE BRAIN AS A VISUAL PATTERN DETECTOR

As a high school teacher and an administrator, and as a national consultant providing professional development in instructional strategies involving brain-based learning and Thinking Maps, I have worked with thousands of educators, like Norm Shuman, who have seen the results of teaching students to use Thinking Maps in all content areas and across all grade levels. The link to best practices is apparent, and the link to present findings in brain research is even more obvious. Thinking Maps work, precisely because they are fundamentally connected to how the brain thinks and learns. Just as the brain seeks patterns of information to network, Thinking Maps teach and supply an explicit visual language for students to find the patterns that exist and to construct their own networks of knowledge.

The experts in brain-based research and learning agree on two aspects of brain theory: The brain is a pattern seeker and is dominantly visual. According to Eric Jensen, in his book *Brain-Based Teaching and Learning,* "Ninety percent of all information that comes into our brain is visual" (Jensen, 1996). The importance of the maps as concrete pictures of abstract concepts is linked to our ability to learn visually and the way they complement the complexity of the structure and processing of our visual cortex. Thinking Maps, which are visual patterns for thinking, are therefore well designed for teaching and learning. Because each map is a visual representation of a thinking process by way of a pattern, teachers can take advantage of a strategy that matches the natural learning tendencies of the brain.

Students in Norm's classroom working on the Native American units had the concrete visual tools to find the patterns embedded in reading and to see their own thinking emerge as they literally connected their ideas on the maps. They didn't have to hold all of the information in their minds or in repetitive, linear notes on a page. The students and teacher could understand each other from the note-making stage to the final presentations by way of the common visual language. When they presented their material, students and teacher had a clear visual picture of their mental processes for understanding and for assessment.

When students repeatedly associate a concrete visual pattern with an abstract thought process, they learn patterns for what thinking looks like. These patterns then automatically signal the brain to recognize and even seek out thought processes in print, discussions, assessments, and across all of the amazing media sources they are now required to access for research purposes. In effect, students have wired together networks of neurons for metacognition. Like Norm's class, students become fluent with these patterns of thinking and begin to recognize them independently of teacher instruction, thus developing their own thinking and learning toward higher levels.

Meaning and Emotion

Brain research has provided many insights into how the brain unconsciously takes in and consciously processes information. What causes the brain to pay attention? How is information learned by the brain? How is that information then stored and later accessed? What role does emotion play? The answers to these questions provide insights into creating better environments for teaching and learning. Based on information from authors including Wolfe, Sylwester, and Sousa, I have created a Flow Map as a guide to the complex interaction of attention, emotion, and memory in the different stages of information processing in the brain (Figure 2.3).

Getting students to pay attention can be a challenge for any teacher. Many of the brain research findings have helped us understand that there are two keys to unlocking the unconscious processes involved in paying attention: *emotion* and *meaning*.

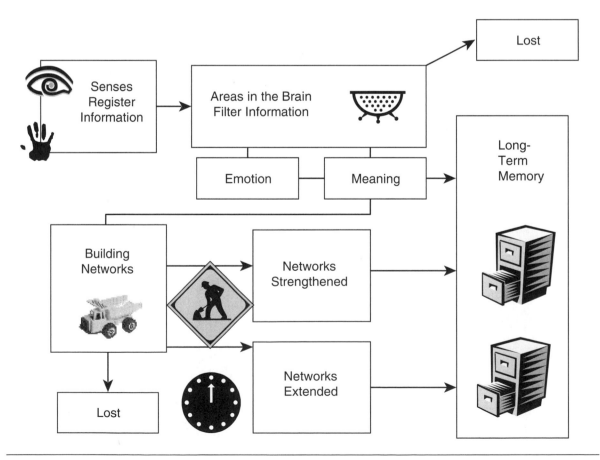

Figure 2.3 How the Brain Processes Information Flow Map

In the classroom, students are bombarded with information throughout the day, much of it novel and not directly connected to their frames of reference. Although students may be trying their best to pay attention, the unconscious brain process makes split decisions about what information it will process. The five senses bring all information to the brain (relevant or not), where the filters in the brain—the thalamus, amygdala, and cortex—determine to what the brain will pay attention. Acting like a relay mechanism, the thalamus sends signals through networks of neurons to the amygdala, the part of the brain responsible for emotion, and the cortex, the part of the brain associated with rational thought, checking to see if this new information has either stored emotional or rational meaning attached to it. Depending on the information sent from either the amygdala or the cortex back to the thalamus, the brain will pay attention to the information. If no emotional or rational connection exists between the new information and prior stored information, the information will be discarded.

Often students are in classes working with new concepts that they might not be interested in or have prior knowledge about. Return to Norm Shuman's class: How many of his students entered his classroom with either interest or basic knowledge about a half dozen Native American tribes? So how will the brain pay attention to the important information when it doesn't know what to look for? How can students attach emotion or meaning to content? The answers to these mysteries can be translated into a better understanding of what causes students to pay attention in a classroom.

Why, for example, do we begin to see a specific car on the highway as soon as we buy one? Why, immediately after meeting someone new, do we seem to begin seeing that person around town? Buying a specific car or meeting someone new stimulates emotional and meaningful connections. Our brain automatically begins to create networks of emotional or meaningful connections to that car or that person. Students will pay attention to what they are learning, such as relatively dry information about a new culture, if the content has an emotional connection or if it has meaning for them.

By learning the Thinking Maps, students create patterns for learning. Students begin to "see" thought processes in text the same way that people see their new car everywhere. Students are able to access the rich and meaningful information in a text because they begin to see the forms embedded in the text. This is true because "most writers present information in the context of an explicit structure, and the more a person is aware of this explicit structure, the better she is able to summarize the information" (Marzano, Pickering, & Pollock, 2002, p. 32). The structures of the content text—richly linked to patterns of thinking—are like the car on the highway, now given meaning and relevance (see Chapter 6, Maps for the Road to Reading Comprehension).

Students in Norm Shuman's class who were familiar with the maps looked for categories of information while reading the text and looked to pattern that information during cooperative learning, class presentations, and discussion. They became connected to the work as they worked with each other to fine tune and give form to the information, thus making it meaningful. As humans, we feel compelled to make sense of our environment, and feelings of self-control, mastery, and understanding come from this experience. Therefore the actual process of engaging in the material and developing the maps evokes an emotional connection, because having tools to manipulate the information is, in and of itself, a validating process.

The role of emotion and its effects on learning is an abstract concept, but critical to student success. In the PBS series *The Secret Life of the Brain,* on the role of emotion in learning, a comment was made that "the brain is not a thinking machine, but a feeling machine that thinks." Every teacher who has worked with a student who shuts down when faced with challenging work will verify this research finding. School is full of novel situations that could create anxiety in students, either enhancing or obstructing the learning process. In a threatening situation, stress triggers an emotional response that interferes with information processing. Neurotransmitters rush through the body to heighten the senses and prepare large muscle groups for action. In this situation, most of the activity in the brain is concentrated on the limbic system, not the cortex, the region of the brain responsible for planning, decision making, and rational thought. This biological stress response is great for survival but not for learning.

Because Thinking Maps are a common visual language used by all teachers across grade levels, they become a familiar set of tools that make the learning process and patterns of information explicit and accessible to students. Teachers have reported a subtle distinction that has a lot of power: Students who work with the Thinking Maps feel safe when faced with challenging work because they have a set of tools for thinking that provide them with a structured framework within which to be creative. The level of fluency with the tools in Norm's class offered students the opportunity to engage with each other and with the teacher's complex questioning and final test without feeling threatened. With questions already linked within the thought processes of the Thinking Maps, students are, in fact, starting with these questions in mind. This invitation to learn, rather than the obligation to know, shifts the entire mood of the learning process. Not knowing is just not knowing *yet.* The automaticity of thinking permits novelty in content without being a threat to the learner.

CHUNKING AND MAPPING

Once the brain chooses to pay attention to the information that has emotion or meaning, the conscious process of storing information begins. The brain continues to process the information for storage and later retrieval by building networks of neurons to pattern the knowledge. The information must first be processed in short-term or working memory, which can hold only a limited amount of information for a limited amount of time before it is called upon to process more information. It is necessary to "chunk" information or else working memory will be overloaded and the information will be lost.

The visual patterns and the cognitive language inherent in the Thinking Maps help the brain pay attention to information at the beginning of information processing and aid students in continuing to meaningfully chunk information in patterns for efficient processing in short-term memory. While working in the cooperative groups to refine the maps, Norm's students created Thinking Maps that patterned the information into chunks, categories about Native American beliefs, customs, agriculture, etc. By consciously making the links on the paper and in their minds, they transformed isolated bits of information, which would have overloaded the capacity of working memory, into a patterned whole.

Thinking Maps gave students a method and a structure that emphasized the relationships of pieces of information to each other. Because the patterns are embedded across the concept, recalling one bit of information on the map essentially fires the retrieval of the entire map. The more these patterns of thinking are rehearsed, the stronger and more efficient are the neural pathways for storage and retrieval of information in long-term memory. Thinking Maps, visual tools that pattern information, support what the brain does naturally to process information by reflecting both its highly structured as well as its adaptive capacities to embed patterns within patterns.

An Engaged and Elaborative Mind

Read any book on "brain-compatible" teaching strategies and you will see graphic organizers on the list of effective practices. For at least 30 years, teachers have been encouraged to use these organizers in their classrooms. Textbooks and school-supply stores have taken this idea and created hundreds upon hundreds of attractive graphics. What seemed like a strategy to get students to think has actually morphed into worksheets with attractive, yet meaningless, triangles and stars. Students who are constantly given these disconnected organizers from day to day and year to year actually become more dependent than independent learners, waiting for their teachers to hand them a black line master, thus affirming a brain research mantra that "dittos don't grow dendrites." In other words, just giving students blanks to fill in does not encourage them to think independently, even if those blanks are drawn in clever clouds or the outline of a shield.

As noted above, Robert Marzano identifies the use of nonlinguistic representations as one of the nine instructional strategies that affect student achievement. However, if we link brain research to this best practice, the nonlinguistic representation must have a critical attribute to be successful: explicit engagement and creation. "It has been shown that *explicitly engaging* students in the creation of nonlinguistic representations stimulates and increases activity in the brain" (Gerlic & Jausovec, 1999). Students who use Thinking Maps are engaged in the creation of their ideas as they elaborate on their basic knowledge from a blank page to their fully developed view of the content. This set of flexible tools actively involves them in the process of meaning making, not simply filling in blanks.

The bottom line is that many best practices teachers are asked to use in their classrooms do not of themselves foster student thinking and learning. When we begin to link these practices to brain research and fundamental cognitive processes, a new level of meaningfulness and emotion becomes evident. Teaching students to be independent, problem-solving, critical thinkers is not a new goal in education, but it has never been more important than it is now. Ruby Payne (1998), writing in *A Framework for Understanding Poverty*, illustrates the need for all students to become critical thinkers: "The true discrimination that comes out of poverty is the lack of cognitive strategies. The lack of these unseen attributes handicaps, in every aspect of life, the individual who does not have them."

Reaching the goal of creating thinking and caring classrooms where all children are successful can be achieved by critically evaluating and meaningfully applying the research we have available to us. Educators must become informed consumers of the information about best practices and brain-based learning. We cannot afford to believe that brain research is just a fad and that "this too shall pass." We have enough research available to us to know that some strategies are better than others and that there are classroom practices that will enhance teaching and learning. I have seen Thinking Maps help students do just what the brain is built to do: to think in patterns of content in order to solve problems. I have seen good teachers become better teachers because they had these valuable tools to engage students' minds. And I have seen schools become places of deeper learning, because they linked best practices and brain research through this common visual language for learning.

3

Leveling the Playing Field for All Students

Bonnie Singer, Ph.D.

Topics to be discussed:

- Thinking Maps® as tools for developing students' executive functioning and metacognitive habits of mind
- a revealing story of one special-needs student's transformation in writing processes, executive functioning, and performance
- improving writing, oral language, and thinking processes in unison

Those of us who are fortunate enough to work with children often find ourselves forever changed by relationships with one or two of them. My life took a definite turn when I met David. He taught me that the mind of an eight-year-old is capable of much more than I had previously thought, and that even children with severe learning disabilities can learn to play the game of school as well as or better than their nondisabled classmates. Through David, I learned just how powerful Thinking Maps can be, and I saw how profoundly they can change a life. The Thinking Maps not only got David back in the academic game, but they also leveled the playing field so that he could emerge as a leader in his classroom.

As a speech-language pathologist in private practice, I have the luxury of being able to work with any student who struggles with language, literacy, or learning. In addition to David, I have had the opportunity to use maps with countless other children who are not diagnosed with learning disabilities but just have trouble learning, the so-called underachievers. Though each story is unique, similar themes emerge from the students and whole schools I have taught to use Thinking Maps. As a result, David's story is worth telling, for it offers us insight into many children who struggle with school and inspires new hope for their futures.

THE STORY OF DAVID

I remember vividly the day I met him. A small second grader with a chip on his shoulder, David sat down at my table, pulled a stack of crumpled papers from his backpack, and exclaimed with indignant exasperation, "Look at what she gives us!" He slapped a stack of graphic organizers on the table with a dramatic flair. "These are stupid," he declared, "and they don't help. I hate writing, and I'm not doing it!" On the table were five graphic organizers—variations on a typical "web." Although they had different shapes, they all depicted the same visual configuration: a circle centered on the page with ovals or lines radiating from it like spokes on a wheel.

This particular set of webs was given to David by his teacher with the intention that they would guide him with planning and writing a story. Attempting to use the only strategies available to him, he dutifully filled in each graphic. In the end, he had five webs on his desk. Rather than help him write his story, they overwhelmed him with information that neither looked like a story nor helped him order his thinking so that he could generate one. As a result, he gave up. This experience reinforced his already growing belief that he wasn't and would never be a good writer, and it strengthened the bad taste he had in his mouth for writing.

Historically, David had always had difficulty producing more than a sentence on his own. His motor skills were compromised, so handwriting was an arduous process for him. By second grade, he was identified as a child who wasn't making academic progress, so he was provided with support from the learning specialist in his school. Though he struggled academically, David was quite talented in some areas. His verbal IQ was 139—in the superior range, as measured by the Wechsler Intelligence Scale for Children-III (WISC-III). But his visual-spatial skills were not nearly as well developed, as evidenced by his below-average WISC-III Performance IQ of 86. Overall, his developmental profile, with a significant (53 point) discrepancy between verbal and visual-spatial abilities, indicated a nonverbal learning disability along with ADHD, attention deficit hyperactivity disorder (for which he took medication). The school psychologist who evaluated him reported that he had difficulty with visual discrimination, motor planning, attention to visual details, and visual-spatial construction. Further, he noted that it was particularly difficult for David to see the relationship of parts to the whole in nonverbal tasks and that he "may need help with sequencing, prioritizing information, and strategies to see the 'big picture' or how details relate to a bigger concept."

David could describe his problem with writing: He had trouble with handwriting, and he didn't know how to plan his ideas or start a piece of writing. Webbing strategies didn't help him because he couldn't determine which idea on his web should go first. Nothing in the visual structure of a web suggested "start here." I suggested to David that his teachers were trying very hard to help him with writing, but they weren't using a graphic that worked very well for his brain. Despite his vehement protests that "graphics don't work," I introduced him to the Flow Map, a Thinking Map for sequencing ideas. Together, we generated ideas for a story, while I modeled how to map them out sequentially. Afterward, I asked David if he thought he could write the story using the ideas on our map. "Sure," he quipped confidently, and he quickly drafted a lovely little story. The next week I began to scaffold the use of the map, starting a new Flow Map, and he finished it and used it to write another story. Over the next few weeks, David practiced making Flow Maps with me before doing his story-writing homework. His attitude toward story writing slowly began to shift as he learned a simple technique that allowed him to see his thoughts before he wrote within a visual structure that looked like the discourse he was attempting to generate. After a break for summer vacation, I asked David if he remembered the Flow Map. He quickly drew a blank map, while cheerfully explaining what it was used for, how to make it, and how to use it for writing. With this visual image now rooted in his mind, narrative writing ceased to be a problem for him. So did his sour attitude about writing.

Gaining Fluency

Over time, as David became more fluent with the maps, his demeanor changed. Though his visual-spatial skills were indeed compromised, he was a quick study. With direct instruction and a good deal of guided practice, he learned the visual array of the maps and the pattern of thought each map represented. I realized we had turned a corner when his mother found him on the couch on a Saturday making a Flow Map of his day. The frustrated, angry, and resistant boy who had first walked into my office evolved into an enthusiastic, creative, and self-confident boy who was truly excited about learning and said, "Thank you for teaching me" at the end of each session. David learned a new language—a language of thinking. It was both a visual language and a verbal one. This language paved the way for explicit consideration of how, when, where, and why to apply specific thinking strategies to support his schoolwork.

In our second year of working together, David became so confident about his ability to think that, when we had extra time in a session, he began to make up Thinking Map games. We took turns creating problem scenarios and quizzing each other on how we would need to think to solve them. Here, he demonstrated that he had truly developed an awareness of his thinking and internalized the language of the maps, as he reported ways to use them that I had never taught him. The maps were now truly tools for thinking, learning, and problem solving, and these tools established a level of metacognition that I had never before seen in a child his age.

At the end of fourth grade, David had an updated neuropsychological evaluation before he moved away to another state. His WISC-III verbal IQ remained in the superior range (138), and his nonverbal IQ score rose 12 points from the below-average to the average range (98) as shown in Figure 3.1. Interestingly, significant gains were evident in some key areas of cognition—namely his attention to visual detail and his ability to perceive part-whole relationships, integrate information, and plan and organize an approach to a task. In our two years of working together, we used Thinking Maps to develop each of these skills in natural and authentic learning contexts. When David moved and began to receive special education services, his learning center teachers could not determine what was wrong with him. Despite significant cognitive discrepancies, he was meta-cognitively, motivationally, and behaviorally active in his own learning process, which masked the severity of his learning disability and allowed him to function on par with his peers.

At this point, David still had a significant discrepancy between his superior verbal skills and his average nonverbal abilities, but his presentation as a learner was dramatically different. First and foremost, he *knew* how he was thinking and could identify what kind of thinking any task demanded of him. As a result, he was highly self-regulated. He demonstrated the three defining features of self-regulated learning (Zimmerman,

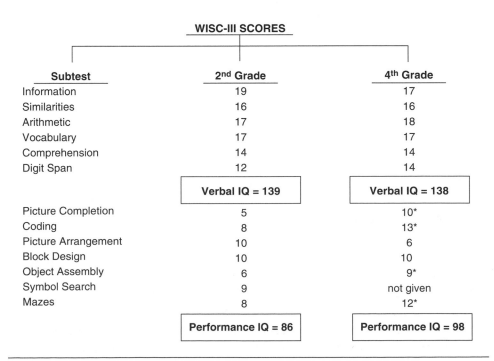

WISC-III SCORES

Subtest	2nd Grade	4th Grade
Information	19	17
Similarities	16	16
Arithmetic	17	18
Vocabulary	17	17
Comprehension	14	14
Digit Span	12	14
	Verbal IQ = 139	**Verbal IQ = 138**
Picture Completion	5	10*
Coding	8	13*
Picture Arrangement	10	6
Block Design	10	10
Object Assembly	6	9*
Symbol Search	9	not given
Mazes	8	12*
	Performance IQ = 86	**Performance IQ = 98**

Figure 3.1   David's WISC-III Scores Before and After Thinking Maps

1989): the ability to self-monitor, self-evaluate, and self-adjust. He had an arsenal of strategies that he could employ in any learning situation, and he readily employed them when tasks demanded complex thinking. Consequently, his self-efficacy for any learning task—even writing—was tremendously strong. David moved from being stuck on the bench to being a varsity player when it came to school.

What Can We Learn From David?

What's interesting about David is that his story is representative of other students who learn Thinking Maps and who have special needs or are underachieving academically. This raises the question of what the maps do for children's minds. Clearly, the maps did not "cure" David of his nonverbal learning disability or his attention deficit disorder. We know that such disabilities are lifelong, and his cognitive profile remained indicative of these disorders even after becoming proficient with the maps. However, the Thinking Maps did significantly affect his cognition as well as other things that aren't measured through standardized tests, namely his *meta*cognition and his day-to-day performance in school. Consequently, they affected his approach to problem solving, his enthusiasm for learning, his willingness to participate, and his beliefs about himself as a learner.

Over the years, I have used Thinking Maps with students who are underachieving academically and with those who have a wide range of disabilities (including cognitive deficits, language disorders, nonverbal learning disabilities, Asperger's syndrome, high functioning autism, and attention deficit hyperactivity disorder [ADHD]). I have yet to encounter a student who cannot learn the maps or use them in productive ways. The question remaining, then, is what exactly do the maps do for kids who struggle?

Seeing Patterns for Organization

First of all, the maps help kids see patterns. As Caine and Caine (1994) note, "The mind is a pattern detector." Many students who struggle in school do so because they fail to detect or intuit patterns. They don't *see* how what they did yesterday links to what they are doing today. They don't *see* the patterns of information that are laid out in a chapter or presented in a lecture. And, like David, though they may know a lot, they don't *see* how to pattern what they know in order to write or tell someone about it. Their failure in school, in part, stems from a fundamental difficulty with representing their thoughts.

Failure to invoke patterns for representing thought frequently results in disorganization. We see this very clearly in students who have ADHD. Individuals with ADHD have trouble with a range of abilities that are subsumed under the umbrella term *executive functions*. When we say someone has difficulty with executive functions, we mean he or she has difficulty planning an approach to a task, organizing a sequence of actions or series of data points, holding action sequences in working memory until they are executed, inhibiting actions that are irrelevant to the task at hand, deciding what to attend to and what to do, shifting when necessary, monitoring and evaluating his or her behavior, and adjusting his or her behavior and emotions in response to perceived success or failure (Denckla, 1998; Singer & Bashir, 1999, in press). In essence, these are the cognitive abilities CEOs tend to be good at.

Students with ADHD, by definition, have compromised executive functions because attention and executive functions are governed by the same part of the brain. However, students *without* ADHD can also have executive function problems. As a result, disorganization is a common characteristic of a broad range of learning disabilities as well as general underachievement. Thinking Maps allow students to see patterns that go beyond the word or sentence—patterns that capture the big picture—they offer students with varied learning abilities and learning styles a means for organizing their thinking and their understanding of the world. Further, they provide a vehicle for such students to represent and share what they know and understand.

Language for Learning: Supporting Oral Communication

In viewing how students represent what they know, the central role of language warrants consideration. Vygotsky (1962) asserts that language and cognition are inextricably intertwined (also see Chapter 6, Maps for the Road to Reading Comprehension). Cognition is limited by language, and vice versa. It is nearly impossible to solve a complex problem without an internal conversation—without talking your way through it. Educators want students to become better thinkers, and they depend upon listening, speaking, reading, and writing (to a far greater degree than other representational systems) for developing as well as assessing student knowledge and understanding. This puts students who struggle with language at a severe disadvantage when it comes to playing the game of school. Those who have strong linguistic abilities tend to do well overall; those who don't tend to struggle inordinately in most academic subjects. Consequently, success or failure in education is largely dependent on language, as it is both the object of knowledge and a principal means through which new knowledge is acquired (Cazden, 1973).

As a speech-language pathologist, what has amazed me most about Thinking Maps is they offer a milieu from which focused language can emerge. They scaffold and integrate multiple systems that support expression. Maps allow for interactions between listening, speaking, reading, and writing within a language of thinking that bridges visual-spatial and verbal representations. Consequently, they profoundly change both the language used *within* the classroom and the language demands *of* the classroom. This allows students who struggle with listening, speaking, reading, or writing, who previously could only stand on the sidelines, to get in the game.

Thinking Maps change the way teachers talk to students, which changes the way students talk to themselves and each other. We hear students and teachers use words like *think, classify, sequence, analogy,* and *brainstorm*. These words represent cognitive processes—internal workings of the mind. In classrooms using Thinking Maps, such cognitive processes are taught to students directly, and the words that represent them are woven through an ongoing conversation about how to do the thinking that school requires. It is truly astounding to hear a first-grade teacher ask her class, "How are you thinking about this?" and have *all* of her students raise their hands confidently with an answer. No longer are students guessing blindly at how to approach a task, hoping they will stumble across a path that will lead to success. Now they are asked to consider what cognitive route(s) they will take before they set out on their journey. That consideration takes place through language—through an *explicit* and *constructive* dialogue between teachers and students about what kind of thinking a task requires and which thinking tools will get the job done. This explicit conversation about thinking fosters the development of metacognition—the seed from which self-regulated learners grow.

Organized Thinking and Coherent Speaking

Thinking Maps explicitly promote student reflection, which is necessary for planning and organizing. In using the maps, students can develop executive functions necessary to support language and scaffold social participation in a learning community. The maps store words and ideas until students decide what to do with them. Because they represent *specific* thought processes, and do so visually, they help students inhibit mental actions that are irrelevant to the task and decide what to attend to and what to do. They cue students to shift their approach when what they are mapping doesn't capture their thinking accurately, and they guide students to monitor and evaluate their behavior and make adjustments as necessary. As one student at the Learning Prep School in Massachusetts (a school for students with severe learning disabilities) once said to me, "The maps are like a brain."

I routinely ask students how the maps help them, and the number one response I get is, "They help me organize my ideas." Often, students and teachers mention the payoff this has with writing. What strikes me more is the payoff it has with talking. Thinking Maps change the way students talk to their teachers, their parents, and each other. Having a place to arrange and store their words helps them. What also helps them are the visual-spatial arrays that represent structured thought and discourse. The maps are devices that allow students to *see* what they think and find the language that will convey that knowledge to their teachers and each other in a clear and organized way. As one fifth-grade student told me, "The maps put my thoughts into action."

Nick, a sixth-grade student with a learning disability attending the Learning Prep School, shared a Double Bubble Map he made to compare and contrast the main characters in two books he read during independent reading (Figure 3.2). He not only read the words and phrases on his map to his classmates, he also elaborated upon each idea by offering details and examples from the two books he read. For example, when discussing the similarities of the characters regarding the making of new friends, Nick explained that Robinson met a native person on his island while Cody met a person in the woods. Both found new friends to help them survive while they were stranded in isolating environments—Robinson on an island and Cody in the arctic forest of Alaska. Nick recalled key facts about each character, and what is more impressive is that making the map helped him to remember, integrate, and understand the books at a very deep level. Talking *from* the map allowed him to share what he knew in nicely organized and coherent discourse. Nick noted that he never would have remembered all those details if he hadn't constructed that kind of map. He went on to explain that the Double Bubble and Tree Maps help him more than the other Thinking Maps because they depict ways of thinking he previously found difficult.

Having trained and mentored faculties of two schools that exclusively serve students with a broad range of learning disabilities (the Norman Howard School in Rochester, NY, and the Learning Prep School in Newton, MA), I have been struck time and time again by how oral communication in the classroom changes. Via the maps, communication literally takes on a whole new shape. Teachers and students have a means for integrating key concepts and conveying new understandings fluidly, grounding them in a spatial realm. It is fascinating to me to watch teachers and students talk about how they will use one map or another. They gesture as they talk; they make circles and boxes and lines in the air, and they "plug" their ideas into these imaginary spaces. Their spoken language

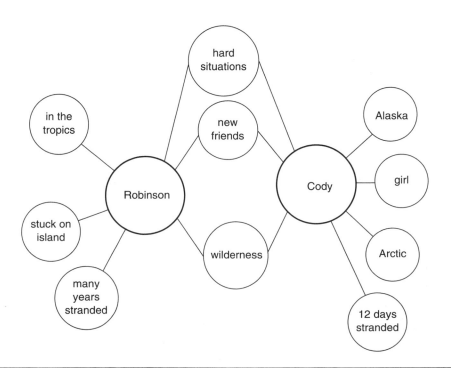

Figure 3.2 Learning Prep Student Comparing and Contrasting Two Characters

piggybacks onto a spatial superstructure. Fluid classroom discourse, then, is born from the marriage of verbal and spatial realms—from the integrated workings of both the right and left hemispheres. I believe this has much to do with why the maps bring about such profound changes in classroom environments and student performance. They level the playing field for students who rely on relative strengths within either the verbal or visual domain, bolstering whichever domain is weaker to bring about a more balanced learner.

Not only does the nature of spoken communication change in classrooms using Thinking Maps, but the amount of spoken language changes. Discussion and debate become more elaborate when students have tools that allow them to see how all of the pieces of curriculum content go together. As their ability to show what they know improves, so does their motivation for and investment in learning. Often, reluctant or reticent students begin to take more risks and participate. After only six months of using Thinking Maps with students, many of the faculty at the Learning Prep School reported that the students' spoken and written output at least doubled. Indeed, one sixth-grade teacher in Chicago noted that she used to do all the talking when she taught. After learning the maps, she talks far less than she used to. Her students do the talking, and she helps them see where their learning conversation is going.

Closing the Gap for Underachievers

Though Thinking Maps have the potential to raise the performance of all learners, they are particularly powerful for students who are functioning in the bottom of the bell curve (i.e., students with identified special needs and those who are not coded but are struggling nonetheless, perhaps due to mild problems with executive functions). Who are these students and what are the implications of using Thinking Maps with them?

In the lower quartile, we find three groups of students. One group has identified disabilities, but they can function quite well when classroom instruction supports and accommodates their unique learning styles and needs. For these students, the maps are strategies that bridge cognitive, visual, and verbal realms, perhaps providing a toolset that allows these students to manage mainstream curriculum demands. Another group has significant learning challenges that require special education services (e.g., students with language disorders, learning disabilities, perceptual disorders, motor disorders, or compromised cognition). The maps provide general and special education teachers serving these students a common language and toolset for teaching, thereby fostering collaboration and partnership among school faculty. Whereas these students generally lack flexibility in their learning styles and have difficulty transferring new learning from one context to another, the maps provide them with a set of tools they can use both in and out of the classroom. They form a bridge between general and special education.

A third group in the bottom quartile consists of students that are poor CEOs of their own learning. Lacking insight about how to meet academic task demands, they are underachieving relative to their potential. As a result, they aren't sure how to get from A to Z when given a task unless they are provided with explicit scaffolds. In some cases, such students fail to make progress in the general education curriculum and are referred for special education services. Too often, they don't qualify for extra support, and the gap between academic expectations and their achievement continues to widen. For all groups in the lower quartile, Thinking Maps can help students self-regulate their own learning and be more successful in the game of school because they serve as a device for mediating thinking, listening, talking, reading, writing, problem solving, and the acquisition of new knowledge and understanding. They can be used for universal instructional design and the successful inclusion of all learners.

The Thinking Maps, then, have the potential for reducing the number of students in special education and allowing more students not only to survive, but to thrive in general education classrooms. Consequently, they have the potential to be a school's most powerful weapon when it comes to closing the achievement gap. As the Flow Map in Figure 3.3 shows, having a small set of flexible thinking tools lessens all students' anxiety and confusion about school work, which brings forth an increased sense of control and self-efficacy, which leads to increased motivation to participate and learn and greater academic success. Success further decreases anxiety and confusion, and the cycle continues. By leveling the playing field, Thinking Maps provide students who are not doing well with the tools they need to win at school.

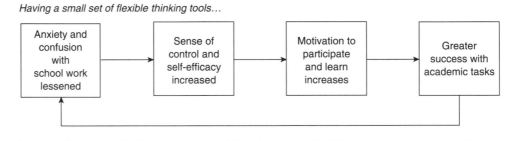

Figure 3.3   Effects of Thinking Maps on Student Learning

4

Tools for Integrating Theories and Differentiating Practice

Alan Cooper, B.Ed.

Topics to be discussed:

- differentiating instruction through student-centered tools in New Zealand
- using a Flow Map for simultaneously enriching habits of mind, multiple intelligences, and learning styles
- facilitating emotional and cognitive development using Thinking Maps®

There are a number of ways in which we enrich the experiences our students have in our classrooms in any given year and over time in our schools. As we grow as teachers and administrators through these changes, we also enrich our learning community. In the short term, new techniques and theories implemented in schools may leverage new learning, but ultimately, a long-term question may remain below the surface and undermine change: In what ways do these practices and theoretical models integrate with the existing approaches we have in place so that the individual efforts are unified? A school may become reactive to yearly changes and become additive, but not integrative. Sustaining a larger vision and creating a coherent educational experience for students requires constant orchestration of the overlapping teaching strategies, student tools, and various theories introduced into the school.

If the leadership of the school community does not address this question, then new processes may not be used together by teachers and students. The educational program risks becoming perceived by all concerned as merely a jumble of discordant instruments sounding off, rather than a richly synchronized, high-quality performance. As the headmaster of St. George's School, a K–8 private school in New Zealand, for 18 years, I had the opportunity to bring many practices and theories together and help facilitate conversations with our faculty, school board, and parents to make sense of this integration. I was equally concerned about both the practical and theoretical integration of models. Over the years of my service I have become particularly intrigued by how Thinking Maps have helped integrate the theories and practices of Goleman's views on emotional intelligence, Howard Gardner's multiple intelligences, the Dunns' learning styles model, and Art Costa's habits of mind in our school.

INTEGRATING TOOLS FOR DIFFERENTIATION

The greatest advantage we as educators can give the wide, diverse range of students we teach is to enable them as learners. The drive toward the twin goals of common content and differentiated processes for individuals is one of the key educational challenges of the twenty-first century. For many school communities, this dilemma can become a point of conflict, driving well-meaning people apart rather than functioning as a point of departure or an opportunity for growth.

In order to maximize learning for all students, individual differences must be sought out and explicitly developed in each of us as teachers and learners. To accomplish this, there is a need not only for the teacher to know how each individual learns but for the student to know that as well. Such information must be raised to the consciousness level. For example, while Thinking Maps are valuable in their own right as flexible tools for differentiating and unifying learning in a classroom, these tools become more useful for learners when they are connected to the other current learning theories and practices. As we found at our school, there are many connections to be made between the use of Thinking Maps in classrooms and emotional intelligence, multiple intelligences, learning styles, and habits of mind. When used together, they develop a synergy that truly benefits both the teacher and the student.

For a very long time now, seeking these connections has been the lifeblood of our school. This is because our school faculty has been particularly influenced by thinkers such as Alvin Toffler, Charles Handy, and Peter Senge. St. George's School has come to perceive itself as a learning organization preparing our students, our teachers, and even our parents for lifelong learning where the only constant would be change and perhaps paradox. We wanted to go beyond teaching the curriculum and attaining high standards, important as they must be, to teaching behaviors that would allow our teachers and our students to be confident problem solvers in areas where they did not know the answers; in areas where they had to ask their own questions; in areas where, as Toffler has offered, they would be required to learn, unlearn, and relearn.

THEORIES INTO PRACTICE

Over a dozen years our faculty has gone through extensive training in the theory and practices mentioned above. None of the training and other forms of professional development were isolated, but were brought into an ongoing conversation about the connections between approaches. Teachers' professional portfolios were an essential place for educators to muse, research, document, and reflect on how new processes integrated with existing structures. A large part of my investigation of how all of these processes worked together was to move in and out of classrooms on a regular basis.

During a span of time when I was observing a middle grade class, the students were studying World War Two and the Holocaust. I began focusing on two boys as a way of looking at how the learning styles approach worked.

One student, Harry, would be described in the Dunn and Dunn Learning Style Profile as a near-extreme "global" learner: He always has his shirt out and constantly chatters, and thus it is no surprise that the sociological line in his profile states that he likes working with peers. As well, he is in constant motion and appears to avoid work. His teacher grasped the important point that it is not work as such that he avoids but analytic work, the factual "stuff" in encyclopedias and textbooks. Another student, Douglas, is the opposite. As an "analytic" learner, he prefers the factual nonfiction, less emotive articles, and encyclopedic information. He wrote up the fact file on Auschwitz and drew the geographical map of Europe with great attention to detail. Harry would have none of this. He started by drawing a barbed wire border—anything to avoid or at least delay getting on with the work. He did read excerpts from the *Diary of Anne Frank*, nonfiction reading, but not in the cold hard fact form. It was the emotional content that motivated him. He wrote a very good emotive poem. Harry constantly discussed research with Douglas that Douglas had found, but the teacher worried at times that neither was really learning because Harry seemed to be interrupting Douglas all the time.

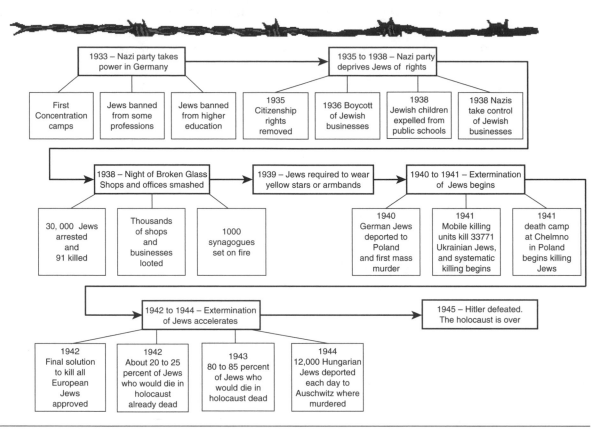

Figure 4.1   The Holocaust Research Flow Map

However, both Harry and Douglas were learning and they were using a common tool—a Flow Map—that served to focus their widely ranging styles (Figure 4.1). One of them was engaged at the global, emotive level and the other at the analytical, factual level, but the information appeared together in the map. The map became a reference point and place that brought their two styles together. When it came to the formal presentation to the class, Harry was quite verbose and could recall fully the information that was required in the study and shown explicitly in the map. This success story is a starting point for investigating, albeit in short form, the linkages made below between the Thinking Maps and very complex theories of emotions, intelligences, habits, and styles. A wider understanding may come about as we consider how teachers and students are becoming conscious and conversant about how these models work together to support deeper learning.

LINKING TO EMOTIONAL INTELLIGENCE

Confidence is necessary for both teachers and students for learning to occur. It can be seen as a by-product of emotional intelligence (Goleman, 1995). Self-awareness and self-management, the first two components of emotional intelligence, are expressed by our abilities to manage ourselves effectively. The teacher of the two boys demonstrated this by having the self-confidence to try something with a risk attached. She did not know the ultimate outcome of allowing two opposites, as Harry and Douglas were, to work together. Many teachers would normally group kids together who seem to work in similar ways, not dissimilar ways. However, it was what Costa and Kalick (2000) call a responsible risk. Confident in her knowledge of the way the boys learned, the teacher was able to seize opportunities and turn the apparent weakness in the divergent learning styles preferences of the boys into a strength. She made the connections by combining her understanding of the boys' learning styles and her internal thought processes with the use of Thinking Maps as the animating center for the boys' work.

Managing relationships effectively is a second component of emotional intelligence. The teacher's knowledge about how individuals learn gave her empathy for the learning styles of both boys, divergent as they were. She made the required organizational changes within the classroom to facilitate these styles, but also she had the social skill to do this effectively. Her empathy was not passive commiseration but active participation. As for the boys, they, too, demonstrated self-awareness. They knew their learning styles as learning strengths, because that was how the learning styles profiles were openly referred to in the school. Consequently, the students had developed a strong and positive sense of self-worth. This aided their ability to self manage: to adapt and to seize a new and quite different working relationship—using a common visual tool—and to manage it in a way that made it work for each of them.

LINKING TO MULTIPLE INTELLIGENCES

There is a range of multiple intelligences, but the focus of this discussion is on intrapersonal and interpersonal forms, linking with Goleman's work. Intrapersonal intelligence is associated with the internal self. Howard Gardner (1993) defines it as "involving the capacity to understand oneself, to have an effective working model of oneself—including one's own desires, fears, and capacities—and to use such information effectively in regulating one's own life." A key word here is capacities, both for teachers and students. It is a teacher's available repertoire, or the knowledge of the available tools and models, that will enable students to work more effectively. Interpersonal intelligence is more concerned with relationships, a key intelligence for teachers as they create a collaborative learning environment. Gardner's definition states that interpersonal intelligence is, "To understand the intentions, motivations, and desires of other people and, consequently, to work effectively with others."

The teacher needs to understand how each individual student learns and to use that knowledge to enable the students to effectively use their individual learning strengths in groups. In so doing, the students, too, need to become aware of their personal intelligences by metacognitive reflection and teacher and peer feedback. The use of Thinking Maps as an open space for co-construction provided a mediating frame for the two boys to act out their styles toward a product that united their styles. The map was a safe place for collaboration. It was evolving and structured, mirroring their thinking, and with no one right answer. The boys were drawing out detailed information in a holistic form and together could evolve the ideas between them on paper.

LINKING LEARNING STYLES

Learning styles (Dunn & Dunn, 1992) are the way in which individuals begin concentrating on and then processing, internalizing, and finally, retaining new and difficult information that they are taught. Integral to this is the realization that learning is individual—that students learn in many different ways, and teaching and learning is most efficient when these differences are taken into account. Just as theories of intelligence are complex, so, too, is the Dunn and Dunn learning styles model, having 21 different categories. However, there is a smaller subset of the whole, where learners are divided into global or analytic learners. It is this subset that Douglas and Harry were clearly exhibiting and their teacher was supporting, as displayed in summary using the Double Bubble Map in Figure 4.2.

Douglas ~~Harry~~, the analytic learner, was the conventional model pupil. He preferred being seated formally; he worked carefully and methodically through factual detail, completing each piece before moving on. Eventually, the details that he had compiled would become the whole—the complete picture. His work was also characterized by persistence, in the sense that he liked to complete what he was doing before moving on. ~~Douglas~~ *Harry*, the global

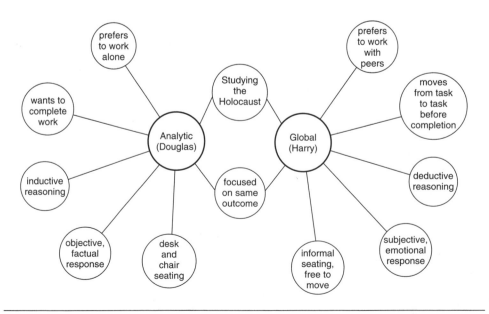

Figure 4.2 Analytic and Global Learner Comparison Double Bubble Map

learner, was the conventional "problem pupil." He needed a more informal seating arrangement, such as soft furniture or being allowed to sprawl on the floor rather than sit at a desk. He needed to be free to move. He focused on the emotional side of things by seeking the big issues, dashing about in this search rather than methodically working from the bottom up. Thus he could be said to lack persistence in that he did not complete what he was doing before turning his attention to something else, searching for the next big picture. Not even his barbed wire border around the Flow Map, an artistic touch, was completed before he was off doing another task. However, in the end, in his own time, he got it completed with Harry.

It was because of the teacher's awareness of and action on these understandings—personal intelligence in action—that these two diverse learning styles were able to be reconciled so successfully.

LINKING HABITS OF MIND

A wide range of habits of mind (Costa & Kalick, 2000) were also activated through this activity, especially when considering this situation from the teacher's perspective. It was the teacher who created this learning pair and took the risk of bringing these boys together with the Flow Map in hand.

One key habit of mind, metacognition, was formally undertaken by the teacher in her professional development portfolio. She brought to a conscious level the personal, practical knowledge that she developed and articulated as it flowed from her classroom interactions. She was thinking flexibly, listening to her students with understanding and empathy, taking responsible risks, asking questions, and above all remaining open to continuous learning. The students were doing likewise. The teacher noted in her portfolio that through this activity the students were beginning "to understand why they worked the way they did." This was clearly facilitating both their intrapersonal and interpersonal intelligences. The understandings of how they learn increased their ability to understand the motivation and abilities of the other students and respond to them in such a way that they achieved a positive outcome. They were learning to self-manage and to manage their relationships—attributes that will produce positive results far beyond the classroom walls. As the teacher noted in her portfolio, "It not only helped them individually, but it also helped them to understand, tolerate and work with one another."

There is a strong match here between the theories of Goleman and Gardner and the Dunns' learning style models. As the students' capacities increased through their understanding of the learning styles of their partners, this internal, intrapersonal growth was transferred to the interpersonal relationships so that it grew, as well. This is ongoing, continual improvement of habits of mind through intrinsic rewards of learning. Jonathan Cohen (1999) describes it this way: "Awareness of ourselves and others provides the foundation for social and emotional competencies: a sense of self worth; the ability to solve problems and make responsible and

Handwritten margin note:

Habits of Mind
1 Persistence
2. Decreasing Impulsivity
3. Flexibility Thinking
4. Metacognition
5. Checking for Accuracy & Precision
6. Questioning & Problem Posing
7. Accessing prior Knowl./Experiences
8. Transference beyond the learning situation
9. Using all senses
10 Listening to others
11 A Sense of Humor
12 Wonderment, Inquisitiveness, Curiosity & the Enjoyment of P.S.
13. Cooperative Thinking
14 Envisioning, Clarifying & Defining a goal prior to embarking on one course of action
15 Exploring consequences of course of action
16 Taking risks

helpful decisions, to communicate and collaborate with others, to become self motivating."

THINKING MAPS: A UNIFYING SET OF TOOLS

Given the short description above of the intersection of emotional and interpersonal intelligences, global and analytic learning styles, and habits of mind, we may begin to see how Thinking Maps provide a unique, unifying language across these four approaches, each of which is theoretically rich. The Thinking Maps provide the "how to" tools that may be both linear and nonlinear, as well as detailed and holistic. Importantly, they are problem-solving tools used for executive processes (see Chapter 3, Leveling The Playing Field for All Students), not just information processors, and in the situation investigated above, the teacher was in the background having created the learning environment. Harry and Douglas did their work and problem solving, in this case with only the one Flow Map as the immediate, mediating agent. By their very nature, Thinking Maps are not content or task bound. They are adaptable and can be easily customized to suit individual learning styles and interdisciplinary problems.

There is considerable appeal in these tools for the global learner because the purpose of the map and the thinking process required are always emphasized. This immediately gives the big picture that global learners need. It becomes a large canvas of one or several thinking processes or multitasks such as comparing and contrasting, describing attributes, categorizing, etc. Thus, the global mind is able to avoid rushing about looking for an organizing purpose as it settles in on it quickly and can then proceed to work deductively down into the detail.

The same map is flexible enough to provide the detailed structure that an analytical mind needs to build inductively, detail by detail, in order to arrive at the main idea. For example, the Flow Map for sequencing a complex event such as a war can be started with an overarching rectangular phase with smaller boxes expanding as stages, leading to ever more refined details shown in substages for each major stage. In the same way, the Tree Map for categorizing can be built with details from the ground up by the analytic learner while the global learner is creating the same map from the top down.

However, there are extra spin-offs from this flexible, evolving, visual structuring of content and processes. The habit of mind Costa calls persistence is one of the major areas separating analytical and global learners in the Dunn and Dunn learning style model. At one end of the persistence continuum are those learners high on responsibility who do not want to stop until they have completed their task. These learners are last to leave the classroom as they copy the homework fully and accurately. They are the students whose parents complain that there is too much homework because they spent two hours completing the half hour's work the teacher thought had been assigned. They are driven to be perfect. Part of that perfection is making sure that the task is completed exactly, with all the details in place. Each of the Thinking Maps has an adaptive structure and consistency so that students who are high on persistence can complete steps before moving on, or they can easily chunk the maps in order to provide for closure when there are time constraints. When several maps are being used in sequence, each map can be completed as a single unit in an overall project. In this way, closure is there at the end of each map, which satisfies those who see completion as an attribute of responsibility and removes the frustration of not completing an assignment.

For global learners, who are often low on persistence, moving from task to task is facilitated. Interestingly, the low-persistence student can keep on working for an extended period just as the high-persistence student can. The difference is that the low-persistence student often needs multiple tasks to work on, thus creating an interplay between focal points, but focusing nonetheless. Thinking Maps provide an alternative way of progressing through assignments. Continuity of task is not essential, so leaving off the work at any stage and then coming back later works. Where a sequence of maps is being used, the global learner can move through the sequence bit by bit, developing single ideas as they arise and moving back and forth between maps. In this way, the multitasking that provides optimum learning for the global learner is also made possible.

REFLECTIONS: EMERGENT THINKERS AND LIFELONG LEARNERS

The integrated habits of mind, emotional intelligences, and learning styles discussed above are obviously evolving well before a child steps into our school and becomes a student. It has become our responsibility, however, as an organization to integrate these theories, so that from the beginning and over time our students come to appreciate their capacities and learn how to use them to work effectively with others in the classroom.

The importance of Thinking Maps as a vehicle by which students are able to discover this is evident. However, the benefits do not stop there. By making these connections, positive attitudes toward learning are nurtured within boys like Harry who are often pigeon-holed as difficult pupils. The maps become a way to get to the holism of their thinking. As a result, these students gain persistence, self-management, and self-efficacy as foundations for differentiated, lifelong learning. The added benefit is that we as educators learn more about ourselves and our students.

Closing the Gap by Connecting Culture, Language, and Cognition

**From an interview with
Yvette Jackson, Ed.D.**

Topics to be discussed:

- urban schooling and the development of cognitive mediation across cultures and language
- revealing "codes of power" through using Thinking Maps® by students in underachieving schools
- literacy results from urban school systems across the country

FINDING LEARNING SOLUTIONS FOR CHILDREN IN URBAN SCHOOLS

I had read about Reuven Feuerstein's (1980) work while I was doing graduate work in New York City in the early 1980s. He describes how he worked with kids who were displaced Jews during the early years of development of the State of Israel, and how he helped them by bringing a deeper assessment of their learning. Knowing that these kids who had been considered low functioning really had more potential than an IQ test was showing changed me.

When I read about those kids, I said, "You know something, it's the same syndrome that my kids from urban settings are going through," meaning they have a lot more potential. They don't have mediators at home full time because they are latchkey kids. Some of the kids were in foster care and others were from poor homes where parents weren't home a lot. So, I looked at Feuerstein's work, and that's when I said to myself, "I can capture the same idea if I know more about mediation." So often students go through something called "remediation," but that is the basic remediation or redelivery of the content information and language skills. What we are talking about is the mediation of their thinking.

If you know about learning and how learning happens, then you can improve the instructional technique, and if you really believe that kids have potential, you set high expectations and have them meet those expectations with the tools that you give them.

Working With the National Urban Alliance for Effective Education

I am now one of the leaders of the National Urban Alliance for Effective Education, and our mission is to substantiate in the public schools of urban America the irrefutable belief in the capacity of all children to reach high levels of learning and thinking demanded by our ever-changing global community. Our focus is on changing teachers' perceptions and expectations of underachieving urban students, and this comes right out of my early interest in mediating learning. Of course, we are also interested in closing the achievement gap between different groups of students.

Many teachers of such students believe that the students are deficient and that their underachievement is the result of limited potential. Yet when we talk about people having undeveloped muscles or physiques, we say they're "out of shape." We don't say, "They're deficient." In our work, we focus on the idea that the brain is like muscle; it requires specific exercises, guided personal training, and relevant and meaningful instruction to build competence and prevent dysfunction. It requires mediation. We address these misperceptions through professional development in strategies and practices based on research in brain-based instruction, cognitive development, and the impact of culture and language on cognition, critical thinking, and higher-order comprehension skills. We believe that when teachers are provided with the tools or strategies that strengthen learning and literacy skills, or what Lisa Delpit (1995) calls "Codes of Power," urban students are able to demonstrate their potential through performance that changes the expectations of the teachers.

Bridging the Gap Between Teachers and Students in Urban Settings

When teachers say there's a gap between themselves and their students, they are referring to a "cultural gap" regarding their frame of reference as well as their language that is different from the students. Many will say, "I can't communicate what I need to with these kids. I can't connect, so the students are resisting learning; they push back and don't want to learn."

The fact is that students do want to learn very badly and their teachers want to teach them. What teachers sometimes interpret as students not wanting to learn is really more what Jabari Mahari (1998) describes as the "out of sync rhythms between the students and their culturally different teachers." So a student may say, "You're not communicating, so I'm pushing back. It's not that I don't want to learn; I'm just going to act this way because we're not connecting." This misunderstanding of the student's intentions inhibits many well-meaning teachers from trying instructional strategies that motivate and support the learning of their culturally different students. Instead, they continuously use methods that not only minimize learning but very often result in students resisting. It's a vicious cycle resulting in underachievement and the achievement gap that we see around this country.

There are three interconnected factors that are key to bridging the gap between teachers and their underachieving urban students. One is addressing the fear that teachers have in not being able to address the needs of their underachieving students so they can meet the standards. The second factor directly relates to the first component of how to address the learning needs. To address learning needs we need to shift the focus from what has to be taught (content) to how learning happens (cognition, metacognition, process) and what affects it. The third factor is to provide teachers and students with a language that enables them to communicate with each other, building the mutual respect and relationship that is so vital to students of color.

I address the first and second factors by trying to simplify the research about learning through an equation that would illustrate the critical targets to address in learning instruction:

$$L = (U + M) (C1 + C2)$$

Learning = (Understanding + Motivation)
(Competence and Confidence)

We know that in order for people to gain academic knowledge they have to understand the concepts of that knowledge. Another equally significant catalyst of learning is motivation. Both understanding and motivation are affected by what Eric Jensen (1998) describes as brain realization of relevance and meaningfulness. But the critical question we have to address in order to stimulate motivation is, "What makes something relevant to an individual?" Well, it's *cultural* experience that makes something relevant and meaningful, thereby stimulating motivation. So we can't ignore that culture affects how one understands something: the perspective one takes on something; the experiences one brings to reading affect how one infers. It's also one's cultural orientation that plays a large part in one's thinking. Reuven Feuerstein (1980) and Vygotsky (1962) point out that the other significant factors in stimulating motivation are competence and confidence. Jensen addresses the importance of confidence in relation to the positive impact challenge has on students when they feel a sense of competence and confidence to meet the challenge. Lisa Delpit (1995) refers to the importance of building confidence through competence as "codes of power" or higher-order thinking and literacy skills.

These understandings about learning and what affects it bring us to the third factor to address to bridge the cultural gap between teachers and students, and that is language. Just as culture shapes relevance, it's important to realize how language is affected by culture and how they both affect cognition, learning, and how one communicates. Culture molds language, and language is a way of thinking. Addressing this interrelationship is critical in bridging the gap, and this is where Thinking Maps play a role of major importance.

I believe that Thinking Maps are essential tools in bridging the cultural gap between teachers and students because they address all three related factors. First of all, each of the eight Thinking Maps facilitates the development of one of the cognitive skills that are critical to learning and are also identified in all the state standards as skills students must have. They need to be able to define and generalize concepts or themes; describe, identify, categorize, and organize details; compare and contrast; sequence; identify cause and effect; analyze parts of a whole; and understand analogies. Second, Thinking Maps provide a language about thinking that allows teachers and students to communicate with precision, bridging the cultural gap. Equally important is that they provide students with the tools for building competence in learning and communicating that learning with confidence. The maps are like tools of power for unlocking the "codes of power" Lisa Delpit (1995) discusses.

The Pedagogy of Confidence

Pedagogy is an art that is developed and refined when teachers are confident in their ability to successfully affect students. Teachers become confident when they know what to do and believe that they have the skills and abilities to do what they know they have to do. When teachers are confident, they communicate to students confidence in students' ability to learn. A confident teacher is aware of the impact of culture on language and learning and uses this understanding to guide the selection of effective learning strategies that enable students to become competent and confident learners. The interplay of these elements and the forces at work in this complex system involving teachers, strategies, culture, and research are represented through the Multi-Flow Map (Figure 5.1). Thinking Maps provide the tools and language for a teacher to confidently address the critical needs of underachieving students.

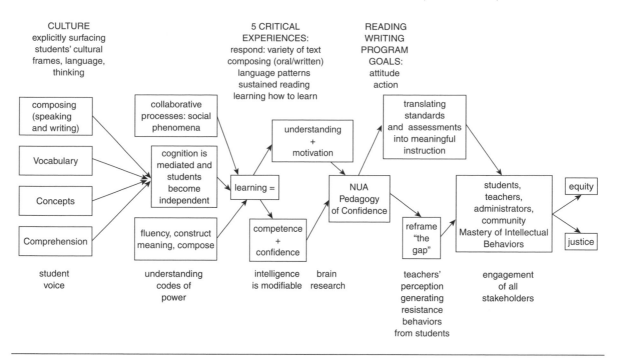

Figure 5.1 NUA Organization Strategy Integration Multi-Flow Map

Critical Learning Needs of Students in Underachieving Schools

In every district in which we work, students who are underachieving have critical needs in verbal knowledge, inference, and academic language usage. These needs are compounded by what I call "learning blockers," things that obstruct the natural learning process, specifically, cognitive, language, and textual blockers.

First of all, there is the cognitive blocker that occurs if students are not guided to identify the understanding, or concept, that should be the focus of the learning. Without this focus, students are unable to differentiate between relevant and irrelevant information, so critical details can't be identified, prioritized, analyzed, hypothesized, evaluated, or compared to personal experiences.

There are also language blockers that are manifested because the language of textbooks is so distinctly different from the language students use at home. Even though students are expected to read these texts with comprehension, very little discussion takes place in the classroom that engages students in using the vocabulary used in textbooks. The result is that the language necessary for comprehending texts is not developed. In high school, this lack of facility or understanding of the language of texts in different subject areas is extremely debilitating. The other language blocker is a lack of knowledge and understanding of patterns of language, from the most obvious one of decoding skills to syntax and understanding parts of speech and grammatical rules.

Last, there are textual blockers. There are two types of textual blockers: semantic and structural. Semantic blockers are words such as pronouns or idioms that are often not identified by teachers as problematic and don't necessarily require a deep understanding of language codes or patterns, yet they can severely inhibit comprehension of text. Structural blockers are the patterns that authors use to communicate information. These include descriptive, cause and effect, problem/solution, compare/contrast, and enumerative (main idea with supporting details). Each structure requires a different set of cognitive skills to analyze and construct meaning from the text.

The Thinking Maps become essential tools to address these learning blockers because they help students and teachers do what Reuven Feuerstein (1980) describes as "mediating learning" through these blockers. If teachers explicitly instruct students in the use of Thinking Maps, they are addressing language and cognitive blockers. All eight maps elicit the use of cognitive terminology and then provide vehicles for capturing the language so that students can go back and refer to that cognitive language, building their verbal repertoire of cognitive skills. If students can name the thinking they are doing, they will notice and seek that language in questions, assignments, and texts, thus owning the language the tool reflects.

While developing a level of fluency with this concrete visual language that represents cognition, Thinking Maps become the mediating tools for students' and teachers' learning and thinking. Thinking Maps mediate learning at many points as represented by Figure 5.2.

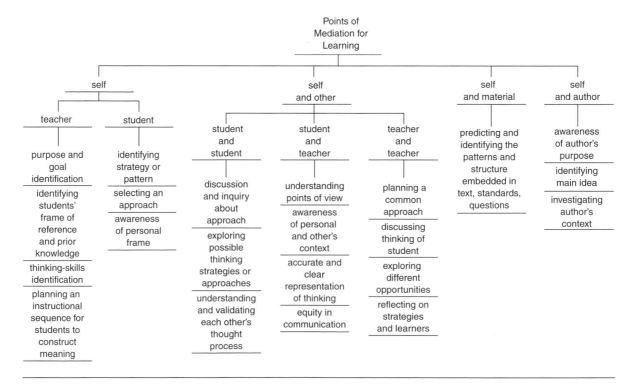

Figure 5.2   Points of Mediation Tree Map

Thinking Maps mediate students' and teachers' individual metacognition as they reflect on their own thinking about thinking. For the teacher, the Thinking Maps encourage teachers to identify the purpose and goals of the lesson before instruction in order to determine what kind of thinking is involved. Teachers' reflective conversations help them establish the prerequisites that students need to be able to construct meaning. Similarly, before students begin a task, they can ask themselves, by using the cognitive language embedded in the Thinking Maps, "How can I approach this task?" or "What do I notice about this assignment?" In both situations, Thinking Maps foster metacognition, the first step in mediating one's own learning.

Besides supporting internal dialogue, Thinking Maps mediate thinking between individuals in the classroom. With the Thinking Maps, a teacher mediates learning by addressing specific learning needs in a way that engages students and activates those cognitive skills involved in the process of constructing meaning. The Circle and Frame Map, used for defining in context, is excellent for guiding students in analyzing and defining the focus of understanding or concept learning critical to guiding underachieving students in constructing meaning. The Thinking Maps encourage discussion between the teacher and the students about the kind of thinking required from the text by analyzing which Thinking Map is best for reflecting that kind of thinking. These explicit conversations about language, process, and cognition develop the focus on thinking, which can be transferred across disciplines. With shared visual representations, teacher and student can understand and communicate in the same language, shifting the power in the classroom.

In addition to understanding and communicating with oneself or with someone else, Thinking Maps mediate learning between student and teacher with text or content. Thinking Maps create a clearer pattern for a teacher to teach with and for students to analyze text and to demonstrate understanding of the text in the pattern required. Thinking Maps guide students in identifying and analyzing the understandings, skills, and the text structures or patterns needed to construct meaning from a reading or unit of study in any discipline. Thinking Maps help teachers identify and analyze the kind of thinking that's going to be required to read a particular text as demanded by the text structure used by the author. The process fosters the great link between reading and writing. So Thinking Maps help students analyze text structure and really internalize the pattern, and then use that pattern to write their thoughts and demonstrate their thinking. This process of transferring between reading and writing is a complementary response to Ernest Boyer's (1983) definition of reading and writing. He said, "Reading is unlocking frozen thoughts and writing is freezing thoughts." Thinking Maps help students unlock the frozen patterns of thoughts as well as take their thoughts and freeze them in a pattern of thinking.

Teaching Inferential Thinking

In regard to inferential thinking, the Thinking Maps are the most useful tools I have found. Teaching inference can be extremely difficult because inference is contingent upon connecting one's prior experience—and culture—with that of the author. Consider that individuals who are asked to author texts have years of expertise in their discipline or area of focus on which to base the ideas they want to convey and the meaning they want to imply. These books are given to students who often don't have any experience that connects to that of the author's, and yet the expectation is that students should be able to infer, or read between the lines, to connect their experience with that of the author to speculate about ideas that are not literally presented. That's what you do when you're inferring. You've got to go from your personal reference to what the author is saying, which is why it's easier to infer with narrative or fiction than expository text.

Fiction is written about themes that everyone has experiences with or can relate to (e.g., love, fear, longing), but in discipline-based textbooks that are nonfiction or expository, concepts are more technical, more remote, and frequently harder for underachieving students to relate to. Guiding students without exposure to experiences that reflect what the author is writing about requires tools to engage the teacher and students in the kind of conceptual discussion that creates bridges for the students so that they can make a connection between the author's experience and their own. Perhaps Thinking Maps can mediate learning at yet another level—between the author of the text and the learner. A tool that engages students in this type of discussion is the Frame of Reference that can be drawn around any of the maps. An example of this would be using a frame around a Bubble Map to develop characterization. In the Bubble Map shown in Figure 5.3, you identify adjectives that describe a character; the frame elicits exploration or inferences of why the adjectives were selected to describe the character. Why is the character the way he or she is? If "angry" is identified as one of the descriptions, in the frame a student would infer why the character was angry. If the character is described as discontented, the frame would elicit why he or she is discontented. What happened in the characters' lives to cause them to be this way? The Frame of Reference enables students to infer ideas, speculations, or theories about who this character really is. It's not just about description; it's the inference behind the description that is the core of characterization.

Developing Memory as Part of the Mediation of a Student's Learning

Unfortunately, memory has been associated with rote learning, and that's not what we're talking about here. Eric Jensen (1998), Mel Levine (1993), and others have written extensively on memory and its impact on learning. The shame is that teachers too often ignore the use of powerful memory devices such as mnemonics to strengthen student learning because they believe that any memory focus is associated with rote learning. The key here is that rote learning is not about patterning, but memory is. Students' achievement has a lot to do with their memory of things. The

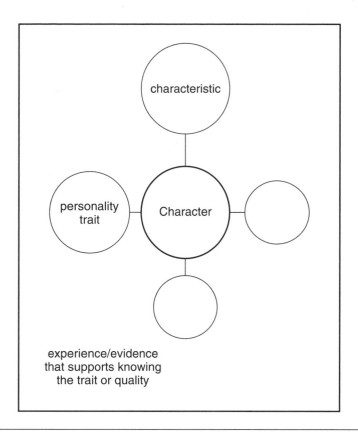

Figure 5.3   Supporting Inferential Thinking With Bubble and Frame Map

Thinking Maps strengthen learning by becoming external memory patterns for students when they use them to freeze their thinking. The maps provide a place where students can refer to all the interrelated ideas and from these ideas make the extractions. If students tried to hold the quantity of ideas their brains explore, they would be expending a lot of their mental energy focusing on just trying to remember all the details instead of generalizing and elaborating on these ideas. Thinking Maps elucidate patterns and function as external memory, so the maps can fortify and expand students' learning that relies on memory. In a sense, first students refer to the pattern of information, then they can infer from that pattern. This is the shift from frozen information to the construction of knowledge.

Reversing Underachievement in Literacy Among Urban Learners

We work to reverse underachievement, predominantly underachievement in reading and writing, the major deficit being identified in inferential thinking, vocabulary, and language usage. We focus our professional development around the acceleration of intellectual performance, specifically in literacy. We know that literacy is the catalyst to empowering students so we go beyond the standard definition of literacy and have embraced the definition described by Elliot Eisner (1994) as the ability of an individual to construct, create, and communicate meaning across disciplines in many forms of representation (e.g., written text, drawing, mathematical symbols, dance). We resonate with this definition because it expands instructional focus to include the cognitive functions that are the prerequisites to accelerating learning and achievement throughout life.

We believe that literacy for urban learners is best developed when the teacher mediates the learning process by providing lessons that foster social interaction for language development and guide the application of cognitive skills that assist students in constructing and communicating meaning. The Thinking Maps are a core component of the cognitive strategies we provide because they are tools that have a direct impact on how students construct, communicate, and create meaning. In each district in which we work, we have witnessed how teachers immediately employ Thinking Maps as one of the most used tools of their instructional repertoire. The result has been what administrators and parents associate with the most impressive and valued impact our literacy initiatives have on learning—significant growth in the achievement of students who have previously been labeled as "low achievers." In Indianapolis, schools have recently experienced a 12-to 20-point jump in scores, which is significant. While across the state of Indiana, scores have fallen since 1998 by 1.2%, the "vanguard schools" in Indianapolis participating in the literacy initiative experienced an average increase of 10.4%, with seven of the elementary schools showing double-digit gains. In Seattle, a study showed that African American students who failed the reading section of the Washington Assessment of Student Learning (WASL) in 1999, and then spent at least two years with teachers who participated in the initiative, passed the 2002 test at twice the rate of those students who spent a year or less with participating teachers.

This evidence has been significant in demonstrating the learning potential of underachieving students, which has in turn altered the expectations of thousands of teachers, but to me there is additional evidence that has great implications regarding the impact of the Thinking Maps. Insights about the benefits of districtwide institutionalization of the use of the Thinking Maps as critical instructional tools have been felt from the classroom to the boardroom.

After our third year in the Indianapolis project, the board of education summoned the assistant superintendent to explain why they should continue to fund the literacy initiative. We decided that the most convincing way to respond would be for teachers from kindergarten through high school to share with the board the effects of the strategies and practices they had been implementing in their classrooms. Every one of the teachers talked about the impact the Thinking Maps had on the achievement of their students: A kindergarten teacher presented samples of her students' studies in science through each of the eight Thinking Maps; middle school literacy teachers shared examples of student expository and narrative writings; and a chemistry teacher demonstrated how he applied the maps in chemistry. Beyond the strong impression these presentations made on the board, the real epiphany was experienced by the high school teacher who exclaimed, "Wait! The kindergarten teachers are using the same maps we are. If every teacher is working on this kind of thinking with their students, think how strong they'll be by the time they get to high school." A similarly impressive revelation was the focus of a story told by a teacher about two brothers doing homework. A kindergartner said to his middle-school brother, "Oh, you're doing a Bubble Map. That's for describing." The older brother asked how he knew that. The younger brother informed him that he learned about that at school, surprising the older brother completely.

Thinking processes are universal and thus the Thinking Maps help students transfer these cognitive skills across content areas and grade levels. Children are born understanding cause and effect. They know how to think sequentially. In urban settings where there may be historic under-achievement, when we provide tools that enable teachers to build on the capacity of the students to think critically through instruction that provides them with tools to fortify their understanding, competence, and confidence, you have students who are motivated to excel and do excel. It becomes part of the common culture of the classroom, of the school, and as we have seen, of whole systems.

SECTION 2

Integrating Content and Process

Maps for the Road to Reading Comprehension

Bridging Reading Text
Structures to Writing Prompts

Thomasina DePinto Piercy, Ph.D.
and David Hyerle, Ed.D.

Topics to be discussed:

- linking reading text structure research to cognitive patterns
- results from first graders' fluency with Thinking Maps®
- multiple Thinking Maps applied to phonics, vocabulary, and reading comprehension

While I am reading, my mind adds to my Thinking Maps all by itself, and suddenly I know more than I knew!

(student in Cristina Smith's
first-grade class, Mt. Airy School, Maryland)

At Mt. Airy Elementary School, in a classroom of first-grade students, on a morning in mid-May, we watched as a third-year teacher read the guiding question for the day: "How will you organize your thinking about this book?" While this may seem to be an unfocused question, the teacher knew the students could meaningfully respond. The book, *How Leo Learned to Be King*, rested on the chalkboard tray with its colorful picture of a crowned lion on the cover, set there after it had been read aloud the day before. This is an inclusive classroom of students in a modest suburban neighborhood school, a school that had experienced a 15% decline in writing scores over the previous two years and mediocre reading scores as the population swelled beyond the original building and into portables.

This year student performance changed significantly upward and was reflected on state tests as scores generally fell across Maryland. Mt. Airy Elementary School has risen to the highest performing school in our county since providing reading and writing instruction with Thinking Maps. Our data supports the observations we see in classrooms: Thinking Maps significantly impact instruction and improve student performance.

While this is important news, a closer look shows that students have changed how they are understanding texts: They are surfacing dynamic patterns of content from the linear landscape, the wall of text. The range of structures bound within line-by-line text becomes unveiled in the form of mental maps as shown in Figure 6.1a–g. They are changing the form, trans-*form*ing text. Step into a classroom and observe a teacher and you will see how this works.

While observing Ms. Crystal Smith's classroom, I sat down behind the students: As principal and instructional leader, I began clacking away notes on my laptop. Students gathered on the floor near their teacher, just below the blank, open space on the chalkboard that held the guiding question for discussion. The book *How Leo Learned to Be King* had been read aloud the day before, but the students and all of the teachers and administrators across our school had learned about Thinking Maps the year before. These excerpts and the related maps may heighten your understanding of Thinking Maps and still underrepresent the richness of the classroom conversation. Here is how first graders organized their thinking about this book:

Erin: You could use the Circle Map . . . put the topic in the middle and all ideas that you get in your mind from that topic, you write down in the circle . . . Leo . . . details about Leo . . . he was mean and he was nice.

Megan: A Bubble Map about a mouse. You say a word about what the mouse is . . . like furry . . . describing words.

Billy: We could do a Double Bubble. We could compare *How Leo Learned to Be King* and *The Lion and the Mouse*. . . . they (both books) both have a lion and a mouse.

Mark: A Tree Map. I am thinking of . . . about Leo . . . what he looks like . . . and, um, I think, and what he is like . . . and what he did.

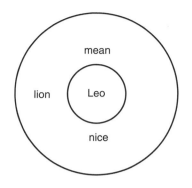

Figure 6.1a   Leo Circle Map

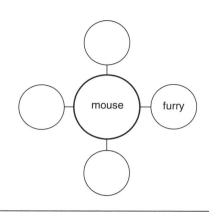

Figure 6.1b   Mouse Bubble Map

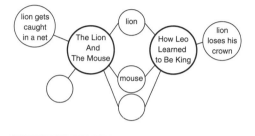

Figure 6.1c   Comparing Two Books Using the Double Bubble Map

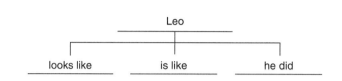

Figure 6.1d   Leo Character Analysis Tree Map

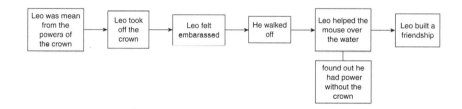

Figure 6.1e   Leo Character Development Flow Map

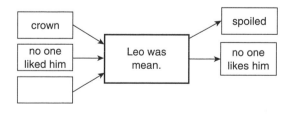

Figure 6.1f   Cause of Leo's Being Mean Multi-Flow Map

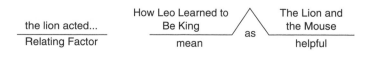

Figure 6.1g   Bridging Qualities of Characters Across Text

Thomas: You could organize it with a Bridge Map. In *The Lion and the Mouse,* the lion was mean to the mouse, but in *How Leo Learned to Be King,* the lion was nice to the mouse by helping him get over the river.

Alexis: You could use a Flow Map. First he was mean. Then when they took off the crown he, like, got a little embarrassed. He walked away, he got surprised, because he met a mouse. And at the end he helped the mouse and *they became friends.*

Regan: Multi-Flow . . . what caused him to be mean. The crown made . . . the crown could have caused him to be mean.

Erin: No one liked him. They took away . . . they didn't want him to be their king.

Shawn: We've got a lot of maps, don't we?

Teacher: That makes me think . . .

Shawn: . . . that we are like second graders!

The discussion among Ms. Smith and her students is within reach of any school, replicable, and may refine and even reframe reading and writing instruction, and even offer a new direction for cognitive science research. This teacher had brought students to such a high level of fluency with Thinking Maps that they could begin to identify text patterns on their own. They were able to use fundamental thinking-skills vocabulary (describing, compare, causes, etc.) and respective cognitive maps (Bubble, Double Bubble, Multi-Flow, etc.) and had the metacognitive awareness of being able to explicitly transfer these processes and tools to reading comprehension through identifying text structures. They were then able to return to their seats with blank sheets of paper and, with varying results, choose a Thinking Map and expand their thinking. They later went on to write about the story using the maps they had chosen to organize their ideas.

This sample of classroom activity is a practical and symbolic representation of a new form of literacy and a transformation of how we perceive the interrelationships between thinking patterns and the fundamentals of reading comprehension.

Thinking and Maps

Thinking Maps are the paper of my mind.

(third-grade student, Mt. Airy)

If text on paper is what we produce for linear communication, Thinking Maps are the paper for the mental mapping that goes on in our brain and through our minds. The U.S. Department of Education–sponsored publication, *Put Reading First* (Armbruster, 2002), targets both semantic maps and graphic organizers as the keys for unlocking text structures and reading comprehension and as bridges to writing prompts. The strength of graphic organizers is the visually scaffolded structure of each form. The weakness is that there is a static nature to many of these templates and an episodic use of the tools by students. There is also a glass ceiling on thinking: Students go from grade to grade, classroom to classroom across schools, often filling in prestructured blanks on a worksheet without much reflection or higher levels of thinking.

As shown above, Thinking Maps provide the dynamic thinking patterns and thus the cognitive link to common text structures. The tools also link these text structures to organization patterns often found in writing prompts, and this is shown in summary form in Figure 6.2. For example, the ability to comprehend a text based on "problem-solution" depends on the student understanding the fundamentals of cause-effect reasoning. Cause-effect reasoning is an essential thinking skill for being able to produce a coherent and well-organized piece of writing in response to a prompt based on prediction (see Chapter 7, Empowering Students).

Reading and Writing: From Phonemic Awareness to Metacognitive Processes

Thinking Maps just happen! They work automatically while I am reading!

(fifth-grade student)

If you accept the premise that we mostly teach and assess using written, spoken, and numeric languages, it is easy to see how we are still caught in the dichotomous debate between phonics and whole language. This debate is nestled within the most heavily researched and publicly financed areas in education, namely, improving literacy. Teachers, researchers, major publishers, and test developers have attempted to synthesize the two sides, yet the practice in the field remains discordant and failed. Our cyclical failures to break through this dichotomy reveal that the problem lies not merely in balancing phonics and whole language or taking a radical swing to one side or the other.

How else does one explain the deficits our nation is experiencing in reading as indicated by National Assessment of Educational Progress (NAEP) scores from 1971 to 2000? NAEP has reported that our at-risk population has improved only slightly despite receiving enormous resources. For our students who are not at risk—those who have the fundamentals of decoding, fluency, and pertinent vocabulary—reading comprehension scores are not much better than they were 25 years ago. It is time to accept the minimal impact on reading comprehension that the present paradigm of research and translations into instruction have made since the 1980s. Why has there been limited change in standardized and performance-assessment scores of reading comprehension despite the enormous effort

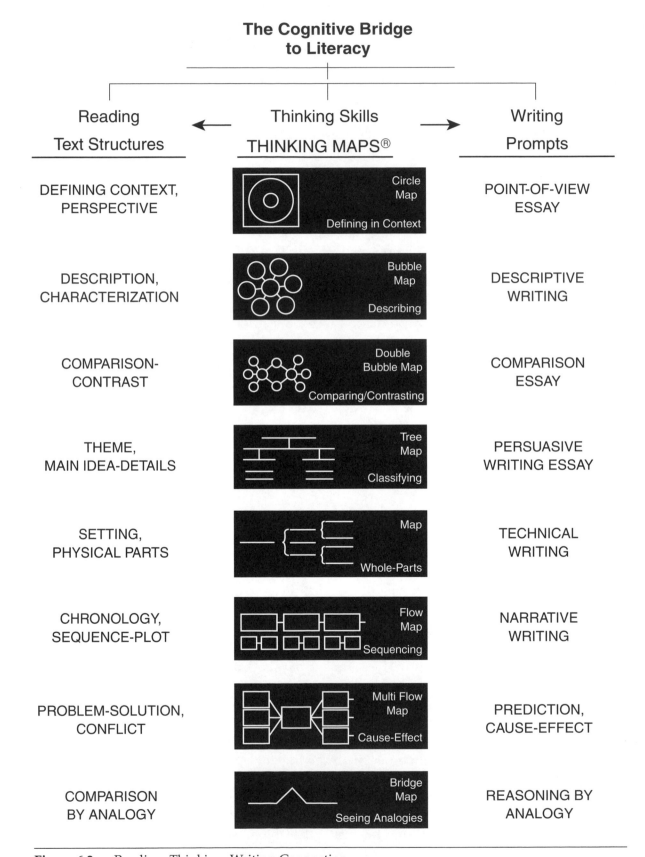

Figure 6.2 Reading, Thinking, Writing Connection

over nearly two decades to overhaul reading comprehension instructional techniques?

Our work with Thinking Maps points to a third way. One missing link is the cognitive *underpinnings, interconnections,* and *interdependencies* between the processes of phonemic awareness, vocabulary learning, and meaning making. Sasha Borenstein (2000), Director of the Kelter Center for Literacy Development that serves students from the Los Angeles region, states that

> ... the recent research in the area of literacy done by the National Institute of Child Health and Human Development has documented the need for explicit, systematic instruction in "breaking the code," phonics and word study, as well as in "making meaning" strategies for comprehension. The research supports an active, thoughtful instructional approach rather than a return to repetitive, passive work. (Hyerle, 2000, pp. 108–109)

Reviewing the three areas of the *Put Reading First* (Armbruster, 2002) report distributed widely by the U.S. Department of Education reveals how Thinking Maps provide a cognitive bridge to phonemic awareness, vocabulary instruction, and text comprehension.

Phonemic Awareness

Sasha Borenstein has found that Thinking Maps are a set of tools for helping students to see, break down, and put words back together. Through her work with students who are at risk and falling behind in the Los Angeles area (for a related story from Los Angeles, see Chapter 10, A First Language for Thinking in a Multilingual School), she and her staff have found that Thinking Maps work as microcognitive tools for seeing how to work with words:

> Thinking Maps are flexible, active tools for exploring literacy. The maps are student-centered, pushing learners to discern patterns and interactions in materials and concepts. Thinking Maps are used in discerning the concepts which organize the expectancies and rules of phonics. Performing the sounds of the past tense, /t/, /d/, and /id/, can lead to the understanding that the sound of this morpheme is based upon the last sound in the root word to which it is affixed. The Brace Map is used by students to identify these **part-whole** relationships. Finding the **similarities and differences** between syllable types using the Double Bubble Maps leads to the understanding that each syllable is defined by its vowel. Creating a Flow Map for **sequencing** the spelling of /ch/, ch or tch, /j/, ge or dge, and /k/ k or ck at the end of a word can lead to the concept that the spelling depends upon what type of vowel is in that word. (Hyerle, 2000, pp. 108–109)

The summary page for phonemic awareness research in *Put Reading First* recommends guiding students to categorize phonemes, see part-whole patterns in words, and put them back together through blending. These are key strategies for developing this one area of early reading development while facilitating language and cognitive skills development.

Vocabulary Instruction

A second area of *Put Reading First* focuses on learning vocabulary. Vocabulary learning is a networking process involving not only direct vocabulary learning through word-learning strategies and repetition but also the indirect acquisition of vocabulary in different contexts. This is because the brain is constantly networking bits of information, and the maps facilitate patterning of related words, which become a context for definitions (see Chapter 2, Linking Brain Research to Best Practices).

Returning to the above reading of *How Leo Learned to Be King,* Thinking Maps create multiple pathways for students and teachers to gather vocabulary from the story into several patterns. These are explicit visual patterns that show a word *in context.* When a student independently voiced that the Circle Map could be used, she stated that you put the topic (Leo) in the center and the details around it. The Circle Map is defined by the visual representation of a circle within a circle and by the thinking skill of defining in context. Students learn to use this tool to look for and gather in the outer circle of the map context words, building vocabulary and meaning around a key topic in the center. Contextualization *requires* that students attempt to give definition to a word not just by what precedes it, but often by reading ahead so that the full context may be brought to bear on the word. All eight Thinking Maps are vocabulary builders: In practical and metaphorical terms, they are the scaffolds for the building process.

Text Comprehension

Correlating with NAEP data is the national report explaining that future implications for reading comprehension include evidence-based assessments. Affirming this concern, Donald Graves (1997) asserts that educators and the public are in a frenzy over how to boost reading comprehension scores.

We must teach students how to synthesize and show their thinking. What we have needed is the physiology of reading comprehension, the actual working parts as a reader interacts with text. But what would the working parts look like? Graves writes that when a reader engages with print, in the past we have had no idea what types of thinking are in process. Over twenty years ago, Lauren Resnick (1983) noted that if we cannot produce a more substantial explanation of the internal events that produce improved comprehension, it will be difficult to develop an instructional training approach. She later suggested that research has located a psychological (metacognitive) space, in which educationally powerful effects seem to occur, but it has not yet adequately explained what happens in that space to produce the effects. A synthesis of these reading researchers (DePinto-Piercy, 1998) confirms the need to change our instructional focus. We must move from the panoramic lens of a wide variety of strategic instructional techniques to include a zoom lens for specific instruction focused directly on what students do during the process of reading.

In the document *Put Reading First* (Armbruster, 2002), proficient readers are described as active and purposeful, and strategies are suggested for guiding students to self-monitoring and metacognition. Central to this section of the report is the focus on graphic organizers and maps that support students in identifying text structures within fictional and non-fictional texts. The report states that these visual tools

- help students focus on text structure as they read
- provide students with tools they can use to examine and visually represent relationships in a text
- help students write well-organized summaries of a text

Dr. Bonnie Armbruster, one of the lead authors of *Put Reading First*, was an early leader in the research on text structures. For example, her work showed that using a problem-solution graphic before reading gave students an advanced organizer of this key structure, and their comprehension improved on those specific texts. Of course, texts are not identified as problem–solution or chronology for students, just as quality responses to open-ended writing prompts are not completed by staying inside the lines of a graphic template (see Chapter 7, Empowering Students). Thinking Maps extend this work by having students become fluent in a cognitive and metacognitive toolset for adapting their thinking to varying contexts.

Readers at Risk: A Map for the Roads to Reading Comprehension

When we are out driving in an unfamiliar region, we need a map. The reading comprehension landscape is much more complex as students' eyes hit the page running. Reading instruction traditionally walks students right up to the road of comprehension and says, "Now you're on your own." After being motivated and developing prior knowledge, students had been expected by teachers to cross the road of comprehension alone, greeted on the other side with comprehension questions. Students, especially at-risk children, so often make a run for it, thinking that the faster they get down the page, the better. Then teachers provide "fix-up" or "remedial" strategies when students can't respond to the questions. Lev Vygotsky's (1962) zone of proximal development is the critical region beyond a learner's immediate, autonomous performance, where instructional guidance is crucial. Yet it is exactly in this zone of comprehension where there are limited instructional strategies available.

Rather than dropping students off at the edge of the road, Thinking Maps help them *see* their way through to the end. By guiding them across an unfamiliar text with Thinking Maps, we are providing direct instruction for using reading strategies independently. Providing direct Thinking Map instruction for use *during* reading allows students to cross the reading comprehension road safely. Ultimately, Thinking Map instruction for reading and writing provides students with instruction beyond what- and how-to-use strategies. Thinking Maps require students to understand why and when to use them. Strategic reading behavior—and writing processes—require that it is the learner who selects an action for a specific purpose. It is the intentional self-selection of and self-regulation of a particular strategy to achieve a specific goal that is the critical component of strategic reading behavior (See Chapter 3, Leveling The Playing Field for All Students).

Literacy in a New Language

My Thinking Maps have power. I have all these ideas and nowhere to put them. Thinking Maps let me get them out!

(first-grade student, Mt. Airy School)

The outcomes described above have been attained because of ongoing professional development commitment within the unit of change that makes a difference for individual students over time: the whole school. The whole faculty of the Mt. Airy school were and still are committed to ongoing training. Teachers left the initial training in Thinking Maps with the goal of explicitly training their students to use these tools independently, in cooperative groups, and for the whole class, thus supporting them in internalizing the tools for direct transfer to content learning and process outcomes. The central outcome of the initial training and ongoing follow-up design is represented not only in the high-quality first-grade classroom conversation at Mt. Airy School, but in the quantitative results on the school's state assessments. Following the first year's implementation of Thinking Maps, writing scores realized a 15% increase on the state-mandated assessment, the Maryland State Performance Assessment Program. Later, Mt. Airy Elementary rose from being a school in the middle of testing to becoming the highest performing school of the 21 elementary schools in Carroll County.

In addition, the No Child Left Behind legislation requires that each state test content knowledge and how well students perform. Maryland meets this requirement by using the new 2003 Maryland School Assessments. The cornerstone for Maryland's accountability system is the measure of Annual Yearly Progress (AYP). Again this year, Mt. Airy Elementary is the highest performing school in the county. Mt. Airy's scores are higher than the Maryland state average and higher than the county average, remarkably achieving AYP in all eight subgroups, including special education. The results across our student population show that literacy and cognitive development work together as teachers help students cross the road to reading comprehension with Thinking Maps as a new language for literacy.

To move beyond the inadequacies of past research and practice and to shift literacy to a new form requires a shift in tools and a mind shift by leaders. Literacy alone is not power in the age of information and technology, multicultural and multilingual communication, and global economies (see Chapter 14, The Singapore Experience). A new critical literacy is required, based on research showing that phonemic awareness and metacognitive strategies must develop together with vocabulary development and comprehension strategies across first *and* second languages. Many students, and unfortunately most at-risk students, are given an overwhelming, repetitious panoply of strategies that merely heighten their awareness of words without deepening their comprehension abilities. From our experiences and results, we have found, however, that students are not left behind on the road to reading comprehension when given tools for actively reflecting on how they are thinking and the patterns emerging from text.

7

Empowering Students From Thinking to Writing

Jane Buckner, Ed.S.

Topics to be discussed:

- writing as thinking from a developmental viewpoint
- the Tree and Flow Maps as organizing structures for developing written expression
- results from Thinking Maps® schools using a common language for thinking and writing

It is time for a writing revolution in America. In September 2002, the College Board—composed of more than 4300 schools and colleges—established the National Commission on Writing in America's Schools and Colleges. The decision to create the Commission was motivated in part because of a decision by the Board to make a writing assessment part of the new SAT beginning in 2005. However, a greater impetus for the study was due to a growing concern within the education and business communities regarding the quality of student writing.

In April 2003, the Commission issued a report, *The Neglected "R,"* that revealed disturbing findings regarding the writing proficiency of students in the United States (the College Board, 2003). Among those finding was the fact that most fourth graders spend less than three hours per week writing. This is 15% of the amount of time they spend watching television each week. At grades four, eight, and twelve, only 50% of students assessed met basic requirements for writing, while only 20% were considered to be proficient. In addition, 66% of high school seniors do not write a three-page paper as often as once a month for their English teachers. Further findings revealed that 50% of college freshmen are not able to produce papers that are relatively free of language errors. It is estimated that these writing weaknesses of incoming college students cost campuses up to one billion dollars annually for remediation. Unfortunately, this writing deficiency is spilling over into the business world as business leaders complain about the writing skills of new employees. This grim picture was the motivation for numerous recommendations presented in *The Neglected "R."*

The Commission called for a major effort to improve teacher training in writing to include all discipline areas, as well as a greater allocation of time devoted to student writing instruction both during the school day and in the form of daily homework assignments. The Commission acknowledged that our problems regarding writing proficiency did not occur overnight and that in order to fix the problem "the amount of time and money devoted to student writing must be dramatically increased in school districts throughout the country, and state and local curriculum guidelines must require writing in every curriculum at all grade levels." In addition, the Commission report suggests that writing has been shortchanged in the school reform movement launched 20 years ago and, since writing has not received the attention it deserves, the acquisition of proficient writing skills now must be put squarely in the center of the school agenda beginning in elementary school.

As schools look to invest effort into developing writing proficiency, they need to find a high-quality writing approach and professional development plan that systematically supports the writing process from idea generation to the final product as well as writing development from the early grades through high school. Currently, schools across the nation have improved whole-school writing performance through comprehensive training in a developmental K–12 writing framework: *Write . . . From the Beginning* (Buckner, 2000) and *Write . . . for the Future* (Buckner & Johnson, 2002). Both frameworks utilize Thinking Maps as the foundational tools to teach the thinking patterns and processes involved in composing in the narrative and expository domains, thus uniting writing *explicitly* with thinking.

DEVELOPING COMPOSITION

Child development experts contend that writing proficiency begins with oral communication well before the elementary grades. From the moment of birth, children use their newly developed lungs to communicate with those around them. Caregivers soon learn to distinguish among the different cries of an infant and to associate those cries with the specific needs of their young charges. As children grow into toddlers, language begins to develop, and the early babbles and coos become decipherable verbiage through which the child learns to communicate. At approximately the same time that language is developing, fine motor control is developing, thereby enabling these youngsters to make their first written marks on the world, often in the form of crayon scribbles in inappropriate places.

By the age of three, a child's scribbles become more decipherable, yet primitive, drawings that represent something or someone in the child's world. For a developmental period, drawing actually becomes the child's form of written communication. Once the child is exposed to picture books, environmental print, and the opportunity to observe adults engaging in writing, an awareness of the distinguishing attributes of written communication develops and the child comes to the understanding that a message is communicated through the written word as well as through pictures. At this point, the child seeks to imitate what he has observed.

The earliest attempts to imitate writing often appear to be squiggles and nonsense to the untrained eye. However, the value of these scribbles and squiggles has been documented as an indicator of early developmental stages in writing. Marie Clay (1975), among others, has studied extensively these early writings of children and has described certain principles children must master in order to make marks that resemble writing. Clay maintains that seven basic principles must be learned by children before they can be said to write, and that many of these principles may be seen emerging in the scribbles of children before anyone notices that they are trying to produce real writing. With repeated writing practice, children will produce marks, according to Clay, that resemble more and more the writing they see in print around them. At first the child's writing will appear as a form of "mock" writing. Over a period of time, and with opportunities for practice, the writing becomes decipherable. For this reason, children in preschool and kindergarten should be encouraged to engage in writing throughout the school day. In some instances the teacher will provide a model for writing, while in other instances the teacher will facilitate spontaneous and self-selected writing engagement.

Once students have begun to communicate with confidence through the written word and can produce several sentences using inventive spelling, they are ready for formal instruction in writing in much the same way that they become ready for formal instruction in reading. Just as a teacher's manual serves as a valuable resource to provide a guide for the how-to of reading instruction, Thinking Maps can and have been used by teachers to facilitate, enhance, and expedite the acquisition of writing proficiency for students from the primary grades through high school. Reading and writing share common text structures, and for this reason each is taught most effectively through a step-by-step cumulative process, vertically aligned from one grade level to the next.

Writing as Thinking

In an effort to alleviate the writing fears of their students, teachers have been known to tell their charges that writing is just "talk written down." This statement is a gross oversimplification of a complex process—writing is actually "thinking written down." Perhaps one reason for inefficiencies in student writing is connected to this misunderstanding. To write well, one must first think well about what is to be communicated. The foundation of formal writing instruction begins with the essential understanding of the purpose for writing, as well as the various organizational patterns that can be used to accomplish this purpose. These patterns correspond to the types of thinking that are involved for a reader to be able to comprehend the writer's message. Each organizational pattern needed for writing can be visually represented by one of the eight Thinking Maps, depending on the specific purpose for writing. For example, the purpose of narrative writing is to entertain through relating a story or memorable experience in sequential order; therefore, a Flow Map would be used to organize the writing. Teachers who consistently model the use of Thinking Maps for organizing writing have witnessed increased writing proficiency in their students and in their schools.

Within the past several years, more and more states have begun to implement an assessment to ensure writing proficiency in their students. In Florida, for example, all fourth-grade students are assessed annually on either narrative writing or expository writing to explain why. A passing score is a 3.0 on a 6-point holistic scale. In 1999, the percentage of fourth-grade students passing the FCAT writing assessment at Brookshire Elementary School in Orange County, Florida, was approximately 84%. The goal of the teachers and administration at this site was to move their overall school grade of C to an A by targeting improvement in their writing scores. Kindergarten through fifth-grade teachers participated in training at the beginning of the school year in the use of Thinking Maps in all curriculum areas. Follow-up sessions focused exclusively on using Thinking Maps for organizing and modeling writing. Teachers were taught the specific attributes of both narrative and expository writing, as well as the thought processes and Thinking Maps to use with each.

Following the training, a spiraled curriculum plan for teaching writing using consistent visual tools was implemented schoolwide. Grade-level training sessions for writing were held to ensure that teachers knew how to model the use of the Thinking Maps for organizing writing with their students and how to demonstrate taking the information "off of the map" and onto the page. All teachers had the opportunity to observe demonstration lessons using Thinking Maps for student writing. The administration monitored and supported the teachers' efforts, providing individual assistance as needed. Within one year, the number of students passing the writing assessment had risen to approximately 97%. At the end of the second year, every student taking the FCAT writing assessment scored at least a passing 3.0 and the school achieved a state grade of A.

This same escalation of writing scores can occur all the way through secondary school as students are taught to plan and organize their writing using Thinking Maps. In 1995, Melba Johnson, a high school English teacher in Brunswick County, North Carolina, attended Thinking Maps training and immediately utilized the maps in her classroom to teach her students how to organize for writing. Within one semester, the scores of her students taking the tenth-grade state English II Writing Examination on literary analysis rose five points. One year later, Melba attended training on the use of Thinking Maps specifically for the teaching of writing, and for the last five semesters of her teaching career, 100% of her students passed the high school English II Writing Examination. The only difference in her instruction was teaching her students how to use Thinking Maps to plan and organize for writing based on the specific purpose and thought processes involved in the assignment. In addition, Melba experienced the same success with her eleventh- and twelfth-grade advanced placement students by using this same process.

Structures for Organization

While single classrooms can experience success, the most effective use of Thinking Maps for teaching writing involves whole-school commitment and vertical alignment of writing instruction. The nonplagiarized, authentic research report that is difficult for many upper elementary and secondary students can be made easier if, beginning in first grade, students learn how to use a Tree Map to organize information by categories prior to writing. For example, a first-grade student has written a report about his favorite vegetable. Prior to writing, the student organized his information on a Tree Map (Figure 7.1) according to the categories of information about which he would be writing. Note the correlation between the categories on the Tree Map and the organization of the writing.

By organizing in this manner, the writer ensures better comprehension by his reader since the writing is set up like a familiar reading text structure. Another familiar text structure found in literature is the presentation of a series of events in sequential order to establish a story line. Another first-grade student uses a Flow Map to organize her writing to tell a story about what her grandmother did when she came home (Figure 7.2). The sequence of the Flow Map will become the sequence of the writing. Writing to "explain why" requires the writer to take a stance or make a choice that is supported with reasons. This type of writing has yet another organizational pattern which can be represented with a partial Multi-Flow Map. Figure 7.3 is a sample of writing by a first-grade student to explain why a certain food is her favorite snack.

The teacher had modeled repeatedly how to use a Circle Map and a partial Multi-Flow Map to develop reasons and to organize for writing. The student began by brainstorming all of her favorite snacks in a Circle Map. Once this was done, the student was instructed to make a choice regarding the food about which she would write and to compose a

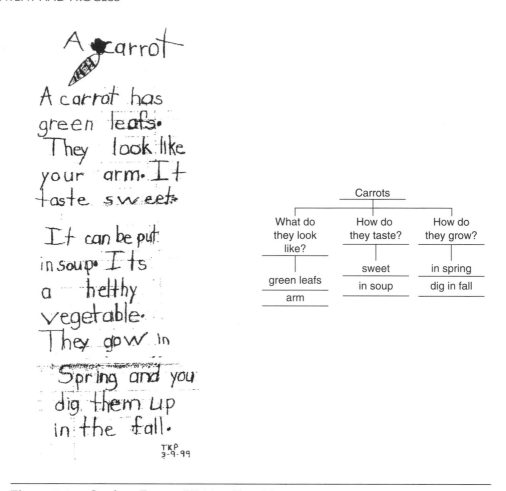

Figure 7.1   Student Report-Writing Tree Map

Figure 7.2   Student Narrative-Writing Flow Map

sentence about her favorite snack and write it in the center box of the partial Multi-Flow Map. Next, the student engaged in thinking about "what caused me to select this snack as my favorite" or "what are the reasons why this snack is my favorite" and then recorded her thoughts in

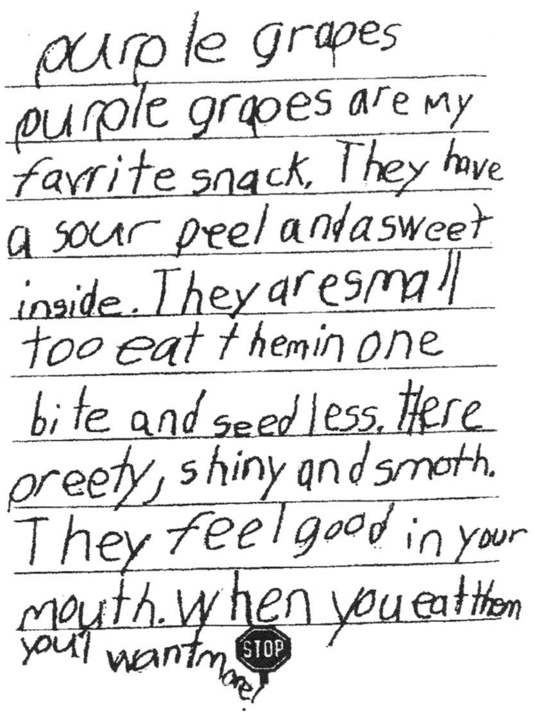

purple grapes
purple grapes are my
favrite snack. They have
a sour peel and a sweet
inside. They are small
too eat them in one
bite and seedless. Here
preety, shiny and smooth.
They feel good in your
mouth. When you eat them
you'l want more!

Figure 7.3   Writing-to-Explain-Why Multi-Flow Map

the small boxes on the left-hand side of the map. The teacher had explained that when others read her writing, they will be thinking about her choice and her reasons for that choice.

An example of narrative writing by a second-grade student who used Thinking Maps to help him plan and organize for writing shows that this student has combined two Thinking Maps to plan his writing by creating a "Flee" Map (Figure 7.4). This is a combination of the Flow Map for sequencing events and the Tree Map for recording details related to those events. The flexibility of the maps allows students to combine maps as needed when engaging in a task that requires more than one thought process. Had the student used only the Flow Map, his writing could become nothing more than a sequence of events that reads like a list. The elaboration or details related to each event are planned on lines borrowed from the Tree Map and located just under each of the stages or events. Note also that the Flow Map is nonlinear in appearance, allowing the student to plan a beginning and ending to his story.

As students mature, the Thinking Maps used for writing become more sophisticated in appearance; however, the correlation between the maps, the thinking, and the writing is still apparent. Figure 7.5 is a recreation of a visual representation of eight-year-old Cagney's thinking about her favorite summer vacation and the reasons why it is her favorite. She begins with a partial Multi-Flow Map to develop her reasons; she then uses a combination of a Flow Map and a Tree Map (Flee Map) to organize the parts of her writing, to decide the most appropriate sequence for presenting her reasons, and to plan

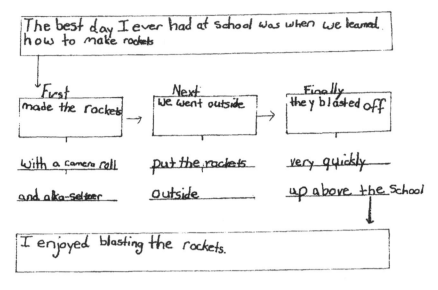

Figure 7.4 Combining Sequence and Details in Narrative Writing

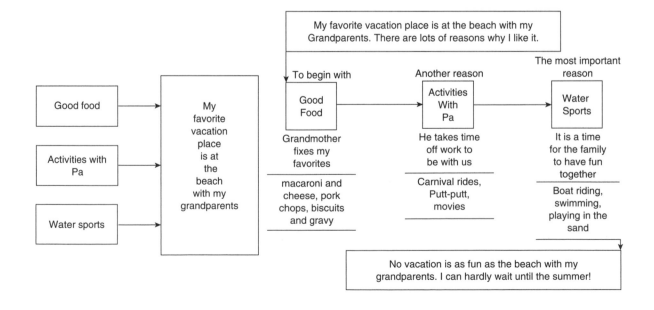

Figure 7.5 Using a Multi-Flow and "Flee" Map to Plan Expository Writing

the elaboration of her selected reasons. By the time Cagney wrote her essay, the hard part, the thinking, had already been done. It is important to notice in this example how multiple patterns of thinking—based on common, well-defined, and flexible graphic structures—are adapted by the student in order to progress to more complex thinking and more elegant writing.

Thinking Maps for writing can be valuable to the global learner as well (see Chapter 4, Tools for Integrating Theories and Differentiating Practice). In every classroom, there are those students who do not grasp the concept of putting together a piece of writing from the part to the whole as it is often modeled by teachers. With these students, teachers can use a process referred to as "reverse mapping," in which the teacher assists the student in analyzing his essay from the whole to its parts. The teacher provides a blank template of the Thinking Map that is used for organizing that particular type of writing, and the student cuts apart a copy of his essay and places the parts on the template. The student can immediately see the "holes" which represent the parts of the essay that are underdeveloped. At this point the student can create the needed information and fill the "holes." The flexibility of the Thinking Maps empowers teachers to adjust instruction to the individual needs of students.

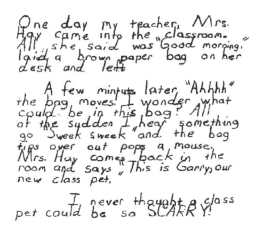

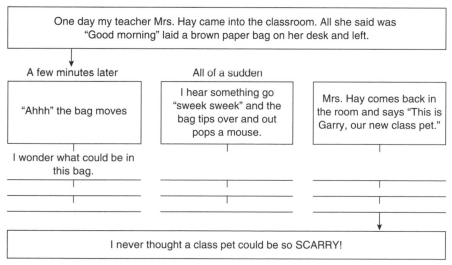

Figure 7.6 Reverse Mapping for Revision and Elaboration

Eight-year-old Alecia was a student who needed individualized assistance in her understanding of the components of narrative writing. She was attentive in class and conscientious about completing her assignments correctly. However, as she tried to use the Thinking Maps modeled by her teacher for organizing writing, she often produced an underdeveloped story. Using the reverse mapping procedure, the teacher was able to instruct Alecia in how to develop her story more fully. Alecia's work has been reverse mapped with teacher assistance (Figure 7.6).

Precision of Thought and Language

Learning the organizational structure for different domains of writing is a first step for students. However, there must be a focus on the quality of the content of that writing as well. Word choice and clear, precise language give life, color, and voice to a piece of writing. One of the 16 habits of mind for developing thinking is defined as *precision of language* (Costa & Kallick, 2000). Many of the Thinking Maps have proven to be effective in helping students to achieve this goal. For example, when a student is contemplating how to describe a noun such as *cactus* in his writing, he must consider two things: the words he could use and the words he should use. As Mark Twain said, "The difference between the right word and almost the right word is the difference between lightning and a lightning bug."

Understandably, upon first sight, teachers often construe the Bubble Map as just another brainstorming web, but as defined within the Thinking Maps model, this tool is based on the cognitive process of identifying and describing the attributes of things, not all of one's associated ideas (which is easily accomplished using the Circle Map). This precision of definition of the cognitive skill of identifying attributes using the Bubble Map guides students to more precise word usage, vocabulary development that then can be used effectively to help the students with this task. In this example, the word *cactus* is placed in the center of the Bubble Map, and the student records adjectives and adjective phrases in the smaller bubbles surrounding it. The immediate goal for the student is to think of as many adjectives as possible that could be used to describe the word *cactus*. The next step is for the student to evaluate the adjectives selected and to determine the most appropriate and precise one to use. The quality of writing will improve when the student uses tools and strategies that help him to ponder and wrestle with language in the same way that a sculptor, singer, or athlete wrestles to develop a particular skill.

Quality Assessment Tools

As governors and legislators incorporate writing into state school standards, a new commitment to measuring writing quality is sure to follow. Multiple choice tests used in the past are likely to disappear, as a new commitment to measuring writing quality will result in requiring students to produce a piece of prose that someone reads and evaluates for quality.

Also on the education horizon lies a swing away from current assessments that dictate the type, or domain, of writing a student must use to respond to a prompt, thereby requiring that the student have a repertoire of writing domains from which to select.

Recently the state of Texas implemented just such a writing assessment that allows students the choice of how to respond to a given prompt. When given either an "on demand" or an "extended time" writing task, success for these students lies in the knowledge of various visual tools for organizing the information they wish to present. Through extended exposure and practice, the student will acquire a repertoire of organizational tools for writing and will be able to select appropriately the organizing tool that best accomplishes the purpose of the writing task. In addition, with practice in the thought processes related to the quality of the content of writing, an overall improvement in writing proficiency will occur.

While Thinking Maps have been used as effective tools for improving writing, the greatest proficiency occurs when the students also understand how to assess quality in their own writing. Most state assessments are scored using a focused, holistic scoring guide. The holistic score that is given assesses a "general impression" and is useful as a snapshot of writing achievement. However, holistic scoring provides little information that can be used to plan and develop subsequent instruction geared to improving writing proficiency. According to a recent publication of the International Reading Association, analytic scoring, unlike holistic general impression scoring, looks at multiple elements or characteristics associated with effective writing and provide the most information from which to draw conclusions about writers and writings. As an assessment system, analytic scoring offers information that can best assist instruction because each element in writing is evaluated separately, with each characteristic marked on a scale that indicates how well it has been presented.

Students who are trained in analytic scoring rubrics and understand the meaning of "quality content" have a better chance to be successful on writing assessments. Giving students the tools such as Thinking Maps to organize their writing and a means to self-evaluate the quality of their content is the very least that teachers should provide during writing instruction.

Sharing the Language of Writing

For years there have been those in education who have believed that writing is a special language owned by English teachers. We know, however, that this can no longer be the case. Writing must now become the responsibility of all grade levels and all curriculum areas. If we view writing as intimately linked to teaching thinking and recognizing organizational patterns in text structure, then teachers of all subjects teach writing. The Thinking Maps provide teachers and student with a visual language for transferring both writing and thinking skills into every content area. Precise language, transition words, and reasons of elaboration are part of expository writing in textbooks that students need to comprehend while reading. If students transferred these writing skills from one subject to another, writing could improve. While this is not an easy task, it is one that can be accomplished with appropriate teacher training and commitment. Teachers must be empowered with knowledge about writing before they can be the most effective models for their students. If we expect students to write effectively, then our job as educators is to model how to build a bridge between what is within the heart and mind of the student and the written word. This bridge can and should be in the form of visual tools that help students construct the information they wish to relate.

Writing is not an easy task; it is a skill that takes time to develop in both teachers and their students. It involves becoming aware of patterns of thinking and knowing how to build a strong organizational structure. It engages students' creative and analytical minds as they audition words for themselves and for their readers. The goal of writing should be always to "go for better" and not settle for *red* when *crimson* is the word you need. Most important, writing is an act of courage, a willingness to share oneself with others. It is that skill that allows us to leave a part of ourselves in the world when we are gone; it is that symphony of sounds that allows us to understand the hearts and minds of those who have gone before us; it is that essential skill that we must give to those students who are entrusted to us.

The Challenge of High-Stakes Testing in Middle School Mathematics

Janie B. MacIntyre, M. Ed.

Topics to be discussed:

- examples of students moving from concrete to abstract mathematical concepts using Thinking Maps®
- multiple-year results from research on Thinking Maps applied to procedural knowledge by special needs students
- fostering clear and meaningful communication between students and teachers in mathematics classrooms

FACING MYSELF AND MY STUDENTS

In the early 1990s, North Carolina initiated major educational reforms that continue to become more rigorous. Student proficiency must be demonstrated on annual statewide math and reading end-of-grade tests for elementary and middle schools. Secondary school assessment is conducted through end of course tests in core areas. Student performance and proficiency is directly linked to promotion, unit credit, and graduation. With the knowledge that students with special needs would have to meet the same standards as their regular education counterparts in order to be eligible to receive a high school diploma, a pivotal personal and professional realization occurred. Morally, and with full awareness that my students were counting on me and others like me, it became essential to find and develop strategies that would allow them to adapt to and compensate for learning difficulties, differences, and deficits in order to have an opportunity to earn what would represent the pinnacle of formal education for many of my students: a high school diploma.

Prior to the reforms, the underachieving students in my seventh-through ninth-grade mathematics classes at George R. Edwards School in Rocky Mount, NC—both those coded learning disabled and those achieving in the lower quartile—performed basic computation for whole numbers and decimals, learned to tell time to the nearest 5 minutes, made change for purchases of under $20, and, perhaps, studied fractions. Today, my students have made cognitive leaps and are successfully mastering concepts of solid and plane geometry, exponents and scientific notation, two-step equations, and graphing linear and nonlinear systems of equations to mention only a few. Students are truly light-years ahead of where they were and are able to access and master those concepts, as our research has shown, because of Thinking Maps.

From the onset of Thinking Maps implementation within the instructional process, I have been astounded by the ease with which learning disabled and regular education students have been able to not only grasp new concepts but also demonstrate comprehension and application with accuracy. For over a decade, our teachers have observed that Thinking Maps provide the vehicle by which special needs students are able to adapt to and effectively compensate for learning difficulties and perceptual deficits with tremendous efficiency and success. This inherently concise, consistent, and flexible visual language transcends age and ability and aids students by providing accurate, concrete connections between that which is already known and new skills to be acquired. For example, by using a Circle and Frame Map with my students (see Figure 8.1), I was able to connect the concrete ideas of coordinate planes within a real-world context for their reference.

While I intuitively knew the value of Thinking Maps from over a decade of results gained from examples as shown in the figure, I also knew that in today's data-driven field of education, increases in student performance need to be stated in observable, measurable, and replicable terms in order to be valid. I used my opportunity as a Christa McAuliffe Fellow in 1999–2000 to conduct a control group study to determine the impact of Thinking Maps on math achievement. I found that after an entire year of Thinking Maps implementation, exceptional and regular education

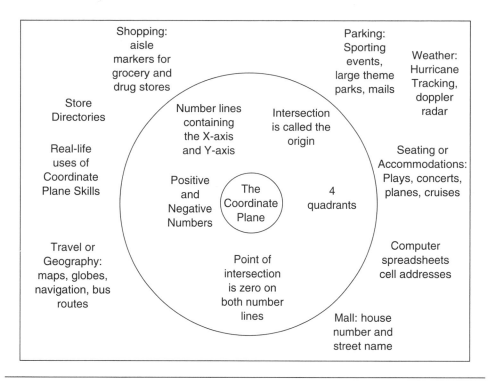

Figure 8.1   Coordinate Plane Circle and Frame Map

students' end-of-grade test results indicated developmental gains of up to four year's growth in one year's time.

BEYOND INTUITION

During the first two years of integrating Thinking Maps, I had a variety of experiences that convinced me that Thinking Maps positively influence student performance. Many times in sharing student accomplishments I was told, "Yes, but Janie, you are a wonderful teacher." In response I would state, "I know I'm a good teacher, but this is not my magic, this is because of Thinking Maps!" I used Thinking Maps throughout all stages of the instructional process: from determining prior knowledge of a given topic through directed and independent instruction, to assessment and self-evaluation of curricular growth. If we were working on a particular skill, I could use the same tool to differentiate instruction depending upon the developmental level of the students involved. In Figures 8.2a and 8.2b, two students were working through a process of how to make a graph using a Flow Map for sequencing. Notice the different levels of sophistication each student applied.

In Figure 8.3, another map, the Bridge Map, used for analogies, was applied to transfer familiar language to the mathematical language needed for this concept. This is just one example in which Thinking Maps scaffold the learning of mathematical language and processes.

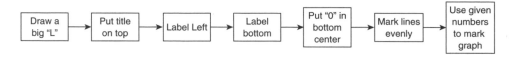

Figure 8.2a How to Create a Graph Level 1 Flow Map

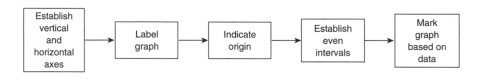

Figure 8.2b How to Create a Graph Level 2 Flow Map

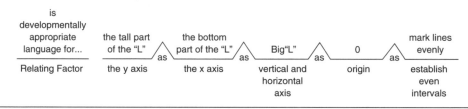

Figure 8.3 Bridge Map for Building Math Language

Not only did the maps foster students' increased personal awareness of their individual cognitive and metacognitive style, but they allowed me to get a glimpse of students' metacognition, thus enabling me to assess areas of inherent student strength and weakness.

As a result of this type of instruction in my math classes, 6 out of 11 special needs students scored "proficient" or "exceeds expectations" in math. Eighth graders were learning 46% beyond what they were expected to learn in one year's time, with one student demonstrating a remarkable 21-point gain in developmental growth. In an even more needy population, in an intensive math remediation class for ninth graders who had previously failed the eighth-grade exit exam, 84% passed the retest. It was apparent that when Thinking Maps applications were incorporated consistently and frequently within the math instructional process, these exceptional students were able to demonstrate, on average, two years' worth of growth in one year.

RESULTS: GAINS IN DEVELOPMENTAL GROWTH

In 1999–2000, I was selected to serve as the North Carolina Christa McAuliffe Fellow. I structured independent research in order to measure the impact and statistical significance of Thinking Maps instruction on North Carolina eighth grade end-of-grade developmental growth of lower-achieving students in math. The research targeted the 291 lower-achieving, rising eighth graders in the Nash-Rocky Mount School System. The schools in Rocky Mount, located in eastern North Carolina, serve both an inner city and rural population of middle to lower class families. Over time the area has changed from an agricultural economy of mainly tobacco farms to a more diverse economy including bank, restaurant, mechanical engineering, and biotechnology headquarters and facilities. The student body also reflects this diversity, with about 50% of students African American and 50% white, including a small migrant and ESL population.

Approximately 30 systemwide eighth-grade math teachers attended Thinking Maps professional development throughout the year, including monthly follow-up sessions that provided model and videotaped demonstration lessons, classroom observations, and coaching opportunities, as well as assistance in the collection of anecdotal evidence and documentation logs indicating the frequency and types of Thinking Maps being used. Participants were provided with over 200 Thinking Maps applications in math that were aligned to all curricular goals and objectives and the state-adopted text.

Due to the pre- and posttest design model used by the state to determine a student's developmental growth, test scores from sixth and seventh grades determined developmental growth prior to Thinking Maps applications. Seventh- and eighth-grade scores determined developmental growth subsequent to the implementation of research strategies. Therefore, North Carolina End-of-Grade Math Tests for three consecutive years were mandatory in order to be included in the project's comparisons. A variety of factors may prevent the administration of a test to individual students, including illness, exemption, transfers into a system, or moving. Of the 291 students identified in the research, 133 students possessed all 3 consecutive years' scores. Based on individual performance, the increases in the developmental growth of these students after Thinking Maps strategies were implemented are significant.

The average developmental growth of the exceptional children as eighth graders at all three school sites for the 1997–1998 and 1998–1999 school years, prior to the implementation of the McAuliffe Fellowship Project in 1999–2000, is shown in Figure 8.5. I included data from the students in my classes ("MacIntyre") who had used the Thinking Maps during both the 1997–1998 and 1998–1999 school years. The students in my classes exceeded exemplary growth in both years, and in one case, almost as much as seven times that of seventh graders at another site. Also shown are the scores that indicate the 1999 pretest and 2000 posttest developmental growth scores for eighth graders who participated in the Thinking Maps implementation during the McAuliffe Fellowship in 1999–2000.

School Sites	Exceptional Children Developmental Growth in Math	
	1997–1998	1998–1999
Expected	5	3.8
Exemplary	5.5	4.3
Edwards	6.25	3.7
Nash Central	4.33	1.6
So. Junior	3.88	2.7
MacIntyre	7.3	7.6

Figure 8.4 Test Results for 7th-Grade Developmental Growth

School Sites	McAuliffe Fellowship Developmental Growth 1999-2000	
	Pretest	Postest
Expected	3.8	3.7
Exemplary	4.3	4.2
Edwards	4.93	8.02
Nash Central	1.28	6.94
So. Junior	1.33	9.71

Figure 8.5 Test Results for 8th-Grade Developmental Growth

At the time of the 1999 pretest, expected developmental growth for these students was 3.8 points, while exemplary developmental growth was 4.3 points. As the graphic indicates, the actual pretest developmental rowth for the students involved in the research was measured at 1.28 points for Nash Central Junior High School and 1.33 points at Southern Nash Junior High School. Therefore, at the time of the pretest, only students at Edwards Junior High School, who had to some extent utilized Thinking Maps, met the expected growth. In fact, they exceeded it.

In the 2000 posttest, given after Thinking Maps implementation, the results show a fivefold increase in the average developmental growth scores of the research participants at Nash Central Junior High School and a sevenfold increase in the average developmental growth scores at Southern Nash Junior High School. As expected, the more profound change in individual developmental growth occurred overall at our sister schools that had not previously used Thinking Maps at all. The less dramatic increase in scores at Edwards could have been due to my six-week absence from my classroom to conduct the Thinking Maps training as part of my fellowship. Of the 133 formerly labeled low-achieving students, 71 demonstrated proficiency on the first trial.

What we have learned about Thinking Maps during this era of high-stakes testing and accountability continues to evolve, but this study confirmed two findings: (1) When Thinking Maps are utilized in daily math instruction, student learning and demonstration of mastery exceeds exemplary developmental growth expectations on state tests; (2) Thinking Map strategies and applications in math are replicable.

THINKING MAPS: A BRIDGE TO SUCCESS

The statistics indicate considerable growth in mathematical achievement, so how and why does applying Thinking Maps in math instruction improve math ability as measured on these tests? Qualitative results in the form of student and teacher anecdotal reports and instructional logs indicate that Thinking Maps support mathematical thinking by enabling students and teachers to clearly and visually explain, understand, monitor, and assess mathematical processes and problems.

Students who typically find math enjoyable and readily grasp new concepts are those who have developed and utilize analytical skills. According to some researchers, "giving students advanced organizers does have the desired effect of increasing recall of critical information" (Deshler, Schumaker, Lenz, & Ellis, 1984). In addition, students with learning disabilities "experience deficits in cognitive processes including disorganization, acquisition, retrieval, integration or association, expression, sequencing, analyzing, and evaluating information," according to Wallace and McLoughlin (1988). With Thinking Maps, teachers are able to graphically demonstrate and model analytical thinking to students, furthering opportunities for them to develop, practice, enhance, and apply the analytical skills necessary to be able to truly understand and apply mathematical concepts.

In addition to analytical skills that may be immaturely developed, some students possess learning difficulties, differences, or disabilities that can directly impact math performance. In the following Tree Map, Cecil Mercer's work (1983) has been expanded to include sample Thinking Maps applications (see Figure 8.6). The application of Thinking Maps is directly targeted to diminish the impact of the acquisitional and behavioral problems experienced by learning disabled students in math. From this Tree Map, we can see that language and procedure play a large role in contributing to mathematical understanding.

Students need support not only with the concepts of math, but with the symbols and multiple steps involved in the construction of the concept. In the following multiple map example (Figure 8.7a–c) introducing and explaining "the coordinate plane," teachers and students work together to understand the language, processes, points, and purposes of plotting and using coordinates.

We also know from theories of brain-based research and theories of emotional intelligence (Goleman, 1995) that in order for learning to occur, new information must have either personal relevance and meaning or an emotional connection to the learner. Through the use of Thinking Maps, particularly the Frame of Reference, graphics can be constructed depicting the relevance of math goals to real-life applications in ways that are compatible with the triune brain's innate, natural preferences for pictures, determining patterns, establishing order, making connections, and completing processes. While students should realize that perhaps only in a

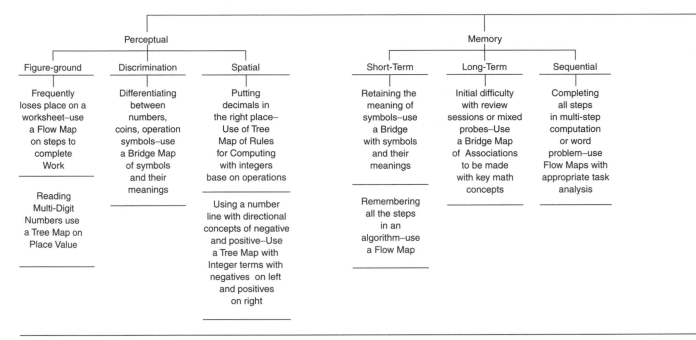

Figure 8.6   Thinking Maps Applications to Diminish Learning Difficulties Tree Map

math class would they be asked to determine the coordinates for a point on the coordinate plane, those skills are utilized often in real-life situations without reference to them specifically by name. Real-life applications can and should be made for every goal and content area to enhance student awareness of personal relevance and the need to acquire those skills.

We can see that Thinking Maps foster clear, deliberate, and meaningful communication between students and teachers. When students are involved in study where instruction is effective, goals are clear, and opportunities for success are frequent, enhanced levels of self-confidence will emerge and render students willing to take more frequent appropriate academic risks leading to upward spirals of student achievement.

In applying the theory that all knowledge is either declarative or procedural to the area of mathematics, declarative knowledge would include content vocabulary, theorems, laws, rules, and contributions of mathematicians—the factually based, continually true information, the absolutes. Procedural knowledge would include everything else: How to bisect an angle or use the Pythagorean theorem to determine a missing measurement of a right triangle; how to graph a point on a coordinate plane; and how to determine the mean, median, mode, and range of a set of data are all examples involving procedural knowledge. Because of the inherent procedural nature of math, the list could go on and on. Using a Flow Map for a procedure, students can guide themselves or can be guided from where they presently function toward the acquisition and subsequent mastery of curricular goals with amazing rates of growth.

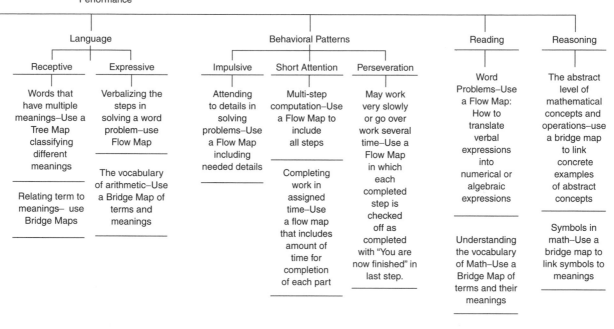

A student from Edwards Junior High explained how Thinking Maps scaffolded her learning by translating abstract thinking processes and mathematical processes into explicit and tangible visual representations: "Thinking Maps help me in math class by explaining something complex or abstract in a simple way. They allow you to see where you have made your mistake, and how TO SHOW your math in words that make sense. I wish someone had taught me math this way before. Now, I can understand exactly what we're doing in class." The student added, "The more we use Thinking Maps, the more I understand, and the easier the work becomes to do."

Teachers also celebrate the changes in student's organizational ability, self-efficacy, and attitude toward learning. "Students get excited and are becoming much better at organizing and maintaining their 'map' notes . . . students are consciously aware of wanting to have their math Thinking Maps with them. The students know the tools are helping and will refer to previous maps to verify their current work. It is very encouraging to me to assist students to develop strategies that enable them to become independent learners." Students and teachers indicated that Thinking Maps fostered students' ability to articulate how they were thinking or to reflect with a metacognitive stance in order to self-assess. Students who previously had trouble organizing now had a predictable road map that they could navigate.

Math teachers in general have a tendency to be highly organized and analytical. Because that can be such a natural part of our way of thinking,

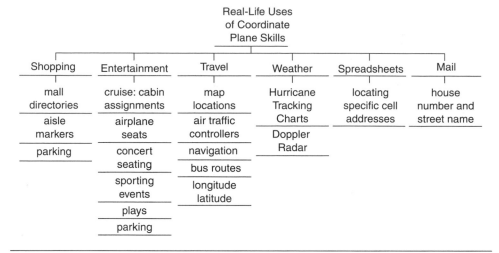

Figure 8.7a Coordinate Plane Tree Map

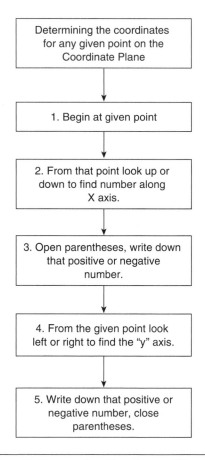

Figure 8.7b Determining Points on the Coordinate Plane Flow Map

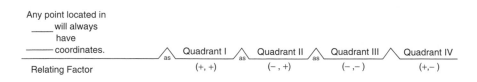

Figure 8.7c Finding Points on the Coordinate Plane Bridge Map

our frame of reference, we sometimes fail to remember that others don't necessarily think that way, particularly adolescents who are still developing cognitively. The use of the Flow Map for procedural knowledge acquisition in math forces that highly organized, analytical teacher to view concepts and skills from the student's perspective in order to determine what is truly needed to ensure student mastery while incorporating the language that is developmentally appropriate for that particular group of students.

The Flow Map used for sequencing is the same graphic design when used in math, English, science, social studies, PE, art, foreign language, or any other class being taught. This repetitive and consistent link to cognition is extremely positive and beneficial in helping students, particularly students identified as having special needs, to become more efficient and organized in their thinking across all facets of educational pursuit. This success breeds increases in self-esteem and the willingness of students to take appropriate academic and responsive risks during the instructional process. Through the use and internalization of this consistent language, students are enabled to quite literally state a more figurative phrase: "I see what you mean."

BEYOND TEST SCORES

Developmental and cognitive gains like this have tremendous implications for instruction, assessment, services, and expectations of this population. By examining data scored in groups with decimal points and percentages, we might forget that those numbers represent individual students. The data validated my suspicions about Thinking Maps as tools for learning. Thinking Maps affirm students' ability to think, with a positive ripple effect upon their sense of self-worth. The gravity of this situation struck me when I told one of my students his test results. Tension filled the air as he approached my desk. Anticipating failure, he lowered his head and said, "I didn't make it, did I?" "As a matter of fact," I replied, "you did." With tears in his eyes, this towering eighth-grade boy picked me up and spun me around. We immediately called to share the great news with his mother. It was during that interaction that I understood the true meaning of my results. Relief and praise washed over this student and his family. He exclaimed, "I am smart, I can do this!"

Thinking Technology

Daniel Cherry, M.Ed.

Topics to be discussed:

- uniting networking capacities in the brain, mind, and machines
- making the explicit connection between higher-order thinking and technology applications
- using a common language of thinking patterns through software for mapping the standards

BRAIN, MIND, AND THE MACHINE

It seems odd to think that soon we will be celebrating the 25th anniversary of the personal computer in public schools. I remember loading programs from the cassette drive on TRS-80s and Commodore PET machines. I was even impressed that I could write a five-line program in BASIC and have my name show up all over the screen. From the time I was an elementary school teacher beginning to use technology, to when I took a position as a districtwide technology coordinator, to my present work as the state director of the Gates Leadership Program, New Hampshire School Administrators Leading with Technology (NHSALT), I have been part of and have observed with a critical eye the slow and, more recently, rapid progression of technology use in our classrooms.

The computer, in one of its earliest and simplest definitions, is an input, process, and output device. Many of these early computers were described as "thinking machines" that would ultimately mimic the sensory input, mental processing, and productive output of the human mind. Artificial intelligence programs were being created to challenge chess champions at a time before the intelligence quotient was being challenged and before a theory of multiple intelligences was offered. This was also a time when the brain was described as a black box, simply broken down into two separate hemispheres, and before we had the new functional MRI brain scanning tools that show that "holism" is a more accurate description of the complex circuitry of the human mind-brain.

When working with computers, our neurons accept visual input through the optic nerve, and our brain processes all of the shapes, colors, and bits of information at lightening speed. An interaction occurs between the user (a strange slang often linked to the addicted) and the machine: a transfer or exchange of data. Amazement and wonder take over. The wiring and firing of neural pathways in the brain is readied as we try to relate to and make conscious sense of the data before us. What does this mean? Thousands of calculations that would take us weeks to accomplish by hand, the ability to accept variables and build projections, answers, answers, and more answers. Think of the possibilities, think of the impact on education, think of . . .

WAIT! HOLD ON. WHAT IMPACT ON EDUCATION?

Now here's a question worth spending some time on. Schools have spent billions of dollars on wires, boxes, routers, hubs, displays, calculators, probes, and printers. Despite this effort and expense, at a time of high-stakes testing, accountability, and financial benefits from research-based best practices, few can respond with deep data when the words "show me the research" are uttered.

There is no way to tie computers to improved student outcomes without taking a great leap of faith. Just to say "kids love computers" gets us only half way. So where can we begin to examine the connections and the impact of technology on higher-order thinking skills?

Jamie McKenzie (2003), a long-time leader and critical reviewer of educational technology, emphasizes that students need to be "info-tectives," savvy with a set of problem-solving tools and adept at moving information around and seeing information in different forms and from different points of view.

One of the keys to instruction and learning is the visual domain. Bridging technology to graphic representations is not something new. In fact, the two fields intimately overlap. Beyond a few bells and whistles and maybe downloaded music playing backup, most of the output from the computer is visual. This means that technology, graphic representations, and the human brain with its dominant visual nature are uniquely bound by visual representations, a meshing of circuitry.

Inspiration and OmniGraffle are now commonly used software programs for webbing and creating visual organizers for content-specific tasks and processes. These are highly flexible, open-ended graphical software programs, with infinite template starters. However, the critique of graphic overload as students and teachers are inundated with graphic organizers (Hyerle, 2000) is mirrored in the graphical creations on these software programs: There are so many graphics that the cognitive load on students (not to mention teachers) ultimately outweighs the benefit. There is little theoretical coherence to most graphic organizers as they show up in many basal texts and books of graphic organizers, and the same is true for graphical software programs through which an infinite number of graphics can be spun out on the screen.

Many of these graphics serve only one aspect of Bloom's taxonomy: They simply capture the factual knowledge within preformed organizational structures that have no real connection to fundamental thinking processes. Often these graphics structure the thinking for students rather than offering students flexible tools that can support them in consciously performing at higher levels of thinking. Chris Moersch (2002) refers to this as "chroming" a lesson: just adding something for the sake of using technology, but not bringing the lesson to any new levels of thinking.

TECHNOLOGY FOR THINKING

As education continues to identify best practices, and cognitive scientists discover more about how people learn and the workings of the brain, educators must focus efforts on delivering quality educational opportunities with tools that are common and transferable to learners in a variety of environments. *Thinking Maps Software* (Hyerle & Gray Matter Software, 1998) having evolved out of the language of Thinking Maps®, is one pathway toward this outcome.

When I started working with teachers and technology through the use of Thinking Maps and *Thinking Maps Software*, I was amazed that, given the same set of tools, first graders and eighth graders were sharing ideas about writing styles of authors. When the work was displayed in a hallway, third-grade students, not familiar with the sixth-grade content, could name the cognitive process that was being used to communicate information through a common Thinking Map. Students were given tools that organized their thinking, allowed them to communicate their thinking, and were motivated by the ability to create graphic representations of their thinking on the computer. We were creating a culture of thinking in our schools that integrated technology as part of the center of the community, improved pedagogy, and promoted thinking.

As a technology coordinator, I saw new effective communication across content areas and grade levels as parents, teachers, and students used a common visual language to teach and share complex thoughts and ideas. We offered *Thinking Maps Software* training to parents. Some parents attended formal instruction in the evening at school, and many parents experienced informal sessions, with their children providing examples and teaching them how to use the software in the labs at schools. Not only were students sharing maps with parents, but parents were sending maps to teachers! Administrators included maps in newsletters to describe processes for student placement. They also used maps to explain the results of programs on high-stakes tests. At open house, parents and children were in front of computers exploring the various uses of the maps. We even had parents bring in examples of maps that they created to be used in their workplace. This seemed to be an integration point, a crossroads for best practices focusing on higher-order thinking, a delivery system using the personal computer, and a common visual language built on the cognitive processes embedded in Thinking Maps. This also produced a systemic change across one of the schools, Hanover Street School, that resulted in improved scores for students on the New Hampshire statewide test.

ELEMENTS OF THINKING MAPS SOFTWARE

Thinking Maps, a visual language, offers common symbols or elements, a flexible structure, and is easily communicated and transferable in the learning community. For teachers, *Thinking Maps Software* creates in the computer environment relevant activities to what is being used in the classroom. By the nature of the visual language, a Thinking Map asks students to define in context, sequence, compare or contrast, describe, identify whole-to-part relationships, determine cause and effect, create or identify analogies, or classify information. Planning units or developing lesson plans takes on a deeper focus when the cognitively based maps are used as a tool to inform instruction. The software is designed for both teachers and students through a three-window approach: a window for lesson planning for the teacher, a window for the dynamic generation of Thinking Maps by students, and a final window for students to transfer their Maps into writing (see Figure 9.1) In the software environment, teachers can use the tools in the same way as students, or they can create plans and assessments or capture and collect evidence of success that can be shared with other educators.

The software is a simple tool that can be used in very complex ways. The software allows for the flexibility to edit, rearrange, highlight, and embed thoughts and ideas throughout the learning.

This means that the students are actively engaged and can interact with the information over time. Just as with word-processing programs, which enable highly flexible movement of text blocks and facilitate editing to create multiple versions of a piece of writing, the software gives students and teachers a common platform for re-visioning information. They can continually return to expand the maps as they assimilate new content knowledge or to transform the maps as they reconceptualize ideas.

From the Individual to the System in New York City

One inner-city school system took the step to use Thinking Maps to unite teaching, learning, and the standards through the software. Community School District 27 in New York City was the largest of the city districts (before a recent reorganization) and was set in a diverse, low socioeconomic area near Kennedy Airport. Nearly 160 languages and dialects are spoken throughout this region. Many of the 37 elementary and junior high schools in the district were underachieving, and the standards movement was just on the horizon. During the 1997 school year—after piloting and evaluating several approaches—the district adopted Thinking Maps as one way to help students, teachers, and schools through this process. With the support and guidance of Ken Grover, Deputy Superintendent of Community School District 27, by the year 2000, most of the teachers had experienced Thinking Maps through direct training.

As an end-of-the-year assessment, all teachers were asked to submit examples of student work and their lesson design, with the New York City Standards that were being met clearly identified on the top of each page. Lynn Kanter, a former reading specialist who became the districtwide Thinking Maps coordinator, produced a compilation of over 400 pages of standards-based Thinking Map lessons spanning all content areas and grade levels . . . all hard copy.

As teachers collected student work and designed engaging activities that integrated technology, the district team facilitated a database development so that any teacher could tap the success of another teacher throughout the district and even see a sample of the type of work generated by a variety of students. *Mapping the Standards* (Curtis, in press) was a pilot for the district, enabling it to continuously build an electronic database of successful learning experiences based on fundamental cognitive processes. The database of selected, high-quality lessons is searchable based on the standard(s) being met, grade, and curriculum area. Figure 9.1 is a partial example of how the three windows enable teachers to create standards-based essential questions, based on thinking processes and leading to the development of Thinking Maps, with a piece of writing as a final product.

The importance and implications of this project are multifold. As teachers experienced success, they were able to communicate the process they used to deliver the instruction, capture evidence of student work, and provide reflections or ideas about the learning they experienced. Within a school, teachers could build a dynamic library of successful lessons and activities that they know work. District 27 then began to share these lesson and maps with teachers throughout the district. Teachers began to dialog and discuss student work and pedagogy. Lessons could be opened up adopted, modified, and exchanged without hard copy, using *Thinking Maps Software.* This is not global "curriculum mapping" but detailed mapping of content-based thinking skills units of study and content standards.

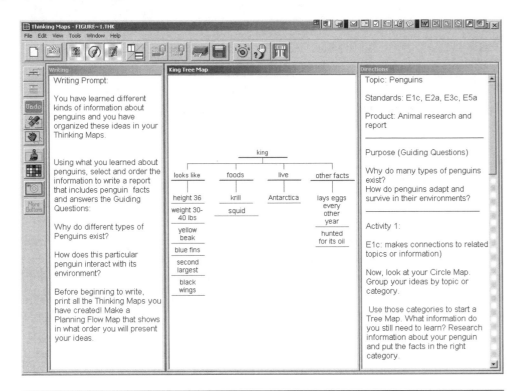

Figure 9.1   Thinking Maps Software With Mapping the Standards

Evolution

Technology in the classroom is still in its infancy. For some teachers in District 27, this was the first time they had used a software program that was directly related to teaching practices and based on something that they were already using interactively in their classrooms. The software thus became a technology for learning, connected to the classroom and teaching experience and not a disconnected process of learning a new technology.

Within our educational systems, advancements in the use of technology must combine with the necessary advancements in school climate, instructional practices, and instructional leadership. It will be in these high-functioning, well coordinated environments that our students will have the greatest opportunity to succeed. Thinking Maps and *Thinking Maps Software* comprise a set of tools to integrate technology with pedagogy focused on higher-order thinking with the potential to create positive, systemic change in education. The dynamic visual circuitry of Thinking Maps creates an overlap between the human brain and the technology of the computer. They provide a crossroads, a nexus between brain, mind, and machine for efficiently and effectively organizing, understanding, and communicating thinking within a classroom, across whole schools, and around the world.

SECTION 3

Uniting Whole Learning Communities

10

A First Language for Thinking in a Multilingual School

Stefanie R. Holzman, Ed.D.

Topics to be discussed:

- results from an inner-city school with students learning a second language while differentiating instruction with a common language
- moving expectations to a higher level across a low-performing school
- changing school climate and culture toward higher-order thinking and literacy development

BREAKING THE RULES FOR CHANGE

"But I already use graphic organizers in my class," was the cry from my staff. As a first-year principal, I was breaking the most basic rule in the book for new administrators. I was immediately changing the mind-set of the culture—the way we do things around here—and I was making all these changes rapidly. A dynamic set of tools for activating the mind and directly influencing performance, Thinking Maps®, was included in these changes. This was not an easy thing to do. Many of the teachers in this urban, inner-city, K–5 school of 1200 minority students (85% of those entering with Spanish as their primary language) thought they were already getting the best out of their students. As the newcomer to the school, I had expectations that students should be achieving at higher levels than current test results indicated.

My high expectations are rooted in an understanding of what many of us who have attempted to learn a second language know: Learning content while learning a second language is a complex process. It is frustrating for a child to have ideas, vocabulary, and rich patterns of thinking in one language that are not immediately translated and understood by teachers in the context of the classroom. This is because the acquisition of a second language obviously gets in the way of our thinking and learning. The Thinking Maps become a translator of language and thinking from one language-mind (Spanish) to another language-mind (English). Thinking Maps became our *first language* for thinking, thus supporting the languages, content learning, and cognitive development of our multilingual population.

My experiences from seeing the maps in use in other schools in Long Beach Unified School District made me believe that our students would learn the maps, and the result of all this would be higher academic achievement. This did happen. The numbers are in from the standardized tests given in California. The state has a very complicated formula to determine expected growth. Roosevelt School was expected to gain 11 points overall. We exceeded that goal with a 60-point gain. Not only did the school as a single unit make growth, but so did our significant subgroups: Hispanic students, English-language learners, and students of low socioeconomic status as determined by free lunches. In addition, with the implementation of the No Child Left Behind legislation, the expectation has been that 13.6% of the students in our school should meet the standards in language arts (including reading, vocabulary, spelling, grammar, and punctuation), and that 16% should meet the standards in math (including basic math facts and word problems). If a school does not meet the expectations, then it is identified as a program-improvement school and must take a number of corrective actions. As of this writing, and with two of our four tracks' test results in (including tracks with literacy classes for retainees and for students who entered school in fourth and fifth grade with no English skills), the results demonstrate that we are clearly not in program improvement.

Ironically, my intent as the instructional leader of Roosevelt School was initially isolated on these tools for a direct and immediate impact on student performance. What I didn't realize and could not foresee were the deeper effects upon the development of teachers across our year-round, multitrack school as a result of the use of Thinking Maps in their classrooms. I discovered that from an administrator's point of view, Thinking Maps did much more than what I had understood from both practical and theoretical points of view. First, there are changes in how teachers learn and teach and evaluate student work, especially with differentiated processes for our second-language learners. Second, there have been shifts in the culture and climate of our school, most obvious in the quality of professional conversations that now rise to the surface (see Chapter 17, Thinking Maps). Third, there is a new level of access and discourse in the areas of teacher evaluation and accountability, which has led to a higher quality of teacher decision making. All of these changes—often referenced as keys to school change—will continue to have a long-term positive outcome on the academic achievement of the students at my school beyond the direct application of these tools by students to academic tasks and tests.

It is important for me to restate that I did not bring Thinking Maps into this school for the purpose of bringing about change in these three areas, but for an immediate shift of student performance that could cascade over time. Below are my discoveries about the interdependent ripple effects that I found in these other areas of teacher learning (including higher-order thinking for English-language learners), school culture, and accountability.

TEACHER LEARNING

The work of teaching is not only difficult, but it is also fast paced. It is the exceptional teacher who is self-reflective and aware of metacognitive processes (see Chapter 15, Inviting Explicit Thinking). Too often teachers are so focused on working with students that they rarely turn inward to notice what and *how* they are thinking. Yet I believe our students should be learning to do what we adults do as we internally process our experiences. Our internal dialogue and thinking is often hidden away as well as our emotional states. In order to do this, teachers need to let students know what is happening in their heads; this can't happen if teachers are not aware of what they are doing. Once my teachers began learning Thinking Maps, they suddenly realized the types of thinking that were flowing through their minds and how the maps can show the students their adult thinking strategies and processes.

When my teachers became aware of their own thinking processes and how the Thinking Maps can communicate this to their students, they were so surprised that they had to check with someone to see if "they were doing it right." One very experienced teacher had an insight during a lesson about "the city and the country" in her first-grade class of English-language learners and came to me to check in. Lots of conversation had happened during her lesson, but at the end of the lesson, she realized that she could have organized this information into a Tree Map.

An example of this is the Tree Map created by a cooperative group about an emotion that surfaced during the reading of a Junie B. Jones book (Figure 10.1). These five students were able to use the map to organize their thinking about anger: what it is, references to characters in other books who show anger (text-to-text connections), what it looks like, and then, things that one would say when angry. "Mr. Angry" is at the top of

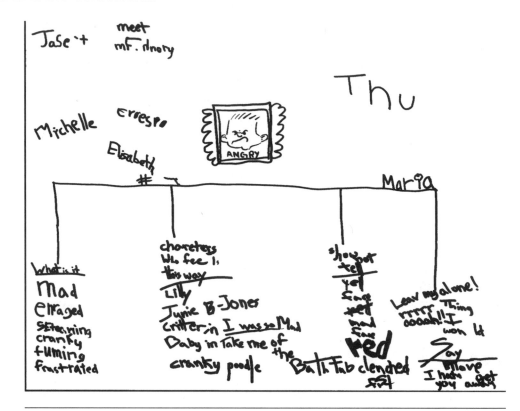

Figure 10.1 "Angry" Tree Map for Writing

the tree. By visually modeling a process for thinking through ideas, and even working through the contents of emotions, a teacher can let her students know how she had organized this information in her head. The students *see* thinking evolve and then use the tools independently and in cooperative groups. Language and cognitive development then go hand in hand.

TEACHERS TEACHING AT A HIGHER ORDER

The capacity for students to be able to apply higher-order thinking skills is referenced everywhere as an ultimate goal of school outcomes in content standards, in textbooks, and on standardized tests. Most teachers are aware of a hierarchy of skills as referenced in Bloom's Taxonomy of Educational Objectives. For example, they know that synthesis-level questions are more complex than knowledge, or fact-based, questions. However, many teachers are not as cognizant of the kinds of thinking associated with higher-level thinking skills. For many, learning the Thinking Maps was the first time teachers actually had a clear understanding of specific types of thinking skills, how they interrelated and transferred across disciplines, and most important, how the skills worked together to engage and sustain higher-order thinking on a day-to-day basis in classroom settings.

After the training, the positive energy from the teachers from this new understanding and related tools immediately transferred itself to the students in their classrooms. This is because these teachers realized that the focus was on immediate use and translation for students. When I walk into classes and I want to know what kinds of thinking the students are learning about and how they are applying these foundational skills to content learning, my teachers can now identify this because they know Thinking Maps. They can also tell what kind of thinking the students are expected to use. Importantly, Thinking Maps were used to promote critical thinking skills even for students who were still acquiring English.

All students in Grades 1–5 were tested on a standardized test in reading and math, and Grades 2–5 were also tested on the California standards test. Much of the math section includes reading. The teachers taught students to analyze the type of math question it was, for example, comparison, whole to part/part to whole, relationships, patterns, etc. and the map associated with each. Once the students understood the five kinds of "story problems," they were able to tease out the critical attributes of these and apply them to the test. For example, in response to a word problem shown in Figure 10.2, one first-grade student selected the key information from the problem using a Circle Map and then used the Flow Map to show the steps and the strategies involved in solving the problem based on the information in the initial Circle Map. The change in students' ability to do these problems made a significant difference between last year's and this year's school scores.

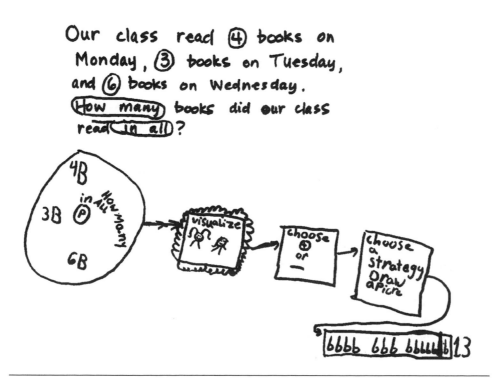

Figure 10.2   Math Problem-Solving Flow Map

In our district, students are also required to take a writing test each year that is scored on a holistic scoring rubric. The task is response to literature, which parallels one of the state's required tasks. Although primarily a reading task, students must read a passage and then respond to a prompt. In Grade 1 at my school, students had to read a story and then demonstrate their understanding of the text by using a Thinking Map to demonstrate the sequence of the story and then show how the characters changed over time. Most students used a Flow Map and then a Bubble Map as their response to the task. This type of task gave us insight into the students' comprehension at both a knowledge level (the sequence) and at deeper levels (how the character changed over time), without burdening them with having to write a complex essay.

This was especially helpful for teachers in analyzing the understanding of the English-language learners. The use of the Thinking Maps for this task also enabled the students to read more critically on the standardized test. Kristin Tucker, a first-grade teacher, reflected that "the Thinking Maps took the English language learner to the highest level of thinking . . . in a very simple way. I didn't have to explain in words what I was doing, instead I just exposed the students to the maps and the students just 'got' them very easily. It was so easy that students quickly learned to combine maps by themselves." This facilitated student learning of content, and the explicit transfer of thinking skills by students also provided her with additional time to teach!

Other teachers commented on how they noticed that the type of thinking used in one curriculum could be used in another. Because the teachers were able to make these connections, they were able to help students make the same connections. The results were that students were able to more quickly learn the content once they understood the underlying types of thinking they needed. Instead of teaching specialized skills and strategies particular to one content, teachers began to generalize these deeply within and across disciplines.

DIFFERENTIATION OF INSTRUCTION AND ENGLISH AS A SECOND LANGUAGE

Over 85% of the students who enter kindergarten in our school speak Spanish as their primary language. By law, we are required to differentiate the instructional practices based on the level of English-language proficiency of students. Theoretically, differentiation seems so simple: Teach differently to different students based on their individual needs. Easier said than done. However, one of the differences that Thinking Maps has made at my school is that teachers teach the same content to various groups in their classroom, but they have begun to provide alternate means for students to access and to show what they know. For example, some teachers expect students to use the Thinking Maps as processes to a final product, while others expect students to use the tools as a final product to demonstrate their thinking and comprehension of the content.

In one of the third-grade classes, the students were expected to understand the similarities and differences between two planets. All students were required to complete a Double Bubble Map comparing and contrasting the two planets, which was the stated outcome of the lesson. However, in order to differentiate the lesson, students who were fluent in English were also expected to write a report that contained this information. Students less fluent in English needed only to create the Double Bubble Map. The teacher was able to evaluate the factual and conceptual learning by every student using either strategy (the map alone or the map and writing). With fluent English speakers, she was also able to evaluate their ability to communicate their learning in writing, something she already knew the less fluent English speakers would not yet be able to do. Of course, it is also essential to have the students who are not fluent in English begin to write from the Thinking Maps, as this provides the bridge from their primary language to the mainstream spoken and written form. As a first language for thinking, the maps became vocabulary builders, visible organizers, and starting points for writing in a second language.

The important point here is that the teachers are able to assess content learning and use student maps as data points to see whether or not it is language that is getting in the way of understanding or if there are content misconceptions that need reteaching. It is often difficult to determine how much limited English-proficient students understand of what is taught. If a teacher wants to know what a second language learner has learned, does the teacher ask the student to use the second-language if the student does not have verbal or written fluency? If assignments ask them to write what they know, these students often drown in the English language. They have to figure out the vocabulary, the syntax, the spelling, and the punctuation of English and at the same time remember the content they have learned. The results are that teachers often evaluate the students' English skills and sentence construction and not their content knowledge or their reasoning. However, when teachers ask students to use Thinking Maps to demonstrate what they know, then the students do not have to focus on English and can use their mental energies to communicate what they know about the content. They do not even have to use words to convey this information. In most cases, Thinking Maps lend themselves to visuals (e.g., drawings or pictures from magazines) to communicate the content.

EVALUATION OF STUDENT WORK

One of the key components of the changes I focused on in my first year was to insist that teachers be able to evaluate the degree to which students learned what was taught. In some cases, such as in mathematics, which has its own universal symbol system, this was easy to do with a pre- and posttest. We did not wait until the results of the state's standardized tests to determine if students achieved growth. Thinking Maps became a powerful strategy that teachers used to evaluate student learning. The results provided teachers with information that was used to monitor student growth and to adjust teaching.

Teachers used Thinking Maps in various ways to determine the quantity and quality of what students learned. Some used Circle Maps as pre- and posttests to determine what they learned. Other teachers gave students an assignment that required them to demonstrate their thinking. For example, one first-grade teacher asked students to retell a story. She was able to evaluate the students' comprehension based on the Flow Maps they created. A third-grade teacher asked students to determine the causes and effects of pollution on the ocean. It was quite evident who "got it" and who didn't. The teacher was able to quickly reteach those who needed it. In all these cases, our English-language learners were able to participate fully in the core curriculum.

CLIMATE AND CULTURE CHANGES

During this initial phase of training, I was impressed by the rapid, contagious nature of the spreading of these tools. The Thinking Maps kept "bobbing up" into other classrooms, even though not all teachers got trained immediately. It appeared that teachers were sharing ideas in the lounge, during grade-level meetings, wherever they met. Teachers actually met on their own time to talk about professional concepts.

I realized that one of the unplanned benefits was that because Thinking Maps were so easy to implement, they could easily become the topic of professional talk. This occurred not only between pairs of teachers, but between teachers who rarely had occasion to share ideas, such as a kindergarten teacher and a third-grade teacher. Suddenly, teachers had a first language for thinking in which to talk about student learning, one that was not dependent on grade level or content area.

Another change that occurred was that the teachers realized that the culture of the school was going to be one in which lifelong learning was not reserved just for students. The expectation was that teachers should be learning new strategies that help accelerate student achievement and that "doing things as we've always done them" was no longer acceptable. The difference between learning the maps and participating in other staff development was that these tools emulated adult thinking and strategies. These were then shared with students. Thus, the strategies were authentic. Rather than teachers learning a "canned program" that did not reflect what they as adults did and did not give them what their students needed, teachers were learning lifelong strategies for themselves and then teaching them to their students. As teachers began to experiment with the Thinking Maps in their own lives—such as making Tree Map shopping lists—they developed into the learning community that I was trying to foster at my school, but never expected to get from these tools.

Another benefit I was surprised and pleased to see was that new teachers could participate in the discussions about high-quality tools as equals. The visual language and the common vocabulary was not a mysteriously complex formula that creates a wall between veteran teachers who have internalized a thoroughly unique and idiosyncratic teaching style and the new teachers and instructional aides who are just learning the ropes. With a common language, veteran teachers could model expert applications along a continuum—one rope—that novice teachers could easily grab onto and make their own (see Chapter 16, Mentoring Mathematics Teaching and Learning).

TEACHER EVALUATION AND ACCOUNTABILITY

Not only can teachers use Thinking Maps to determine the depth of learning of their students, but this language also creates an easy opportunity for an administrator to determine teachers' depth of learning and implementation of Thinking Maps. This is because these tools are visual and become a running record of application, and because the ultimate end user is the student, not the teacher. Often teachers go to staff development workshops and come back excited about what they have learned. However, it is difficult to determine the quality and consistency of the applications over the short and long term.

A quick walk through a classroom looking for evidence of the Thinking Maps and talking with students gave me a good feel for how well they were being used, in what content the maps were being used, and the level of thinking at which they were used. However, the evidence became much more clear as we looked at student work, especially in writing.

As a school, we analyze student writing once a month. Teachers from the same grade level get together, score student work against a district-created rubric, and then analyze the work as to what the students do well and what still needs to be taught. Teachers who taught Thinking Maps to students as aids in writing found that the quality of student writing improved (see Chapter 7, Empowering Students). These results were similar for students in kindergarten and in Grade 3. Teachers used these data to make professional decisions as to how to adjust their teaching to better meet the needs of their students. This was done without any intervention or pressure on my part. Teachers made these types of professional decisions based on the results from the student work—the holistic thinking translated into linear writing—from their class.

IMPLICATIONS FOR IMPLEMENTATION

The implementation of Thinking Maps at my school has brought changes that not only affect student performance as shown in our results presented above, but also the quality of instruction and the culture of the school. I know that over time, I will continue to have the same high-level results as other schools in terms of academic performance for my students. I also know that the changes I see as Thinking Maps become a regular part of the instructional program will also become more deeply embedded in the culture of the school.

There are several dramatic changes I put forward during my first year as a principal that I regret. The implementation of Thinking Maps was not one of them. I asked my staff what they thought accounted for the growth in student achievement. Obviously, I wanted to make sure that we repeated these successful strategies. Every member of my staff responded that it was the implementation of Thinking Maps that made a significant difference in student outcomes. When we analyzed exactly how teachers used the maps, we found two patterns throughout the school. First, Thinking Maps were used across the curriculum in all grade levels including kindergarten. Second, Thinking Maps were used to promote critical thinking skills even for students who were still acquiring English.

Heather Krstich (who taught the third-grade combination literacy class with all the third-grade retainees and fourth-grade very limited English-language learners) suggested that the reason that the Thinking Maps helped was because it gave the students a cohesive feeling across all the curriculums. "The students did not feel [that the curriculum] was so segmented. They were able to focus on their thinking instead of on individual activities in each of the curricula. Thinking Maps gave the students a systematic approach to thinking that they can use over the years." She added that the English-language learners in her classroom had a cohesive strategy built on the language of the maps. "The maps have such a consistent language that students were able to concentrate on their thinking rather than what they were doing."

With this experience of implementing Thinking Maps, I also now have a standard by which I can compare other professional development trainings and other changes I plan to promote at Roosevelt Elementary School. This standard includes implementing changes that successfully affect student academic outcomes, teacher learning, reflection, accountability, and the school climate as effectively as this common language for learning, teaching, and assessing.

We now have this new standard in our school—including for our students—because we have a first language for thinking, whether it be in a first or second language for speaking and writing. This language will help us to think and act on complex problems—such as how to transform and continually grow in an inner-city environment—with the confidence that we will be able to see more clearly each other's thinking.

Feeder Patterns and Feeding the Flame at Blalack Middle School

Edward V. Chevallier, M.Ed.

Topics to be discussed:

- uniting students from an elementary feeder pattern using a common language for thinking and learning
- using Circle Maps and Frames of Reference for identifying author's tone, mood, and style
- note-taking and thinking-skills development using multiple Thinking Maps®

After 10 years as a classroom teacher, I was offered two wonderful and challenging experiences, first as an elementary principal and then as a middle school principal. Through these positions I deepened my understandings of the complexity of instruction. I watched teachers lay a foundation for learning for elementary students, and as I entered my present position, I also saw that many of our middle school students needed a stronger foundation in skills to improve their learning that would stay with them throughout their educational and work careers.

My awareness of this deeper need grew over time from my classroom visits, walk-throughs, and supervision processes. I frequently heard the expectation from frustrated teachers directing students to "take notes" as they were introduced to new information. I also heard my teachers lament that students didn't know "how to think" as their students were challenged with new information and concepts. Over time I realized I couldn't recall any clear examples of explicit instruction in those two important areas—note-taking skills and thinking skills—even though teachers could well identify and articulate these problem areas.

It did become clear that the very core of learning that I began to seek out was rarely found in these classrooms. I came to believe that the issue was larger than the individual teachers: They had never had a unified, consistent way of addressing thinking skills for learning that required sustained, consistent, direct, and differentiated instruction in these skills for all students across multiple years. The absent foundation was missing not because of isolated negligence, but because of an institutional blind spot that so many schools inherit from a structural problem of schooling. We have focused on content knowledge and content-specific processes in schools. The missing piece is a quality mental resource for explicitly addressing transferable learning-processing skills that transcend any one teacher's curriculum or the set, vertical path in a content area.

Through an event that can best be described as good fate, at a time when I was seeking solutions to these problems, I was introduced to Thinking Maps. This solution has not been a quick fix, but a systematic implementation over the past six years that has brought a unified language to this school. This is underscored by the successes I see on a daily basis and at the end of each year in test scores. In advocating for the adoption of Thinking Maps, my goal was to give individual students a set of tools they could learn as they came from different elementary school experiences and take with them as they continued their educational career. What I did not foresee was that over the long term our campus would experience a less obvious, schoolwide benefit: the development of a community language through which all of us could mature as individuals into a learning organization.

LIGHTING THE FIRE IN A MIDDLE SCHOOL SETTING

Blalack Middle School is a campus of approximately 1100 students located in Carrollton, Texas, a city just northwest of Dallas. As the city of Dallas continues to grow, Carrollton-Farmers Branch Independent School District has been quickly changing from a suburban, middle class district that was once predominantly Caucasian to a diverse school district serving many different ethnic groups and a range of socioeconomic levels, with students in the district speaking 46 languages and dialects and representing 53 countries. Four very different elementary campuses feed into Blalack, creating a diverse mix across socioeconomic, racial, and cultural groups.

When the approximately four hundred new students enter sixth grade at Blalack every year, our challenge is immediate: We must provide opportunities that allow all students to become a cohesive group—ready to learn and ready to succeed. We must help our students respect diversity and appreciate the strengths of their new classmates. Thus one characteristic of Thinking Maps that became an immediate enticement was the opportunity to develop a common language for our students. The phrase "and many shall become one" is incredibly apparent to a middle school educator. In *Leadership for Differentiating Schools and Classrooms* (2000), Tomlinson and Allan identify a stark reality: Every three years, middle schools have a nearly complete turnover of their student populations and families, and thus new challenges for parental involvement.

My participation in an initial Thinking Maps training, before my faculty was trained, was an eye-opening experience. Three specific outcomes of using these tools were identified, and each has proven to be true over our years of implementation. I believe that these three outcomes have significant answers to many of the needs we have at our middle school and possibly most middle schools around this country:

Thinking Maps help students actively process information. The use of the maps creates immediate and specific questions. In a middle school classroom, the constant challenge is maximum engagement. Used in even their most limited form, Thinking Maps ensure eight "ready" questions—questions associated with each of the eight thinking skills. Thinking Maps build a bridge from concrete knowledge to abstract concepts.

Thinking Maps bridge the divide between concrete facts and abstract thinking as a developmental necessity for adolescents. Thinking Maps give students a flexible structure for creating their own vision of knowledge as they create their own maps from blank paper. Because no map is ever complete, this flexibility ensures that students at all levels of growth can be consistently challenged in their thinking, building from concrete information to concept formation.

Thinking Maps work as teaching, learning, and assessment tools. The flexible configurations of the maps allow all teachers to contribute to creating applications within and across content areas. Students can successfully use maps as independent learners and thinkers to organize their thoughts for note taking, on formative assessments, and on summative assessments. Many of my teachers regularly ask students to create one or several Thinking Maps to show what they know as they are developing ideas, structuring an essay, or responding to the typical questions that appear at the end of most chapters.

EARLY LEVELS OF CHANGE AND CONCERN

In *Taking Charge of Change* (Hord, Rutherford, Huling-Austin, & Hall, 1987), considered by some to be the seminal work on change in education, the authors introduce the concerns-based adoption model (CBAM). In this model, a levels-of-use continuum gauges how people are using an innovation, from nonuse and orientation, through the middle stages of preparation, mechanical and routine use, to the upper stages of refinement, integration, and renewal. Our implementation of Thinking Maps has followed such a pattern.

In the early stages, the comfort level and range of implementation varied. Some teachers jumped in with full excitement and energy, while many teachers quickly moved from a level of orientation to a level of refinement and even integration within a very short period of time. Others were more reluctant. Their inconsistent use caused them to remain at the routine level. Nonetheless, as the implementation was campuswide, all teachers incorporated the maps into their classrooms in varying degrees because of the training that was focused on students' developing automaticity with the tools.

The student-centered dimension of implementing the maps was never more evident than when one of our administrators confiscated a "slam book" early in the school year. A slam book begins when middle school students identify their "best friend for life." Using a notebook, the students begin corresponding on a regular basis, usually passing the notebook to one another in the cafeteria or hallway. At one point, an administrator came into possession of a slam book and found three high-quality examples of Thinking Maps as shown in Figures 11.1a – c. The student had begun the process of planning a party by identifying her "perfect circle" of friends by using a Circle Map and then used two Tree Maps to organize couples. As an administrator I could not have been more excited. I had been seeking an initiative through which adolescent students could learn tools for independently organizing notes and applying thinking skills, and I had found these tools.

Figure 11.1a Slam Book Circle Map for Automaticity

Figure 11.1b Slam Book Tree Map for Automaticity

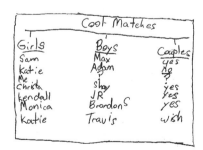

Figure 11.1c Slam Book Tree Map for Automaticity

COMMUNICATION FOR DIFFERENTIATION

All of these early events helped us to shift to the real challenge of implementation: moving from igniting the fire for a new initiative to fanning the flame. To increase effectiveness, the fanning process had to be ongoing, promote excitement, and document successes. In *Leadership for Differentiating Schools and Classrooms*, Tomlinson and Allan address the importance of communication as a factor in sustaining change. The issue of communication is addressed as it specifically pertains to parents and the public. The five qualities of effective communication are that communication should avoid jargon and focus on effects for students, be consistent, be persistent, be interactive, and take many forms. An exemplar of these interdependent qualities is clearly shown through the sustained efforts of implementing Thinking Maps at our school.

1. Avoid Jargon and Focus on Effects for Students

In this era of standards-based, test-driven education, it is important that we not lose sight of the fact that students must be given opportunities to be successful and leave us prepared to be successful at the next level. Educators in Texas and around the country are often driven by concerns about test results and the No Child Left Behind initiative. It is reassuring that we support our students to use Thinking Maps, knowing that these skills enable them to deeply process information while also ensuring that these same tools directly impact their performance on state and other standardized tests. To verify this understanding with our staff, we utilized a professional development opportunity to review specific state curriculum standards and identify specific Thinking Maps that can be used to teach and assess the standard.

Teachers were asked to review the curriculum for the subject and grade level that they teach. For each curriculum indicator (or standard), teachers were asked to identify the underlying thinking skill and Thinking Map (or Maps) that would be helpful in ensuring that students mastered the indicator. One example comes from Jennifer Farlow, a sixth-grade social studies teacher, and her students. By using the Tree Map as presented in Figure 11.2, students were able to categorize information and get a visual depiction (and understanding) of three stages of economic development as they apply to countries. They were also able to clearly see specific factors of production as they apply to these stages. Using Bloom's Taxonomy of Educational Objectives as a guide, teachers were also able to identify the kind of thinking required by students in test questions and the direct application of the maps by students to the curriculum indicators that must be mastered.

2. Be Consistent

While we encourage creative use and flexibility of the maps, we also ensure that the common visual language has the consistency that enables

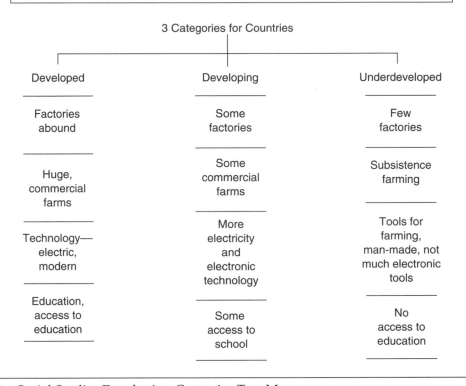

Grade 6 Social Studies [from Texas Administrative Code (TAC), Title 19, Part II Chapter 113. Texas Essential Knowledge and Skills for Social Studies]: explain factors such as location, physical features, transporation corridors and barriers, distribution of natural resources that influence the economic development and foreign policies of societies.

3 Categories for Countries

Developed	Developing	Underdeveloped
Factories abound	Some factories	Few factories
Huge, commercial farms	Some commercial farms	Subsistence farming
Technology— electric, modern	More electricity and electronic technology	Tools for farming, man-made, not much electronic tools
Education, access to education	Some access to school	No access to education

Figure 11.2   Social Studies Developing Countries Tree Map

complex applications. For example, when a question concerning sequencing is asked in a test situation—such as "What are the steps in the process of a bill becoming a law?"—we want students to identify the Flow Map as a common tool for understanding this process.

Brittnie Bragg, a language arts teacher, shared two examples that she regularly utilizes in her classroom. As students come into her room each day, they are asked to complete a warm-up Thinking Map on something they learned, read, or did in the previous class period. Over time, the directions progress from her assigning a specific Thinking Map to her instructions to "use any of the eight Thinking Maps to show me something you remember from the story we read last class period." These warm-up activities provide opportunities for practicing the maps and for practicing fluent, autonomous transfer of thought processes.

A second example stretches the students to even higher levels of thinking. In teaching and reviewing the challenging concept of recognizing the author's style, tone, and mood, Mrs. Bragg asks students to create a Circle Map divided into three parts as shown in Figure 11.3. In the center circle, the students write the title of the story. One third of the circle is segmented for style, one for tone, and one for mood. The students are directed to define each of the three components as they are used in the story, and in the Frame of Reference, prove their definitions by identifying direct quotes or examples from the story to support their thoughts. Such an example underscores the importance of developing a common and consistent vocabulary in a middle school setting for foundational thinking skills and tools. Even with a common district curriculum, the abstract concepts of author's tone, mood, and style lend themselves to a variety of instructional interpretations across the four elementary schools that feed into our community.

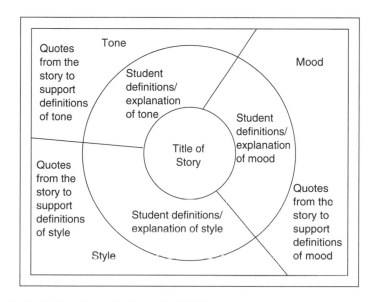

Figure 11.3   Tone, Mood, and Style in Language Arts Circle Map

3. Be Persistent

The importance of persistence as a habit of mind (Costa & Kallick, 2000) for improved thinking and communication has been vital to the success of our campus implementation. Our efforts with Thinking Maps have been sustained over a period of six years, and in order to achieve this, several publicly stated expectations are emphasized and acted upon each year.

First, implementation is schoolwide. All students, Grades 6 through 8, are reintroduced to the eight cognitive skills and maps during the first six weeks of every school year. Second, all teachers new to the campus are required to complete the introductory "Day One" Thinking Maps session conducted by a certified trainer. Third, the campus principal participates in all training. As an active participant in training, campus administrators are positioned to serve as coaches in supporting teachers to sustain implementation.

4. Be Interactive in Implementation

The quality of implementation is sustained by interaction among all stakeholders in the process. Over the past six years, discussions have occurred within departments, in leadership teams, and in planning groups regarding the effectiveness of the maps. Teachers have assumed ownership of the implementation as they have created activities for classroom instruction. A yearly campus improvement plan, developed by a team of teachers and parents, includes specific references to the use of the maps throughout the instructional program.

In recent years, map activities have been used for our own leadership and professional development tools. For example, we have used the tools for a study of current professional literature, data disaggregation of state test scores, and schoolwide goal setting. In the past few years, an ongoing process of "plan, implement, study, and revise" resulted in the adoption of the Thinking Maps language by the elementary campuses that feed into Blalack. Each year, a transition meeting of elementary fifth-grade teachers and middle school sixth-grade teachers is held, and Blalack sixth-grade teachers excitedly share the benefits of the Thinking Maps and the contribution they make to helping students achieve at higher levels. As a result, all of the feeder elementary campuses moved toward implementation, and now almost all students entering Blalack as sixth graders are Thinking Maps veterans.

5. Use Many Different Forms for Sharing and Celebrating

A visitor to our campus cannot leave without seeing the maps affixed to classroom bulletin boards, sprinkled throughout student notebooks, and displayed throughout the hallways. The integrated use of *Thinking Maps Software* (Hyerle & Gray Matter Software, 1998) ensures that students can apply their knowledge in new ways and save an electronic portfolio of their thinking and content knowledge. Parent newsletters are another form of communication that is frequently utilized.

The power of sharing with parents surfaced during a Thinking Maps training I conducted for paraprofessionals who assist at-risk students in our inclusive classrooms. One of the Learning Center managers, who happened to be the parent of a former Blalack student, came to ask for a clarification of something that was discussed. During the conversation, she asked me if her daughter would be able to tell her what Thinking Maps were. Being a proud principal, I assured her that that would be the case. A few days later, I happened to see this parent again and she excitedly shared with me that her daughter could indeed identify the maps as well as the thinking process for each map. My confidence in these maps as tools that would stay with students beyond our school was cemented.

FEEDING THE FIRE: CONFIDENCE AND CONTINUED SUCCESS

As our campus population has continued to change and our challenges have grown, the success levels of our students have continued to rise. This feeds the fire and our confidence as teachers, students, and administrators. Our teachers are ensuring that every child is challenged to succeed and is given the internal, intrinsic, mental resources to contribute to that success. Mary LeRoy, a math teacher at Blalack and a Thinking Maps trainer, expressed this belief:

> When I see a student who has had a history of struggling with math attack a problem with confidence, both the student and I feel the success. Thinking Maps have created this confidence in many of my students. The maps have given my students a means of organization and a strategy to set up and solve a multi-step problem, outline a project, and much more. Once upon a time, a struggling student would see a math test as a white sheet of paper with black letters and numbers and an automatic failure. Now, they see the same test as separate problems, each giving a clue to the map to be used.

From that day, over seven years ago, when I realized that the twin problems voiced by teachers about the lack of note taking and thinking skills by students might be resolved through Thinking Maps, I never imagined that this focus on fundamental thinking processes as and tools could, from the ground up, help transform our school into a much richer learning organization. It took perseverance as educators to see the forest of diverse students also as individual trees growing with common needs. This common language enabled a special education student in another math class, who was struggling with a task assigned by his teacher, to finally look to the teacher with a simple question, "Can I use a Thinking Map to get started?"

12

Embracing Change: The Evolution of Thinking in a K-12 School

Gill Hubble, M.A.

Topics to be discussed:

- the 10-year development of a whole-school, integrated thinking-skills approach in New Zealand
- using multiple maps for scientific problem solving
- how Thinking Maps® changed collaboration, communication, and performance across a K–12 single-sex girls' school

Over 10 years ago, our school began an evolutionary process that finally envisioned a community of learners who could move beyond "tacit use" of thinking skills. Through research, practice, personal discoveries, and many rich conversations, we made a multiyear commitment to integrating the Thinking Maps language into our community. Over the past four years, we believe that our school has achieved "reflective use" of these tools—a sophisticated metacognitive use involving reflection and evaluation (Swartz & Perkins, 1989). We have come to believe that if our students functioned as reflective users of Thinking Maps, this would increase their thinking-skills repertoire and encourage autonomy of thinking and collaboration, certainly important if not essential outcomes for every school in a democratic society.

An assumption underlying the explicit teaching of thinking is that instruction in thinking skills can enhance the development of a student's thinking-skills repertoire (e.g., you can identify and teach the skills required for conscious decision making). In a narrow sense, it is always possible to teach thinking-skill strategies and tools and to test a student's cognitive comprehension of these skills or even his or her ability to apply these skills to a given problem. In a broader sense, the vision of many educators and researchers of the thinking-skills movement of the past few decades has been that the direct teaching of thinking is possible and is a necessary next step in the evolution of teaching and learning toward transfer of thinking-skills across—and deeply into—content areas, for interdisciplinary problem solving and lifelong learning. Our story is of a school wanting it both ways: direct, formal teaching of thinking-skills and explicit transfer into content areas.

St. Cuthbert's College, in Auckland, New Zealand, is a unique, single-sex, independent school spanning the K–12 grade levels, with a student population of 1500 girls aged 5–18. The college is expected to provide an outstanding education that encompasses not only academic, sporting, and cultural excellence, but also adds the dimensions of character and values education. Thus, the long-term development of a systematic, fully integrated use of thinking-skills, ultimately leading to our use of Thinking Maps, took a continuous focus and persistent attention to the goal.

There is a high expectation of all involved that we must provide for individual needs and produce graduates who can gain entry to the universities and courses of their choice and approach tertiary studies, and life, with the attitudes and skills that encourage success and personal fulfillment. Parents expect of the school that it retain its traditions and at the same time be innovative. Through the process of our evolution, we have moved from being a high-quality school with strong academic outcomes to being a true learning organization unified by a focus on developing high-quality thinking. Along the way, our academic results have moved us to the top rungs of the educational ladder in New Zealand, but this seems a sidebar to our evolving capacities to seek deeper understandings of how our minds work and to treasure the intrinsic rewards gained from becoming a school as a home for the mind.

PHASE 1: DISCOVERING TOO MANY POSSIBILITIES

In 1992, staff and management began this process by reviewing the school philosophy guided by the following questions: What kind of learners do we want to produce in this college? What behaviors, attitudes, skills, and knowledge would they have? We agreed that we wanted our students to become adults who were lifelong, independent learners, who approached life's situations and problems positively and persevered to find resolutions and answers. It had been the norm in schools such as ours for teachers to be responsible for writing superb lessons. They were expected to supply students with books of resource notes and to test, train, and in general, provide opportunities for students to learn. The focus was disseminating information and expecting students to study and memorize all this valuable knowledge so they could have success in national examinations.

While our school did well in the national rankings of senior secondary examination results, there was a nagging feeling among some staff that our teaching methods were producing graduates who were dependent learners: students who had excellent recall skills, who were prepared to read and study hard, but whose work was careful, methodical, and pedestrian rather than original, inventive, and risk taking. This idea was supported by the fact that many good students gained fine marks of around 75–85%, but relatively few broke into the 90s at university scholarship level. We decided that we had a responsibility to make a change for our students. We embarked on a project in 1992, which we hoped would lead our students toward being autonomous learners.

First, we made a list of all the qualities such a learner would have. What developed from this was the conviction that effective learners are good thinkers who have a range of internalized strategies they can use to do their work. Then we debated these questions, in order to achieve the changes required to create the learning community we had described:

- How would this change our teaching practice?
- How would this change how students apply themselves to education?
- What skills or strategies would they need, if "better thinking" were our goal?
- From the range of theorists and practitioners who wrote on thinking, learning, and best educational practice, which should we use as our models, and which of the many strategies should be chosen?

By 1992, a range of exciting strategies and methodologies, frameworks and programs, were becoming available for teachers who were interested in encouraging their students to think deeply and independently. A group of our staff read through the available literature and attended courses on best practices. The problem soon emerged: too many possibilities. Everyone who went to a course or read one of these books came to school converted and full of enthusiasm to try out the new ideas. We were all over the place. Across our K–12 school could be found pockets of teachers "doing" such processes as Edward de Bono's CORT program, mind mapping, multiple intelligences, or learning styles.

This was all terribly exciting to those of us involved. We held many personal development–training sessions for the whole staff between 1993 and 1994, and some of us became specialists in one process or another. However, by 1994 it became obvious that we had made a great change to individual teaching practice, but done nothing that impacted schoolwide for students. An individual student could have had some very good lessons from innovative teachers but not have recognized the strategies used or their application elsewhere. In addition, students' thinking patterns or habits would have remained unchanged, and they would not have developed a set of strategies they could regularly use to do their work more meaningfully. We were also quite aware that there was very little conceptual transfer or internalization of the strategies.

PHASE 2: FOCUS ON TRANSFER AND "DOUBLE PROCESSING"

As a staff, we decided to focus on transfer: We would all focus on a selection of strategies, teach them across all disciplines at the same time, practice them, and explicitly identify them, so students could see the transfer links and see how useful they could be in different situations. We selected some of the lessons from several programs and had developed the firm belief that students who processed work in a number of different ways gained a deeper understanding of the content. We called this "double processing": If a lesson involved written notes in linear form, then homework could be to talk to parents about it. If a graphic organizer was used in class, then linear notes could be used for follow-up. At this stage, the graphic organizers we used were such things as the fishbone, Venn diagram, sequence boxes, and mind mapping (or concept mapping). None of us had really associated these wide ranging, disconnected graphics with a cognitive function as they were used by staff to sort content information given in class or for homework. They were prescriptive: Students were told to fill them in.

In 1998, we again reviewed our thinking program. So much had been done, but somehow it still seemed more like a personal development program for staff to improve teaching strategies than for the explicit development of autonomous learning for students. Had we gone wrong? Better teaching had led to better marks for all, but it seemed to us that we were not making enough of a difference for *all* students. We referred again to Costa's (1991) vision of a school as a home for the mind as a reference point. Here was a vision of everybody in a school community working together to put thinking central to the way everything was done. What we needed was a common, schoolwide language that we could all use, which could be built on from ages 5 to 18 in greater depth. We had a unique opportunity to introduce good thinking skills early and develop them over the years so they really made a difference, but which approaches were out there that could do this?

PHASE 3: UNITING THE SCHOOL WITH A COMMON LANGUAGE

In 1999, we decided to have a research year where interested staff would examine the various approaches, programs, and strategies that could form the basis of an effective thinking program. We focused on the primary elements of thinking from the critical, creative, and caring/affective domains. Thinking Maps appeared to be an excellent way to focus on eight basic cognitive processes and the use of the Frame of Reference for metacognitive development. The challenge for us was to get both staff and students to see each of these as an effective thinking process, united together as a language, rather than as isolated graphic organizers. Our goal was to gradually teach and implement these over three to five years so students would have a range of strategies to employ.

Year 1: Introducing Thinking Maps in 1999

To introduce a common visual thinking language to the whole K–12 continuum of St. Cuthbert's teaching and learning needs was an ambitious undertaking. We chose to introduce Thinking Maps through a three-year implementation cycle, by first teaching the use of Thinking Maps explicitly within noncurricular contexts. We chose this method of introduction since research (Perkins & Salomon, 1989) revealed that cognitive skills are not automatically acquired if they are not taught explicitly. This was a formal approach carried out by everybody: expected, planned, agreed on by staff. Following the initial training, teachers were grouped into departments to find applications within subjects and units and supported by follow-up sessions as they gained confidence. They began with a narrow view of what an isolated map could do—and what the maps can do together—and we encouraged them to focus on students gaining confidence and experience in use across the curriculum.

We also established a Department of Thinking and employed a thinking coordinator to manage the program and write the lessons using a six-step methodology: Label the strategy (the cognitive skills and map), explain purpose, practice (provide practice experience and feedback), transfer (put into different content contexts), evaluate, and reflect. Teacher attitude was crucial, and where the teacher was confident and prepared, the lessons proved very successful in teaching the strategy.

While the primary school staff and students had a positive attitude toward the Thinking Maps approach, some secondary staff expressed reservations. Secondary staff had concerns about teaching skills in non-curricular contexts; they disliked the imposition of creating "artificial or forced" opportunities for conceptual transfer. In turn, some secondary students questioned the need to learn about the maps separately because "the teacher shows us how to do them in class anyway." These older students said, "We already know how to think and we don't need you to tell us." Generally, this is a situation easily overcome by confident, persuasive teachers who believe that the processes they are teaching can make a difference, but it is very difficult when the teachers themselves are unsure as they integrate the tools into their repertoire.

Despite these difficulties, we achieved our goal of having every child in the school introduced to the maps in an explicit way. Students are able to use all the maps as required in a range of situations and when use of the maps is genuinely integrated and flexible. Most staff model metacognitive processes by saying, "I need to analyze this information—which maps do you think would be useful here?" Consequently, we see much greater choice and flexibility of use, including the use of a range of maps to reach a decision or to extend an idea.

We believe that our earlier work of encouraging teachers to get students to double process notes also paid off: During some lessons, students were only to take notes in map form, then for homework write up the information in linear form, and vice versa. We saw excellent collaborative work develop, as some groups elected to take class notes in map form and work as teams to develop the ideas as fully as possible. It is much easier to see ideas being extended when they can be seen visually, and students enjoy adding to a collaborative map.

We also had considerable success in working meaningfully with departments to help them create units and lessons that used the maps in subjects. These "transfer" lessons were almost always valued highly by staff and students. The goal was to demonstrate how a thinking tool could be used right across the curriculum, how it could be used for homework and study, used in assessments, and used to help make real-life evaluations of problems in context and make decisions.

Teachers began to see how useful a map was in eliciting prior knowledge. Students are now often asked to draw a map early in a topic, which is then repeated at the end of the topic. By comparing the maps, students see and evaluate their own progress, thereby developing a sense of personal efficacy of themselves as learners. Metacognition and evaluation! Students also feel positive as they choose which maps to use when given a task. Secondary staff who initially were not enthusiastic about the maps because they said they had their own subject-specific processes became more positive when they saw that the maps could clearly reveal where thinking had gone wrong. All students benefited from this opportunity to analyze the merits of each other's thinking processes.

Year 2: Evidence of Independent Use in 2000

In the second year, we were confident that students knew what a Thinking Map was (tacit use), but we were uncertain of the degree to which students used the Thinking Maps independently. We wanted to know the extent to which students had moved from tacit use of Thinking Maps, to aware use or even strategic use. Students could use the maps when asked, but we suspected that they did it without clear intent. The challenge for the year 2000 was to gather evidence of the existing students' independent use of the Thinking Maps.

To determine the extent to which a fluent and "reflective" student use of maps occurred in problem-solving situations, we had students use their 20-minute thinking-skills time to collaboratively solve a long-term problem using Thinking Maps. For example, one teacher created a challenging activity on endangered animals playfully presented through a Gary Larson cartoon and asked students to

> Imagine you are a member of a team of researchers charged with reversing the population decline of the endangered "balloon" animals that have a hard time surviving in a harsh landscape. Use Thinking Maps as tools for generating, organizing, and assessing factors that might affect the population size of the balloon animals (e.g., physical factors, catastrophic events, food supply, disease, competition, eco-tourism, etc.). Develop an action plan, based around your Thinking Maps, to help reverse the population decline.

The students' efforts were assessed, and prizes for fluent and flexible use of Thinking Maps were awarded. One group of four students created the example, shown in Figures 12.1 through 12.5, of using multiple maps to analyze this problem.

The purpose of the activity was to evaluate how students, working in cooperative groups, could apply multiple thinking processes via Thinking Maps to gain a solution to the scientific problem found in cartoons and nature. This sample of student work is representative of the quality of work received and reveals how these students could employ the tools for multistep problem solving and decision making. Although some students showed strategic and even reflective use of maps, the majority still struggled to show the fluency we expected in their map use.

Year 3: Reviewing and Moving Forward in 2001

Our review of student applications revealed that there was still a need for more explicit teaching of these tools. The development of autonomous transfer of thinking skills does not happen over just a year or two. It happens during the evolution of a student's educational career and lifetime. Our evaluation of student map use in the year 2000 indicated that many students and some staff were not as confident or competent in the use of Thinking Maps as we believed possible and necessary to reach the goal of being authentic, independent thinkers. We needed to revisit individual maps for fluency.

Though there was a risk of repetition for both teachers and students— the risk that many schools do not take for long-term change—we created a more authentic, thematic learning experience for senior students based on their reflections on the "Big Day Out," a 12-hour music festival that many students and their friends had attended. We also carried out in-school

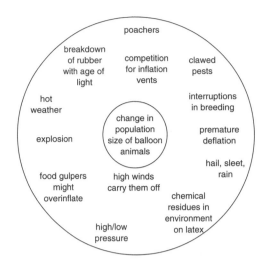

Figure 12.1   Factors Affecting Size of
Population of Balloon Animals

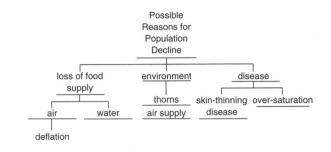

Figure 12.2   Categorizing Factors Affecting Size
of Population of Balloon Animals

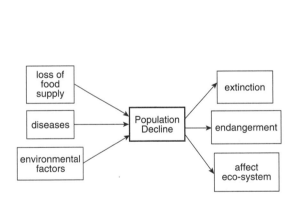

Figure 12.3   Causes and Effects of
Population Decline of Balloon
Animals

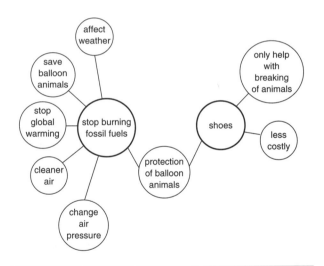

Figure 12.4   Comparing Possible Solutions to
Population Decline

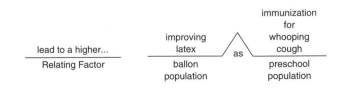

Figure 12.5   Making an Analogous Relationship With a
Possible Solution

research during the year using a questionnaire to ask students about the maps they had used, the subjects in which they used different maps, if they had used maps to organize their thoughts in situations outside of school, and whether they believed their thinking had been developed through learning about Thinking Maps.

In the junior school, students were positive about Thinking Maps, had experienced their use in many different settings, and almost uniformly enjoyed using them to enhance their thinking both at school and at home. In the senior school, the results were predictable: Students who had experienced staff who valued the maps and provided opportunities for transfer into several different curriculum areas were positive about the usefulness of the maps and optimistic about map-related improvements in the way they solved problems or sorted issues. In contrast, students who had been provided with few opportunities to use the maps in curriculum areas or who had had teachers who avowed "grudging compliance" saw the maps, and the thinking-skills lessons, as "boring and a waste of my time." Without opportunities for transfer, senior students marginalized the maps and considered them pointless.

Once again, it was evident that teachers make the difference to the implementation and effective use of a learning strategy. In 2001, in the senior school, we also moved toward more departmental autonomy. Secondary departments were asked questions such as, What kinds of thinking do you most value in your department? What are the most powerful experiences to encourage this thinking for students? What Thinking Map activities will you use to develop these skills? How might you show the effectiveness and value of your thinking-skill focus for students' learning?

Departments were required to add their "thinking focus" to their departmental plan, and staff could choose to be apprised about this thinking focus. Individual departmental choice was interesting. The technology department chose to improve their students' metacognitive thinking through developing links between the sequencing (Flow Maps) and the design process. The art department wanted to use maps to strengthen problem finding and meta-perception. In social sciences, pattern finding was valued, with a focus on Flow Maps for sequencing and Double Bubble Maps for comparing and contrasting, and in the music department, there was exploration of the use of Brace Maps to better teach musical notation and intervals.

Years 4–5: A Common Language in 2003

Through our continued focus and retraining, by 2003 we had achieved a common visual-thinking language across the school, with staff and student competence with the maps much increased. The Department of Thinking expanded to two full-time teachers supported by a team of staff. Examples of student use of Thinking Maps continued to be displayed in every teaching space. They were regularly used in assessments and curriculum lessons. In the secondary school, we saw more experimentation in flexible map use than in the early years, with several maps being linked and used to process a task. In the junior school, the majority of students showed fluent map use by Year 6, and students were adept users of the *Thinking Map Software* (Hyerle & Gray Matter Software, 1998) (See Chapter 9, Thinking Technology).

Thinking Maps continued to be explicitly introduced in the junior school. However, after three years' implementation, the map knowledge base in the senior school was considered to be such that teaching of individual maps was no longer required for any but new students. Flexible catch-up training for new students and new staff was provided each year, and ongoing support from the thinking coordinators was provided on an individual and departmental basis.

By 2003, we have been able to recognize some significant advances in the way the maps are used, especially since St. Cuthbert's College has expanded its professional development time to one and a half hours a week. There has been planned training for teachers in how to link the maps to other thinking or learning strategies. This encourages students to use a wider range of strategies together to engage with the content knowledge. When several approaches are used together—such as linking Costa's 16 habits of mind (1991) with Thinking Maps—the emphasis on isolated tools lessens and changes to an emphasis on the whole thinking and learning processes. It also extends the quality of thinking involved. Here is a sampling of some of the spin-off benefits of our evolution. Teachers have been experimenting with

- developing a metacognitive lesson plan, where teachers identify a specific learning goal, and the questions they can ask students that will allow them to identify for themselves appropriate Thinking Maps to use
- encouraging greater infusion by creating intranet-based learning activities. Students can call up a page of lesson activities available for a task, click on a hyperlink, and be presented with a range of links to higher-order thinking, Thinking Maps, and Multiple Intelligence-differentiation activities. They can then download these directly into their responses.
- encouraging flexible use by having a schoolwide focus on "applied thinking," where a philosophical real-life problem is analyzed using the maps and inquiry techniques

These examples reflect the inherent rigor and flexibility of Thinking Maps and the empowering nature of the change process that was allowed to mature naturally over time. The learning outcomes for our students based on fundamental thinking processes and learning approaches have been remarkable. Academic results in New Zealand's national league tables have risen consistently, with the college a national academic leader, placing 1st or 2nd in New Zealand in every senior external examination category for the past five years, up from 12th at the start of our evolutionary process.

We have also seen improved results on international tests and PATs (reading, listening, and comprehension test), the high level of acceptance and approval from students and parents, and the continued use of double processing using the maps and linear writing from our students who now attend universities.

Yet the most powerful outcome has been the move to collaborative and interactive classrooms where students—and teachers—are confident to discuss their learning and to learn from each other. We now know that students are much more willing to share their work with the class when it is developed visually, collaboratively, and through a flexible, common language for thinking that is the foundation for the evolution of our community. And, as teachers and school leaders, we are able to work deeply in our own content areas, with focused collaboration in teams. After 10 years, we are still living the never-ending ebb and flow of change and thriving as an evolving school as a home for the mind.

13

The Mississippi Story

Marjann Kalehoff Ball, Ed.D.

Topics to be discussed:

- research and significant reading test score results at the junior college level
- from kindergarten to college applications of the Brace Map for part-whole reasoning
- changes in writing performance at the secondary level in formerly underachieving schools

BEYOND EXPECTATIONS

Diana entered my reading and study skills college class at Jones County Junior College with all the reservations of an older, returning student. She appeared bright but unsure of her ability to do well after being out of school for many years. At 16 years of age, she had been diagnosed with arthritis, and by her late twenties had been diagnosed with multiple sclerosis. Diana had been told she could never be an effective learner because of her disabling conditions, but despite the time lapse since her previous formal education, and her lack of confidence, she excelled in the activities in my class. Through the use of Thinking Maps®, she was able to organize content material for discussions and tests. As time passed, Diana shared her joy from successes experienced as a result of using Thinking Maps, not only in my class but also in other areas. She believed she had found a tool by which her limitations and negative predictions could be overcome.

From her achievement in the basic classes, she set a goal of becoming a licensed practical nurse and entered the nurse's aide program. However, after only two weeks into her new endeavor, she sadly informed me that she was withdrawing from college. Surprised, I questioned why, and she answered, "I failed my first nurse's aide test. Now I realize the predictions have come true—I am too limited to meet college requirements." I was not as convinced as she for I had seen her potential. Answering my question about which technique she was using to study, she said, "The Notetaking System of Learning, SQ3R, and Thinking Maps." "How often have you used Thinking Maps?" I asked. To which she replied, "A little." My response was, "Don't use them a little—use them a lot!" She left my office that day with her spirits lifted and a promise to apply Thinking Maps to her studies.

After two weeks, she appeared with a smile on her face and the declaration that she had decided to stay in college. When asked what had changed her mind (and hoping it was success), she replied "I have been using Thinking Maps daily." As a result, she had made an A on her last nurse's aide test. She was absolutely elated, and from that day on, she experienced success on tests in that program, leading to her entry into the Licensed Practical Nursing (LPN) Program, where she excelled. As she progressed in her studies, she began assisting her peers in learning how to organize their material. Not only did she win the gratitude of her fellow students, but the instructors were impressed with Diana's outstanding performance on tests, class work, and State Board examinations. Diana completed her LPN training as an outstanding student and quickly secured a position in a hospital as an LPN. As a result, the nursing staff proposed and established a pilot program in which all entering LPNs would learn how to use Thinking Maps.

COLLEGE-LEVEL TRANSFER

Diana's story helps validate my confidence in Thinking Maps, which I employ in my reading, study skills, and English classes at Jones County Junior College (JCJC) in Ellisville, Mississippi. As a faculty member of the college since 1981, I have faced the challenge of how to address the individual needs of students, transcending their differences while maintaining the purported integrity of the college curriculum. The setting is a melting pot for ability levels, potential courses, and advanced educational plans. Because most community/junior colleges are committed to the open-door policy of admitting students regardless of their ability, age, experiential background, or career aspirations, they are faced with the profound problem of how to treat such diversity. ACT composite scores may range from 8 to 32, while a profile of personal characteristics of these students presents a new, less traditional type of student clamoring to be taught. Supported by civil rights litigation and generous government and scholarship aid and buttressed by a prevailing confidence in the efficacy of advanced education as well as the demands of a complicated technological society, these students have come in unprecedented numbers.

When I began teaching at JCJC, I was baffled by the apparent failure of the students to transfer thinking skills learned in my classes to other academic areas. After nearly 10 years of frustrating efforts to find more effective strategies, I discovered Thinking Maps, which have produced amazing results over the years from K–12 into college. As I began using the maps, my colleagues from other academic areas informed me, "Your students are doodling in my class. They are drawing circles and squares while I am lecturing." "Oh no," I confidently replied, "They are not doodling—they are thinking!" I realized that I had a tool for learning, a vehicle I needed to help students develop and transfer critical thinking skills to various academic areas.

As the use of Thinking Maps continued, a change occurred in the way students approached learning. They no longer looked at the magnitude of their textbooks, but instead they organized and simplified the material by mapping assigned readings. They began to recognize patterns of organization in paragraphs and passages by applying the appropriate Thinking Map to specific reading selections. Making further connections of the thought process to Thinking Maps enabled them to see the type of thinking required to complete a particular task. One of my college students had been diagnosed with attention deficit disorder as a young girl and had been sent to numerous tutors who equipped her with a variety of study strategies that did not work. After being taught Thinking Maps, she commented, "I like Thinking Maps because they are how I think anyway; now I have ways to organize all that information." She proceeded to make a 100 on her first American History test after mapping the material.

EFFECTIVE STRATEGIES FOR READING COMPREHENSION

After I used the maps for several years in my college classes, it was deemed feasible to determine whether or not the maps, interwoven with an existing college reading course, would have a significant effect on reading scores or be affected by the status (traditional/nontraditional) of the student. The investigation was conducted over two semesters with a sample of 92 students forming the control and experimental groups. Determination was made as to whether the treatment of mapping had resulted in a significant difference in reading scores as well as on which variables of fast reading, phonics, comprehension, scanning, structure, vocabulary, and word parts the mapping and no-mapping groups differed. Necessary calculations were made using the multivariate analysis of covariance (MANCOVA) using the Wilk's lambda criterion. Follow-up univariate analyses were utilized to clarify any significant multivariate results.

Statistically significant main effects were found for the treatment. There were no significant main effects for status, nor was there a significant interaction between treatment (mapping/no mapping) and status (traditional/nontraditional). Significant differences at the .01 level were found for five out of seven subtests of fast reading, comprehension, structure, vocabulary, and word parts, with the mapping group outperforming the no-mapping group on each of the five variables. The findings of the univariate treatment by status analysis of covariance were consistent with the results of the multivariate analysis, which found that only the main effects of treatment were statistically significant. No statistically significant effects were found for status, nor was interaction between treatment and status statistically significant. *It may be concluded that mapping made a significant difference on reading test scores.* Whether a person is characterized by age, social roles assumed, or other criteria such as traditional or nontraditional made no significant impact on reading test scores.

These findings were published in my dissertation at the University of Southern Mississippi (Ball, 1998). The research findings along with improved student performance and satisfaction reinforced my confidence in Thinking Maps as an indispensable teaching tool. Each semester I survey my students at the end of the term as to which strategies used were most beneficial, and over the past 10 years, 90% of the students have chosen Thinking Maps as most helpful in studying textbooks, organizing material, retrieving information, and taking tests. Their responses include, "Why did I have to be in college before I learned about Thinking Maps?" "Thinking Maps are really useful and have brought my grades up." "Thinking Maps move me right into what I am doing."

FROM PILOT PROJECT
TO CAMPUSWIDE APPLICATIONS

The ripple effect from the utilization of Thinking Maps is amazing. Based on the success of students in my college classes as well as the achievements of my student Diana and the interest of other nursing students and the nursing instructors, a pilot program was set up in spring 2002 at JCJC by which entering LPN students would be instructed in the use of Thinking Maps in their nursing courses. Upon taking the exit exam at the conclusion of the structure and function course, 100% of the students passed the exam, the first time this had occurred in 17 years. Another group of entering LPN students was taught Thinking Maps in spring 2003, with a 100% passing rate on the Comprehensive Fundamentals of Nursing Exam (Educational Resource Inc., Fundamentals of Nursing) given at the end of the semester. Sandra Waldrup, the director of practical nursing, said, "The Practical Nursing faculty is constantly trying to identify methods which would make learning and retention easier for our students. The volume of information they need can be overwhelming. Thinking Maps provide a consistent way to organize and link related concepts into a manageable system. Our students benefit from Thinking Maps as indicated in their evaluations."

As I began the fourth semester of Thinking Maps training for LPNs in fall 2003, one of my students remained after class to say, "My mother is working successfully as an LPN after completing the course at JCJC. When I told her you were teaching me about Thinking Maps, she shared with me that she had profited from using Diana's nursing notes, which were all in Maps. I feel confident that I will make it using the Thinking Maps, which my mother passed on to me."

Another student in the fourth-semester training, Heather Lewis, wrote, "I am using Thinking Maps for the LPN program, and wanted you to know that my grades have gone from C's and B's to high B's and A's. I'm so glad, and now I am using the Maps in everything." Based on the successful use of Thinking Maps in the basic college courses and other curriculum courses such as the LPN training, the president of JCJC, Dr. Ronald Whitehead, has instructed the Department of Information and Research to pursue means by which Thinking Maps may be secured for use in other academic and vocational areas of the college in 2003–2004.

FROM COLLEGE TO KINDERGARTEN

After using Thinking Maps in my classes and seeing positive results from their application, I felt compelled to share these visual tools with others. I thought that if college students who believed they could not perform satisfactorily were succeeding with the help of Thinking Maps, could not this tool also make a difference in the lives of K–12 school children before they became frustrated and deemed themselves failures?

My outreach began as I presented the results I had experienced from the use of Thinking Maps at conferences and workshops, including the 1999 and the 2000 National Association for Developmental Education Conferences as well as the Mississippi Association for Developmental Education Conference. I contacted school districts from which many JCJC students come, discussing the benefits of teaching Thinking Maps to their students before they enter college. In Jones County, a district I call "the pioneer of Thinking Maps in Mississippi" indicated its willingness to introduce the tools to its K–12 teachers. Located in a largely rural area of the state, the Jones County School District, composed of seven elementary, three middle, and three high schools, piloted Thinking Maps across the district in Grade 4. Twenty-five fourth-grade teachers utilized the maps, and after one year, the district's score increased from level 3.5 to 4.3 (with 5.0 being the highest), with the fourth grade's scores increasing most significantly. Because of this improvement in fourth-grade students' scores, implementation for the whole district began. Eight years later, Jones County continues to show growth and maintain high achievement, scoring a level 4.0 in 2003. Thomas Prine, superintendent of Jones County School District, states, "Thinking Maps allow children when confronted with a problem to have a process that they can use to organize their thoughts enabling them to solve that problem. As a result, the students in our district have excelled district-wide."

By the mid-1990s, as the successful use of Thinking Maps became better known, interest grew. During the 1995–1996 school year, Dr. Susan Rucker, principal at Brandon Middle School, implemented Thinking Maps in Grades 4–8 in her school. Dr. Rucker, currently Associate Superintendent for Innovation and School Improvement at the Mississippi Department of Education, states, "As former principal of Brandon Middle School, I saw the use of Thinking Maps as a way to help students organize their thinking processes. The program proved to be a success for students who had difficulty with performance-based thinking skills. Students of all ability levels showed improvement."

Throughout Dr. Rucker's school, maps were evident everywhere: on the floor, on the ceiling, in display cabinets, in the hallways, in the classrooms, even in the cafeteria. After the introductory Thinking Maps training, Dr. Rucker's expectations included having teachers explain in their lesson plans how the maps would be used and show evidence of dialogue between teacher and student, teacher and teacher, and student and student on Thinking Maps as well as evidence of student and teacher utilization of the maps. When the statewide performance-based scores were published that year, Brandon Middle School students had significantly increased by 10 performance-based points in all but one grade level, leading Brandon Middle School to be named one of only five Blue Ribbon Schools in the state that year.

FROM READING COMPREHENSION TO WRITING PROFICIENCY

At Nicholson, a K–6 school in Picayune School District, a mid-size rural district on the Mississippi-Louisiana border, as teachers utilized the maps, they noted significant improvement in scores on teacher-made and standardized tests. This success peaked an interest in *Write From the Beginning*, (Buckner, 2000), a K–5 writing program based on Thinking Maps (see Chapter 7, Empowering Students From Thinking to Writing). At the end of a year, the writing scores of the students from this school on the state writing test were the highest in the district. Nicholson Elementary exceeded the state's average in both 2002 (0.4 higher) and 2003 (0.5 higher). Roseland Park, which was Picayune's second-year Thinking Maps school, and Westside, a third-year Thinking Maps school, achieved adequate yearly progress (AYP) in all areas (reading, language, math, social studies, and other indicators-growth index) as per federal guidelines in 2003. As a result of the increase in test scores, as well as teacher and student satisfaction, Thinking Maps were expanded to the remainder of the elementary schools and to the junior high and senior high schools. Advanced training tailored to all content areas and grade levels is taking place during the 2003–2004 school year.

Dr. Penny Wallin, presently Superintendent of the Picayune School District, was one of the first National Board-certified teachers in

Mississippi and in the nation and used Thinking Maps when she was a classroom teacher. She states, "In my roles as National Board Certified Teacher, college professor, and now administrator, I understand the importance of equipping learners with pathways to learning. Although all students do not learn in the same way or at the same rate, they must think and process. I began using Thinking Maps in my classroom and as an administrator continue to embrace them. Thinking Maps are truly useful for a lifetime providing consistent, common visual tools that support the eight thinking processes as identified by research."

Another school district, Pass Christian, a small district (two elementary, one middle, and one high school) located on the Mississippi Gulf Coast, began training their middle school teachers along with some high school teachers in the use of the maps. After a little over a year using the maps, the writing scores of seventh-grade students on the state writing assessment increased from level 2.2 to level 3.0 (with 4.0 being the highest level). Only two students received level 4 in 2002, while 40 students attained level 4 in 2003. Upon investigation of what had made such a difference, it was noted that most of the students achieving level 4 had been instructed in Thinking Maps and had been using them in their classrooms. As a result of these successes, additional training took place in both elementary schools and the high school to insure districtwide immersion in Thinking Maps for all levels.

Perhaps one of the most significant implementations in Mississippi is the magnitude at which the maps have been implemented in the Jackson Public Schools, the largest school district in Mississippi, with 60 schools. In 1999, seven of the elementary schools served as the pilot for Thinking Maps implementation. By the second year, another seven elementary schools had been added, and by the third year, all but two elementary schools had received training. In the fourth year, some teachers from each middle school had received map training, while *Write From the Beginning* (Buckner, 2000) had been introduced to some elementary teachers. During the fifth year, the goal is to extend Thinking Maps training to all the high school teachers as well as to train all elementary and special education teachers in *Write From the Beginning*.

The impact Thinking Maps have had on the education of Mississippi's students is impressive. To date, approximately 215 schools (129 elementary, 49 middle, and 37 high schools), 10,400 teachers, and 312,000 students have been exposed to the maps. Dr. Tressie Harper, Superintendent of Moss Point schools, where Thinking Maps have been used districtwide for two years, says, "Students can look at Thinking Maps as tools in a tool box. They can bring out whichever Map to do whichever thinking task they are embracing."

THE RIVER RUNS DEEP AND WIDE

It appears that one of the reasons for the outstanding results and longevity of Thinking Maps in Mississippi schools is the depth of training followed by the degree to which the maps are implemented. After a school has used Thinking Maps for one year, teachers from each school are selected to become expert trainers for their school. Criteria of selection include expertise in the use of the maps, the employment of innovative methods, and the ability to communicate and collaborate effectively with colleagues. A network of Thinking Maps trainers across the state has been established, and meetings are conducted to keep these individuals updated and to provide additional curriculum ideas for their schools.

As an extension of the development of an expert teacher-based training group, the first annual Thinking Maps Conference was held at JCJC in October 2002. This gathering brought together over 300 educators, from kindergarten to college, from all over the state to experience the power of these common visual tools. Keynote addresses were given, but most important, teachers presented a range of Thinking Maps applications in break-out sessions. The "Thinking Maps Gallery" highlighting student and teacher projects provided an opportunity for educators to share ideas and to see integration of the maps with all levels and areas of curriculum.

This gallery of work from K–12 schools from across the state showed that this common visual language has the capacity to connect all learners. Much like the examples shown in the gallery, the examples shown here (Figures 13.1a – d) illustrate the developmental range of the use of just one tool, the Brace Map, focused on only one piece of content knowledge, the structural parts of the eye.

These examples show how the same concept created at varying levels of vocabulary and difficulty may be presented using Thinking Maps as a common visual language to enhance depth of learning, bonding students from kindergarten to fifth and eighth grade, to the college levels.

BRIDGING THE GENERATION GAP

As a professor and now a change agent in schools, I am continually made aware of the far-reaching implications and possibilities of the maps for students and teachers. Traveling to numerous school districts across the state, I have seen Thinking Maps used in classrooms from kindergarten to twelfth grade. Not only do I share with these teachers what I have learned about Thinking Maps, but I also take away many new and exciting ways to use maps in my college classroom. Throughout my 25 years of teaching, I have tried many interventions to help students become more successful learners and have often changed strategies and texts. One thing, however, has not been altered—use of Thinking Maps. When my students ask, "May I take these home to my children?" or say, "I helped my child with his Bubble Map last night and he helped me with mine," then I am certain that Thinking Maps are not only the bridge from subject to subject but also from generation to generation.

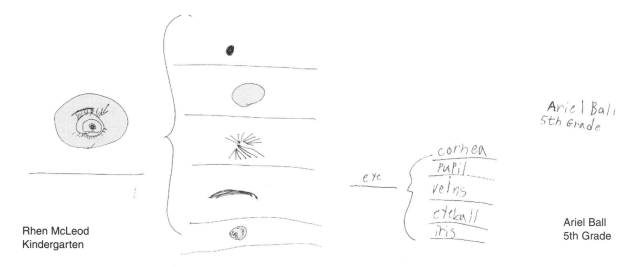

Rhen McLeod
Kindergarten

Figure 13.1a Kindergarten Brace Map of the Eye

Ariel Ball
5th Grade

Figure 13.1b Fifth-Grader Brace Map of the Eye

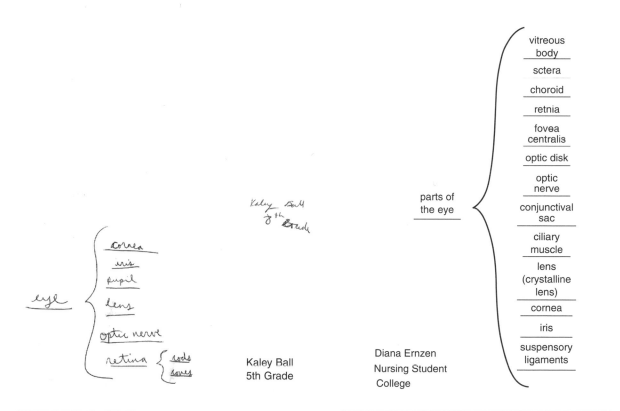

Kaley Ball
5th Grade

Figure 13.1c Eighth-Grader Brace Map of the Eye

Diana Ernzen
Nursing Student
College

Figure 13.1d College Nursing Student Brace Map of the Eye

14

The Singapore Experience: Student-Centered Fluency

Ho Po Chun, M.Ed.

Topics to be discussed:

- Thinking Maps® in a multilingual country focused on thinking processes and information literacy
- using Chinese language characters within a Multi-Flow Map for facilitating cause-and-effect reasoning
- bringing students to fluency through direct instruction in Thinking Maps and software

Singapore is a small city-state nation with a rich, diverse history as a major trading center in the heart of the Asian oceans. As a crossroads island for commerce it has been conquered and colonized many times over hundreds of years, with the British relinquishing authority to Singaporeans just a few decades ago. Understandably, it has a diverse population with many cultures and languages, from Chinese, Indian, and Malaysian to British influences. Singapore is just four times the size of Washington, DC, with a population of approximately four million. Our main language is English. Our country has also become one of the Asian economic powers in the past decade, mostly through finance and technology, not through its natural resources. Unlike its Asian neighbors, Singapore has no significant stores of natural resources from which an industrial, manufacturing economy can thrive, even needing to import fresh drinking water from Malaysia. It is understandable, then, that in the twenty-first century, our only true natural resources are the minds of our citizens. Singapore is quickly becoming an information nation.

With this background, it makes sense that the Singapore government hosted the Fourth International Thinking Conference in 1997. This conference is convened every two years in locales from M.I.T. in Cambridge, Massachusetts, to Auckland, New Zealand, and has been coordinated by leaders in the field of thinking-skills development. The theme of the Singapore conference was appropriately titled "Thinking Schools, Learning Nation." This event has been used as one leverage point for shifting the mindset of our educational system—and country—from a more traditional focus on rote learning to include the facilitation of thinking as an integral part of learning.

At the opening ceremonies of the conference, the president of Singapore spoke eloquently about the need—the necessity—for Singaporeans to reinvent themselves in pursuit of the highest quality education based on consciously and systematically developing the creative and analytical thinking of Singapore's people. While the conference participants from all over the world, including over 400 Singaporean principals, listened, it became clear that the speaker could have been any president of any country in the world, as the world now turns on the capacities of its citizenry to think, problem solve, use technology, and collaborate effectively across the globe.

Aziz Tyebally, a teacher and head of the Department for Humanities at Chung Cheng High School, a school that has successfully implemented Thinking Maps, recently delivered a research paper at a nationwide symposium that revealed this need: "In a knowledge-based economy, information is abundant. What made one person more successful than the other was not the information alone, but rather how effectively he made use of the information. Therefore, our program is designed to prepare the pupils for the economy of the future."

The president and this teacher both made the point that all Singaporeans, including parents of the future workers and citizens of the country, need to improve their thinking. This focus became our entry point into directly training students to become fluent in the use of Thinking Maps.

THINKING MAPS IMPLEMENTATION: STUDENT-CENTERED TRAINING

Presenters at the conference such as Peter Senge, Edward de Bono, and Art Costa spoke about the need for systems thinking, approaching problems from multiple points of view, and activating habits of mind such as reflectiveness and metacognition. The Thinking Maps model was also presented by Dr. David Hyerle as a way to integrate thinking-skills instruction with content learning, habits of mind with technology, and teaching and learning with assessment. By the end of the conference, many educators in

Singapore were excited about many new directions and processes, including Thinking Maps. As one first step, the Singapore branch of the Association for Supervision and Curriculum Development invited Dr. Hyerle to return the following year to present the theoretical and practical foundations for using visual tools, generally, and Thinking Maps, specifically, to about 400 teachers from primary and secondary schools and junior colleges over three days.

While our early results of implementation a year later in a few pilot schools revealed that the Thinking Maps were effective, the model of whole-school training and follow-up with teachers that is used in the United States for implementing Thinking Maps did not mesh with the existing organizational structures in Singapore. The schools and class sizes are large, the time-sensitive curriculum well defined, and the teachers are focused on the continuing efforts to achieve consistently high content-based test score results, placing Singapore very high on international rankings in mathematics and science. So we went in a significantly different direction than most professional development designs: We focused on students as the first target population for training. We also proceeded to draw on the strength of our country that the president had pointed to in his opening address: the complete commitment by every parent to give their children a world-class education.

In most countries, professional development focuses on the training of teachers first, who then use new instructional methods with their students. However, because Thinking Maps are also student centered—and given the structure of our schools and funding—we offered a unique plan: Our consultants would directly train classrooms full of students in how to use Thinking Maps and *Thinking Maps Software* on a weekly basis over one or two semesters. Schools are given $160.00 per student annually that may be used by the school for enrichment courses for its students. However, the school has to seek the approval of the parents before signing a student up for a course. Each school is also allotted $80.00 for each student. This money is to be used solely on the students to meet their particular learning needs. The funding was available, and many parents enrolled their students in our Thinking Maps courses.

Through our targeted training courses, students become fluent with the maps much more quickly than if teachers had to integrate the approach into their day-to-day lessons. This is much like the use of computers: Often students may be more open to new technologies, as they don't have to consider what they need to change or replace in a complex and content-laden curriculum. In addition, and this may seem odd to an outsider, unlike teachers in other countries, where the students move from classroom to classroom at the secondary level, here, the teachers are the "rovers" and the students stay in the home base for most of their lessons, except perhaps for Mother Tongue (Chinese, Malay, or Tamil), Music, Art, Computer, and P.E. lessons. This means that a teacher does not have the exclusive use of a particular classroom and the students remain the center of attention.

At this point, 11,594 primary school students and 1,629 secondary school students have gone through direct training by our consultants, and a total of 730 teachers have gone through an intensive course of 12 hours over 3 days to become experts for their schools. Through this whole process, we have learned that the ultimate power of these tools lies in the hands and minds of the learner.

Student Workshops

The student workshop model turned out to be every bit as successful as we had envisioned. After every course, we would ask students to fill out an evaluation. Below are the comments of some Primary 6 students who have attended our workshops:

"Thinking Maps help me in my Reading Comprehension. I'm able to sequence ideas in a passage."

"In Composition, using the Multi-Flow Map helps me look at the bigger picture."

"Thinking Maps help me expand my vocabulary."

"Thinking Maps help me keep to the point—no 'straying.'"

"The use of Thinking Maps helps me save time."

"My vocabulary has improved after using Thinking Maps."

These comments came from students actively integrating Thinking Maps into their daily work in school through activities that we used to develop fluency of thinking processes. The activities are explicit, systematic, developmental, content deep, and directly train students how to independently employ multiple maps to products such as essay and creative writing that are required by their teachers. The infusion activities that we created are on a continuum, building from introduction to each cognitive skill, the respective map, and multimap use toward products in every content area. Importantly, these levels of fluid, flexible, and novel applications demonstrated by our students exceeded our expectations. We believe this is because we started our work in Singapore focused on student fluency and not on teachers, becoming slowly comfortable with sharing the maps with students over months and years.

An example of an infusion activity that we developed in order to scaffold student thinking and bring fluency to students is shown in an abbreviated form (Figure 14.1). This activity is conducted in Session 10 with Primary 4 students. The previous nine one-hour sessions introduced students to each of the eight maps and the Frame of Reference. This lesson is designed to support students in generating their own story using multiple maps of their choosing. The lead activity in this lesson is to show four pictures of the process of burglars breaking into an apartment, with the final panel showing the family coming home to find the house a wreck and a beautiful vase shattered and in pieces on the floor. The defined outcomes

Session 10   Theme: A Burglary

Primary 4 Lesson Plan   Picture Composition

Objective: To revise the use of Circle, Bubble, and Flow Maps

1. Pupils to study the pictures and come up with different scenarios. (5 Mins) (Robbers are not necessarily strangers. May be an inside job)

2. Pupils brainstorm for ideas and write in Circle Map. (5 Mins) (broke into the house, wore black outfits, would not be seen in the dark, ransacked the house, sound of the breaking vase woke the family, armed with baseball bats and brooms)

3. Pupils use Bubble Map to describe the scene and feelings of the characters. (5 Mins) (Remember to use the frame of reference)

   Example: Scene—late night, quiet house, messy, broken vase, loud crash, thorough search
   Feelings—*burglars:* nervous, disappointed, scared, panic, alarmed, frantic, daring
   physical appearance: black outfits, suspicious looking
   family: shocked, puzzled, angry, suspicious, nervous, scared, worried

4. Pupils sequence the story using the Flow Map. (5 Mins)

5. The conclusion can be a surprise ending. (5 Mins)

   - Something left by the robbers, whom they knew
   - Discovered that she had found something in the vase that she had forgotten
   - Invaluable vase
   - Found long-lost heirloom

(35 Minutes)
Pupils write out the Maps on their own.

***Pupils write draft 2. To be handed in next session.

Figure 14.1   Lesson Planning

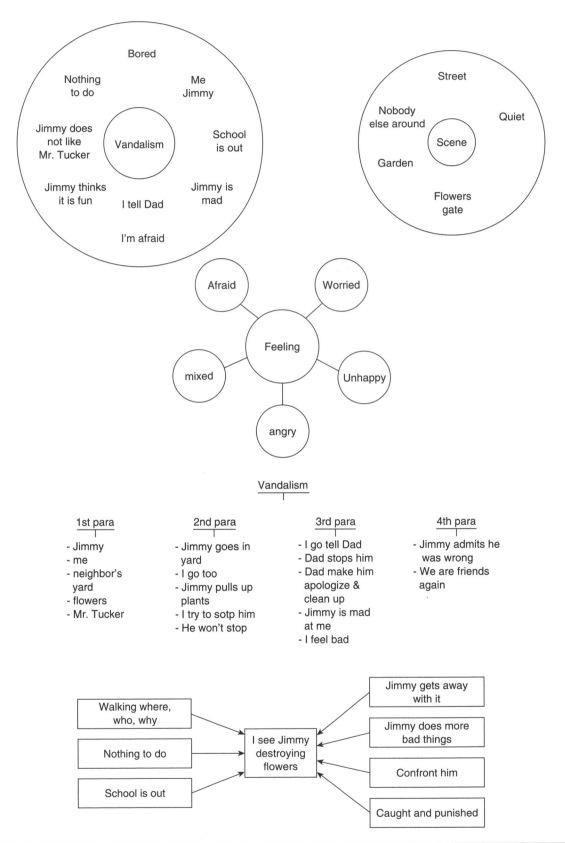

Figure 14.2a Student Maps

Vandalism

School was over for the day. Jimmy, my brother, and I were bored. We wandered down the street looking for something to do. We were the best of friends and always did things together, sometimes with some other kids, too, but today nobody else was around.

"Hey, look! There's old man Tucker's garden. Looks like he's not home. Let's go see it." Jimmy pointed down the street. Mr. Tucker was very old and lived alone. He loved working in his garden and had a lot of flowers and potted plants.

Jimmy ran through the open gate and I followed, hesitantly. Our parents always told us not to go on other people's property without being invited. Jimmy went over to a large bush with bright red flowers. With a sly grin, he pulled off a handful of flowers and threw them over his head, laughing.

"Jimmy! Don't do that! You know not to do things like that!"

"So? I'm just having fun. The flowers will die and fall off anyway."

"But you shouldn't tear them up. Mr. Tucker will be mad with you."

"Yeah? Well he won't know who did it. Unless somebody tells him. And nobody knows except you, and you never tell on me for anything."

He was right. I had never told on him before, since most of the stuff we did together wasn't bad. Maybe annoying, but nothing like stealing or wrecking somebody's else's property. I watched him for a minute as he pulled up some green leafy plants and tossed them around. I just couldn't let him continue.

"Jimmy! Stop it!!"

"You gonna make me?" he said.

I turned and ran home. Dad was in his study reading the newspaper. "Dad, you better come see what Jimmy's doing." I felt bad by telling on him, and was worried that he would be mad and not be my best friend anymore. But I just couldn't let him get away with it. If he got caught, Old Mr. Tucker might call the police, and that would be worse than telling Dad.

Dad brought Jimmy home and told him that when Mr. Tucker came home they would both go over and Jimmy would apologize and clean up what he had done, and then he would work for Mr. Tucker helping him in his garden for two weeks after school to pay for his mischief.

Jimmy scowled at me angrily. I wanted to sink through the floor. But the next day he admitted that I had done the right thing, and he felt bad about what he had done. We were pals again.

Figure 14.2b Story Writing to Accompany Maps

of this activity are for students to be able to independently develop ideas and suitable phrases using the Circle Map, become fluent in developing descriptors of emotional responses of characters using the Bubble Map, and then create a logical progression of events with a surprise using the Flow Map. The product was the use of the maps to write a story about the events.

This lesson was followed in Session 11 by a creative writing assignment using the setting of a conflict in which they are involved. The students were told that they did not have to replicate the use of three maps from the three lessons, nor were they expected to use the maps in the same way. Figure. 14.2b shows a piece of writing about an imaginary situation in which a boy is with his brother, who decides to tear up a neighbor's garden. The page of prewriting using five different maps in very unique ways is an exemplary use of the tools (Figure 14.2a). As you can see, information is actually scaffolded in the maps, moving from a general Circle Map on "vandalism" and then focusing in on the crime "scene." The emotional state of having a brother involved in such an escapade is described in a Bubble Map, using revealing adjectives such as "afraid," "worried," and "unhappy." The next shift is to a Tree Map for organizing the details of each paragraph. The prewriting process is completed by using a Multi-Flow Map to think about the causes and effects of this event. The final essay directly reflects the culminating Tree Map, where everything is put together in detail and information is grouped by paragraphs.

If you look closely at the prewriting and the product (Figure 14.2b) it is easy to see that not all of the information in the maps makes it into this story. This is because we trained students not to merely replicate the information from their prewriting maps in a formal way, but to use the maps as a grounding for the essay. Often when students use static graphic organizers for writing, the writing becomes static. In this case, the writing flows nicely, even without a Flow Map, because the author has generated the rich, holistic ideas and vocabulary that enable flexible and creative writing.

Teacher Training

Of course, to give this attention to student fluency and transfer in the classroom, we knew that our model had to target teachers as well as students. While our initial focus was on the students, we did not neglect the training needs of the teachers. As mentioned above, many teachers went through 12 hours of professional development, but often class teachers would be observing and learning along with the students during our student workshops. This supported teachers' understanding of the tools in real time, using the deep examples and modeling shown above, rather than sitting through long hours of workshop trainings. The teachers are happy that they are able to teach with the Thinking Maps as soon as they are trained because their students already know the maps. Many teachers initially believed that there was no need to take the extra time in teaching the maps to their students, so our work offered them dual support. By taking over one of their classes, we not only taught the maps to the students, but the teachers were able to learn the maps at the same time.

Our consultants also conducted follow-up visits to the school to offer advice and support in the school's implementation efforts in integrating Thinking Maps into the curriculum. The number of visits and the kind of help offered depends upon the needs of the school. This ensures that the school is continually supported in its implementation process. During these visits, issues such as monitoring of student work, provision of assistance to the heads of departments, and any other matters related to learning and teaching with the maps are addressed. Below are comments by teachers who have used Thinking Maps in their lessons:

"My pupils are better at organizing their writing. I see more descriptive words used in their writing."

"Excellent! They can control their time better in the sense that they can complete a story within the composition time limit. This must be due to their efficiency in their organization skills."

"The pupils are more confident and are able to use the TMs to generate ideas in some activities. In Comprehension, pupils are able to pick out/highlight important ideas and not lift out sentences from the passage."

"Thinking Maps helped students to focus better."

"Pupils more aware of flow of ideas."

"Pupils have improved in ideas and vocabulary. Pupils attempting to use newly acquired vocabulary."

"They are more confident in the use of it as a thinking tool. Showed better organization of ideas as they have a standard framework to work on."

Thought and Languages

In response to the call from our Ministry of Education to systematically support creative and analytical thinking, many teachers, for the first time, have a flexible structure that enables them to develop their students' thinking processes. Aziz Tyebally, quoted earlier, describes how their department used the high level of student fluency with the maps to engender a new way to assess students:

The pupils are required to use Thinking Maps to represent the development of their group discussions as well as their individual thought process. The Thinking Maps are dynamic, as they can be constantly built upon over a period of time, hence, a measure of their development of thought could be seen. The school has also incorporated a write-up on Thinking Maps in their Humanities Handbook and uses it as a means of assessment. The Maps were simple enough to learn, so the opportunities for use in complex situations were immense. This was further supported by user-friendly software, which the students could use to enhance their projects. The feedback from students, using a feedback form, was highly positive from the first course conducted. We noted that the number of times per week students say they use Thinking Maps in class and on their own has increased over the years. This seems to indicate that Thinking Maps are becoming more extensively used as a common visual language.

The ease of use, the fluid quality of students' use of the tools, and the flexible structure leading to a new way of assessing thinking and learning have all been essential to the use of Thinking Maps across subject areas and grade levels. The metacognitive skills of the students in these schools are also more evident when the teachers are more fluent in each of the maps, and in particular the Frame of Reference. When teachers systematically keep a portfolio of their students' work using the maps, they are better able to track the development of their students' thinking processes.

There is something powerful as well as subtle about this common visual language for learning that transcends other models of thinking and best practices. We have found that these tools are not bound by language or culture. There were some initial concerns voiced by some principals that the Mother Tongue (Chinese, Tamil, Malay) teachers would not adapt to the use of Thinking Maps as well as the other subject teachers. Just the opposite transpired. We see examples all the time of Chinese characters and other languages embedded naturally within the patterns of thinking represented in the maps. For example, a student has created a Multi-Flow Map showing the causes and effects of throwing things from tall buildings (Figure 14.3), a real concern in Singapore since many families live in high-rise apartment buildings. These second-language, Mother Tongue teachers have surpassed all expectations by demonstrating how innovative and creative they are in integrating the maps into their lessons.

We believe that this is because the cognitive patterns such as sequencing, categorization, and analogies are universal processes of humankind and of the human mind. The visual maps become a common reference point for communicating, expressing, and uniting thought and language. In a country such as Singapore, where East *has met* West, our island culture may be best understood as an embodiment of layers of languages and cultures from generations. We need common tools such as Thinking Maps that help us communicate through the often impenetrable barriers of language and culture that have the potential of separating us. There may be a lesson here for every country at the beginning of the twenty-first century. We, as global citizens, are increasingly in need of common ways of communicating as our world becomes ever more connected and globalized, as technologies web us together, and as we seek to find common ground through understanding about how different people think around the world. As many have said, we may have much more in common than we think.

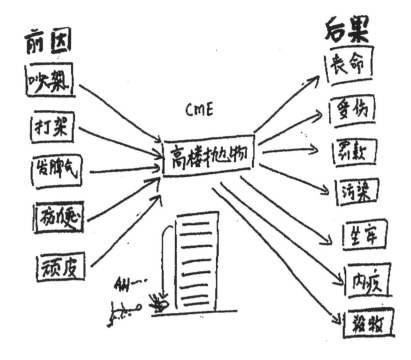

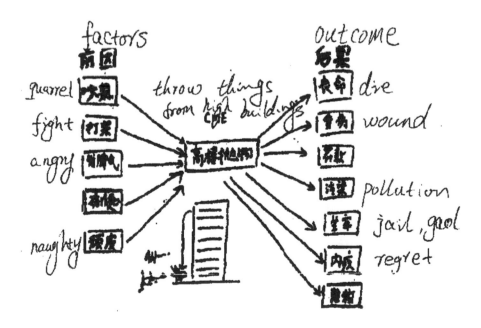

Figure 14.3 Chinese "Highrise" Multi-Flow Map and Translation

SECTION 4

Transforming Professional Development

15

Inviting Explicit Thinking

Sarah Curtis, M.Ed.

Topics to be discussed:

- facilitating reflective practice by teachers through a training of trainers model
- using student-centered work to heighten teachers' understandings of teaching, learning, and assessment
- flexibility with Thinking Maps® for planning and in-the-moment teaching

RESPONSIBLE AND RESPONSIVE PROFESSIONAL DEVELOPMENT

Reacting to the urgency to improve student performance, schools have implemented program upon program and offered workshop after workshop with few opportunities and insufficient time for teachers to deeply learn, integrate, or reflect upon these approaches. Educators of the early twenty-first century face a daunting challenge of trying to meet the needs of all students, of all languages, ethnicities, abilities, and socioeconomic backgrounds, while being held to new standards of achievement. An increase in accountability and a leveling of support leave many educators feeling overwhelmed, undirected, and unprepared. Michael Fullan, a researcher of change processes, states that "the greatest problem faced by school districts and schools is not resistance to innovation, *but the fragmentation, overload and incoherence resulting from the uncritical acceptance of too many different innovations*" (Sparks, 1997).

As a teacher, I felt burdened and exhausted because everywhere I turned it seemed like I had to teach one more unit of content, administer another test, or address the state standards. Buried under district initiatives, school memos, the new math program, and a recently adopted curriculum, I could barely see through to the real purpose for all these improvements: student achievement. After spending weeks wading through a topic driven curriculum and figuratively traveling the globe and spanning centuries of time to reteach myself Renaissance history, the ancient cultures of Meso-America, and the principles of force and motion, I wondered, how could I integrate these isolated topics, and how would my students be able to jump from stone to stone constructing a pathway of understanding?

My unsettling experience with fragmentation was transformed as I began to apply Thinking Maps as learning and thinking tools for myself and for my students. While constructing a whole from the pieces, it became apparent to me that educators need tools and processes to meaningfully translate these initiatives into practice and to support and engage teacher thinking through the implementation process. As a result of my experiences with Thinking Maps, engaging educators in reflective thinking about teaching and learning through the use of this language became the focus of my professional inquiry and practice.

With the goal to improve teaching for student improvement, educators are now seeing that there must be a systemic plan in place for school improvement. Schools need to engage in professional development that really develops the professional so that teachers, just as students, have time to reflect on their own learning processes. Donald Schon, a leading author on reflective practice, describes expert practice as "an artful inquiry into situations of uncertainty" (Schon, 1983). Reflective practitioners ask themselves, "What am I doing and why? What worked and what didn't and why?" Providing occasions for teachers "to reflect critically on their practice and to fashion new knowledge and beliefs about content, pedagogy, and learners" are key components of a new vision for staff development (Sparks, 1997). In its standards, the National Staff Development Council recommends "organizing adults into learning communities," "guiding continuous instructional improvement," and emphasizing collaboration with colleagues to engage the entire school culture in reflections about teaching and learning. Defining the broad goals of professional development is one component of this new vision, but we also need to identify best models, not merely a laundry list of best practices, that will explicitly integrate theory, practice, and reflection and directly impact student learning.

THINKING MAPS: A MODEL FOR REFLECTIVE PRACTICE

As my teaching progressed in the early 1990s, my school in Lebanon, New Hampshire, as a whole faculty began to implement Thinking Maps as tools for learning, planning, and instruction. Our principal was very interested in the facilitation of metacognition over the long term, not just for students, but also for teachers and administrators. As the first year of using these tools progressed, I began to see student discourse and meaning making reflected in the types of thinking inherent in the Thinking Maps. These tools also helped me reflect on the content in a holistic and connected way and design units of study focusing on threading concepts rather than streaming content. Simultaneously, I gained insights into student learning and my own instruction. Students who previously had trouble learning new and difficult content now had a means of connecting new information, processes, and interactions with prior knowledge. They were very capable of thinking deeply about the subject matter but needed an explicit way to examine it and express their thinking. I realized that instead of modifying the content, I needed to fortify their tools for learning.

The students were not alone in their growth. By using Thinking Maps in planning and instruction, my own patterns of thinking improved. The avalanche of curriculum, assessments, district programs, and school memos that buried me in September now seemed more manageable. I could understand and articulate concepts more coherently, synthesize the fragmented curriculum, and feel confident about my ability to help students be successful learners. My professional and personal experiences applying Thinking Maps fueled my curiosity to see what happened in other classrooms, and more specifically, what happens in the minds of teachers as they use Thinking Maps with their students. How do Thinking Maps, tools that facilitate both continuous cognitive development and explicit visual representations of metacognition, promote teacher reflection?

After leaving the classroom to begin providing in-depth Thinking Maps professional development training and follow-up, I wanted to examine these issues in depth. My teaching experiences were exclusively in rural settings in New England, so I also became interested in how this model would work in inner-city classrooms with teachers who worked with diverse populations, in low socioeconomic neighborhoods, and in schools with historically low achievement. I conducted action research as part of a master's project during the 2000–2001 school year, working with two groups of 15 educators: one group from the Syracuse City School District in Syracuse, NY, and another located in Community School District 27 in Queens, NY.

What I found mirrored my experiences; not only did the Thinking Maps improve teaching and student performance, but the model itself deepened teachers' reflection on their own teaching and instruction and produced richer reflections about their students' thinking. For one fifth-grade teacher of particularly challenging students in Syracuse, Thinking Maps were tools that linked together student and teacher success. "I was teaching a lesson in social studies and I must have asked a question every conceivable way I could think of. Nobody participated. So I drew a Multi-Flow Map on the board and got where I wanted to go! Thinking Maps not only seized the teachable moment, they *created* the teachable moment." Ultimately, I came to see that these deeper levels of reflection and performance changes developed because the Thinking Maps invite explicit thinking and thus reflection, bringing a clarity that inspires confidence and competence.

RESULTS OF TEACHER-REPORTED REFLECTIONS

My study focused on those teachers who participated in the Thinking Maps Training of Trainers professional development sessions. Although I was primarily interested in how teachers created Thinking Maps for the purpose of engaging in reflection about learning and instruction aside from their daily classroom interactions with students, I also found that teachers used students' Thinking Maps examples and teacher-generated Thinking Maps lesson plans as visual references that generated reflection about student learning, instruction, and planning. Teacher-reported data revealed positive changes in both student behavior and performance and teacher curriculum and instruction as a result of Thinking Maps implementation.

Figure 15.1 shows the categories of what teachers most frequently identified as having improved as a result of Thinking Maps implementation. Data collected about student performance focused on themes regarding improvement in students' thinking, particularly relating to task persistence and organization in writing; improvement in student behaviors including attention, motivation, and participation; and an increase in student-directed learning. Teachers reported greater clarity in instruction, increased awareness of purpose in lessons, and a greater degree of effectiveness in teaching. These student and teacher findings, separately and collectively, demonstrated how all learners in the classroom used the same set of tools, Thinking Maps, to visually represent their thinking, which led to a greater level of understanding and efficacy.

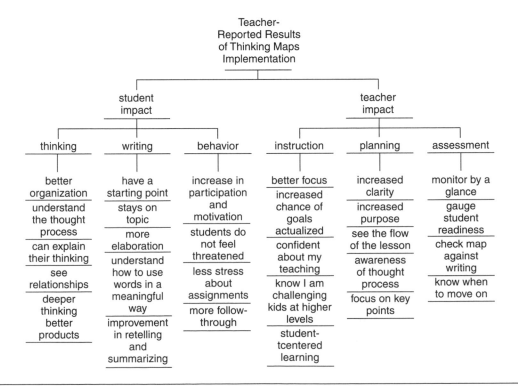

Figure 15.1 Teacher Reflection Results Tree Map

The qualitative findings offer valuable information about the climate and creation of classroom environments in which teachers design and present clear and meaningful instruction and students can understand, attend to, and participate in learning tasks in challenging urban settings. It was through teacher reflection about Thinking Maps experiences that these urban educators gained insight into student learning, teacher instruction, and curriculum planning.

REFLECTIONS ON STUDENT LEARNING AND BEHAVIOR

Being able to see their own and others' thinking afforded students and teachers new understandings about themselves and each other as learners. Having a visual representation system for knowledge created confidence and competence for the learner (see Chapter 5, Closing the Gap by Connecting Culture, Language and Cognition), whether that person was a student or a teacher. A third-grade teacher from Syracuse shared a story involving a child who frequently misbehaved in class, didn't finish his assignments, and totally avoided writing. He loved Tuesdays because the school counselor visited with him during the writing period on that day. Every Tuesday, the child glanced at the door, eagerly anticipating the counselor's arrival and his free ticket out of the writing assignment. However, one particular Tuesday, following a Thinking Maps training session, his teacher used a Circle and Flow Map to explain the assignment to the class and to demonstrate how to organize ideas on the way to a piece of writing. Focusing intently on the lesson and adding his ideas to the class map, the boy hadn't noticed the counselor entering the room. The student explained that he was busy working on something and couldn't leave right then.

Observing the student's level of engagement encouraged the teacher to examine why this lesson was effective and what caused inattention with this student and others in the classroom. The teacher thought the lesson was successful because using the maps in her lesson gave students a cognitive and visual cue to follow the process of writing. As the teacher used the Flow Map to organize and sequence the ideas in the story, her verbal explanations of processes were supported by the visual representation of the map, thus making the thinking processes explicit to the students. Students could follow not only the steps, but also the mental dynamics of idea formation. Teacher clarity and a concrete model of the abstract thinking processes invited this student's participation and understanding.

What does an improvement in motivation and the level of engagement tell us about learning? One Training of Trainers cohort group noted how often negative behavior is a defense mechanism for confusion or fear or the result of frustration with traditional models of instruction and production of work. Perhaps, they posited, this student wanted to participate in writing but couldn't organize his ideas or sequence his thoughts. These improvements in behavior might indicate that students have the ability but not the means to represent ideas clearly and proceed to writing.

During one training session, in the middle of a discussion of the success stories about students with behavioral issues and attention problems, one participant exclaimed, "Thinking Maps can replace Ritalin!" (see Chapter 3, Leveling the Playing Field for All Students). After the initial laughter died down, the teachers began to seriously explore the plausibility of this exclamation. One teacher stated that Thinking Maps would be a viable alternative therapy:

> Thinking Maps works for these kids because it is consistent when nothing else in their life is. They go home to a place without rules, responsibility, and consequences. Their home life is chaotic. No routine, no schedule. Sometimes Mom is home, sometimes not. No one is looking out for them. They can do whatever they want, whenever they want. Although they might like the freedom, they don't have a sense of order or control. They come to school wanting that power and sense of control. The consistency of Thinking Maps can give them a sense of ownership. "I can do this. I know how to do this." They feel like they are good at something.

In her reflections, this teacher considered from within her own cultural experiences and assumptions, aspects of how the familial and socioeconomic context of the students might surface within this learning community: consistency, control, and ownership. She was sensitive to the underlying emotional currents in the classroom and understood how Thinking Maps could alleviate the tension. As she examined the effectiveness of Thinking Maps, she identified permeating, perhaps universal, needs.

Other teachers remarked how Thinking Maps had supported the emotional as well as the cognitive development of students by appealing to students' sense of safety. "They [students] feel comfortable, not confined to a certain number of responses . . . add to them as lessons progress . . . and use them on their own as well as in a group." Another teacher noted that, "If I reflect for a minute, I think it [using the Thinking Maps] has widened our horizons because kids are empowered over their learning. They are more willing to take risks because with a map nothing is wrong. You can show your thinking how you want. It doesn't have to be the same as the next person's."

Listening to these observations, there was a common recognition that one's knowledge and its expression don't necessarily coexist. Just because students knew information didn't mean they would share it. In the complex climate of preadolescent, urban classrooms—where the culture of the students does not necessarily match the cultural background of the teacher—the expression of knowledge by students may be double-edged, as their ideas are subject to outside expectations and scrutiny. The Thinking Maps, a flexible, consistent, common visual language, supporting both the process and product of thinking, were understood by these teachers as a safe venue to show what you know (see Chapter 5, Closing the Gap by Connecting Culture, Language, and Cognition).

TEACHER INSTRUCTION AND PLANNING

Although a considerable amount of teacher-reported data focused on student learning, teachers discussed some of the same ideas of competency and confidence surrounding their own instruction and planning. Teachers' reflections about Thinking Maps integration identified that Thinking Maps helped them to become more flexible, responsive, clear, and purposeful in their instruction and planning.

In-the-Moment Instruction

At the third Training of Trainers session, a kindergarten teacher couldn't wait to share what she had learned with the group. In preparation for a lesson comparing and contrasting two books about George Washington, she had drawn a Double Bubble Map with four bubbles for the similarities and three bubbles on each side for the differences. During the lesson, she recorded the children's responses, but within moments, they had exhausted her template. "You need more bubbles!" they chorused. Their powers of observation and attention to detail astounded her. She learned how attentive her students were and planned to use those responses as a rubric by which to judge their future work. The map was an unexpected assessment tool. Moreover, her students reminded her not to predetermine their capacity for information. "My thinking could have limited their thinking!" Reflecting about this experience led her to question her expectations of her students and their proficiency with observation and comprehension skills.

Whereas the kindergarten teacher used the Double Bubble Map to facilitate comprehension after reading, a second-grade teacher applied the Thinking Maps to support students' thinking during math computation. Working at a low-performing elementary school, this teacher found herself in an anxiety-producing situation when an outside group of consultants selected her for observation. The school had purchased a very specific program aimed to improve mathematical computation skills and hopefully release the school from the state's probationary status. In order to guarantee results, the company structured quality checks at participating sites. This teacher was slated to teach a lesson on subtraction and feared their presence because the children were having a difficult time with subtracting two-digit whole numbers. "I was thinking what the kids had problems with. In the middle of the problem, they seemed to forget the next step."

She decided to use a Flow Map to show the sequence of steps in subtraction. The next day, the students accurately completed the problems using the Flow Maps at their desks. The observer thought the lesson was sensational and asked if she could keep a copy of the Flow Map. "The Thinking Map helped me get my ideas in order and really think about subtraction." The Flow Map clarified her own thinking as well as the students'. Relating to the sharing of this example at the training session, another teacher later reported in the postsession survey nearly exactly the same sentiment. "They [Thinking Maps] help me organize, and lessons involving the use of Thinking Maps have a far greater chance of reaching their objective."

Planning

Reaching her objective, rather than repeating last year's abysmal performance, was exactly what a sixth-grade teacher was determined to do with her unit on fairy tales (Figure 15.2). Unlike the previously mentioned situations, this teacher used the Circle Map during the initial planning stages as a reflective tool to help her analyze the unit and plan for success. First she brainstormed all the tasks, materials, and understandings necessary for students to be able to write the final product, an original version of "Cinderella." Looking at the Circle Map while simultaneously recalling the problems from last year's narratives, she anticipated some obstacles and consequently selected the most important ideas, including defining elements of a fairy tale that would support students in the development of their final piece. She asked herself, "What do I want them to learn? Which Thinking Maps would help them notice the patterns in various versions of Cinderella?" She selected the multitiered Bridge Map (Figure 15.3) as the tool to isolate the elements of a fairy tale and help students see the pattern of elements across many versions.

She then used a Flow Map (Figure 15.4) to sequence the progression of tasks to ensure that students actively processed the material. She decided to have students apply specific Thinking Maps at different times during the reading process in order to scaffold their comprehension. In her planning, she became very animated, discussing how she could incorporate cooperative learning and sharing among groups. Her work demonstrates her understanding of the learning process of her students and the need for students to first deconstruct fairy tales during reading in order to later reconstruct the elements in their own fashion while writing their own original Cinderella story. With the maps, she had a built-in, ongoing assessment of their comprehension and could adjust her instruction accordingly. As she decided about both the progression and nature of instruction for this unit, she had to adopt the learner's perspective and anticipate where her students might have difficulty. Applying the maps as both a lesson-design technique and a student tool, this teacher was deeply reflective, shifting her perspective from the end product to the processes required in her students' minds. As she left the training session that day, she felt very confident in her ability and in her students' abilities to find the essentials within a Cinderella story.

This teacher's mapping of her Cinderella unit exemplifies how Thinking Maps aid teachers' understandings of the topics they teach and how using the maps promotes reflection about instruction. To effectively plan a unit, teachers need to clearly articulate their outcome and decide on an effective course of instruction. For example, they need to anticipate how students would know what the elements of a fairy tale are and identify the variations in elements due to the geographical and cultural background of

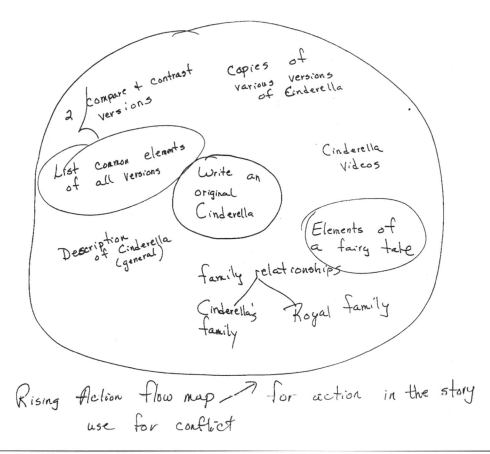

Figure 15.2 Cinderella Lesson Planning Circle Map

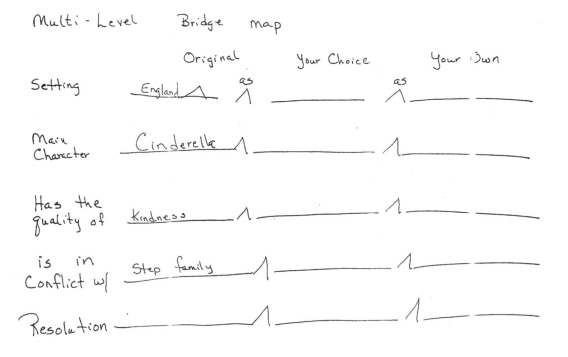

Figure 15.3 Elements of a Fairy Tale Bridge Map

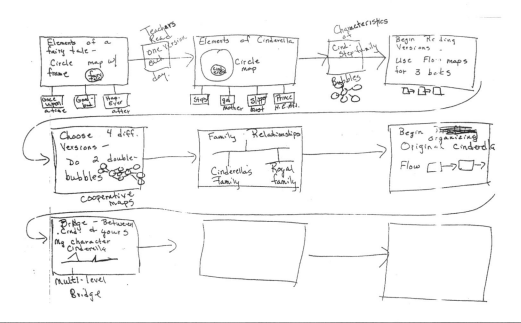

Figure 15.4 Cinderella Unit Plan Sequence With Multiple Map Integration

particular tales. Thinking Maps thus provide teachers with a means of questioning themselves in order to look for certain patterns of knowledge.

Beyond the Classroom

In addition to their teaching positions in the classroom, these Training of Trainers participants used Thinking Maps to help in their other roles within the school organization. As curriculum coordinators and teachers on special assignment, half of the educators were responsible for evaluating, presenting, or integrating new programs into current practice. Under the pressure of time, money, test results, and district demands, these educators had to present ideas to administrators and faculty members who were at times highly skeptical about new approaches. In order to understand and present the key points clearly, concisely, and convincingly, these educators used the same tools that fostered understanding and participation in the classroom to communicate their ideas. One teacher remarked, "Thinking Maps were most helpful in creating a clear and concise outline for staff of the requirements and concepts to be covered in the New York State core curriculum."

It is interesting to note that at the beginning of the sessions the participants were constantly asking how to integrate the Thinking Maps with the New York State English Language Arts Assessment. They wanted to know how they could immediately use Thinking Maps to support the writing process and other comprehension skills tested on the assessment. If they didn't teach writing, they asked, "How does this help math problem solving?" or "How can we make this work with our reading framework?" or "What maps would you use with conflict or equality?" Initially, the stress wore a "V" in their brows as they worked hard to bring the Thinking Maps onto their overcrowded plates, because previous professional development experiences had brought another program to implement rather than tools for integrating what was already on their plates.

Over the course of the training, they learned how the Thinking Maps would actually help students learn the patterns of thinking embedded in reading and writing across all subject areas and existing in programs they were using. The discussions and feedback changed from knowledge questions about the maps to understandings about effective integration of the maps into existing programs and processes. "Now I am much more aware of the thought process I am working on with each assignment. I know I am reaching higher levels of thinking." Another teacher remarked, "The *thinking* is the process and the *maps* are the language." So by the end of the training process, the maps were an effective and efficient set of tools for integrating layers of instruction.

In the same way the participants' students had taken ownership of the maps and become fluent with the tools, the educators I followed had become more fluent and reflective thinkers. They seemed much more capable and confident about asking and answering questions about learning in the context of their complex, challenging, and often changing educational environment.

CREATING A CULTURE OF CHANGE THROUGH INVITING EXPLICIT THINKING

When I consider the layers of pressures placed upon teachers in the classroom—and the shifts made by these educators I was able to observe and question during this study—I think about the intrinsic personal and professional rewards of working in a school in which faculty members are reflective practitioners. Imagine whole schools in which students, teachers, and administrators utilize tools to understand content, context, their colleagues, and themselves. As demonstrated in this study, Thinking Maps implementation and the Training of Trainers process provided both a language and a model for thinking deeply and reflectively about student learning, teacher instruction, and planning. "Thinking Maps," observed one of the participants, "ensure that thinking is the focus of teaching." This focus on inviting explicit thinking through Thinking Maps animates reflective practice—the process of thinking about the complex nature of teaching and learning—and ensures that responding, relating, and renewing are at the center of creating the unique culture of schools.

16

Mentoring Mathematics Teaching and Learning

Kathy Ernst, M.S.

Topics to be discussed:

- using Thinking Maps® for classroom observations and coaching
- mentoring multiple levels of mathematics staff development using a reflective Flow Map
- guiding reflection and mentoring National Council of Teachers of Mathematics standards-based lessons for understanding

Milo Novelo and I walked briskly through the corridors of the New York City public school, one of four in which he worked as a mathematics staff developer. Milo was one of my graduate students in the Leadership in Mathematics Education Program at Bank Street College of Education. I had been his advisor, teacher, coach, and mentor for more than a year. My visit on this blustery November day was in fulfillment of his supervised fieldwork. Milo looked forward to these site visits because they enabled him to do what effective educators *must* do but are rarely supported in doing: reflect on, discuss, analyze, question, and improve their practices. I looked forward to these visits because they gave me an opportunity to learn—to deepen my own understanding of mathematics teaching and learning and to reflect on and improve my skills as coach and facilitator.

My primary purpose in conducting classroom observations is to reveal to teachers (i.e., classroom teachers, staff developers, and coaches) the ways in which their questions, prompts, actions, and classroom environment impact student learning and understanding of mathematics. As Milo put it, "When you spend a day walking in my shoes, you put a mirror to my work so I can stand back and look at it. You challenge me to examine what I'm doing and to question *why* I do what I do." I have learned from experience that a classroom observation can stimulate reflection and transformative learning if its content is descriptive, accurate, and above all, purposeful, to the teacher being observed. The focus of my observation, therefore, is that which the teacher has previously identified as being important to observe—the understandings or misconceptions of a particular student, the teacher's questioning techniques, the management of "choice time."

The postobservation conversation between the teacher and me is an opportunity to reflect on and delve deeply into the teaching and learning—to examine student work and dialogue in response to the teacher's questions and prompts. This focused analysis invites teachers to probe such questions as, What does the child know and understand about mathematics? What evidence supports my thinking about what the child knows and understands? What questions and prompts did I or could I pose to assess, support, and extend the child's thinking and understanding? What changes can I make in my teaching to more effectively support student learning? At the heart of these conversations are an examination of student work and an analysis of the lesson itself—the intricate flow of dialogue and action between and among students and teacher. Essential to the integrity of these conversations are not only descriptive, accurate, and purposeful observations of the lesson, but observations that are readily accessible.

Milo informed me that our destination was a fourth-grade class, taught by Anna, a novice and struggling teacher. It was only this morning that he had touched base with her, introduced himself, and arranged for us to come into her class during the math lesson. Observations and consultations by several curriculum experts with disparate directives had failed to yield improvement in her ability to manage and teach her students. The little self-confidence and joy she had once had in teaching was rapidly eroding. As we entered her room, Milo tried to put Anna at ease by introducing me with his usual line: "Kathy's my advisor from Bank Street. She's here for the day to observe *me* and to help me do a better job as math staff developer . . ."

Until today, I had been dissatisfied with my ways of documenting classroom observations and sharing my data with teachers. At the beginning of each postlesson conversation, I would typically ask for the teacher's input, with questions such as, What stood out for you regarding the children's work and thinking? What aspects of the lesson were you pleased with? Although I was often successful at building upon and deepening the discussion with references to the teacher's observations and samples of children's work, there existed an uncomfortable disconnect between my observations, written in the moment, and those of the teacher, recalled after the fact. Upon reflection, I discovered some interesting patterns in my work.

In spite of the fact that my classroom observations often yielded pages of descriptive and accurate accounts of meaningful dialogue and action, they were not readily accessible to me or anyone else. Whenever I needed to retrieve an anecdote that was relevant to my follow-up conversation with a teacher, the flow of our discussion was usually interrupted while I hurriedly scanned pages of my notes, searching for the "gem" I knew was buried somewhere between the mountains of lines. There sat the teacher, passively, while I sat in control of the data (after all, it was written in my own "chicken scratch"—who else could make sense of it?). Unfortunately, these awkward interruptions often caused anxiety in the teacher, giving rise to a cloud of tension that threatened to stifle our conversation. I'd occasionally catch the teacher glancing uneasily at my notes, trying to decipher what I'd written. I sometimes found myself trying to reassure the teacher that my purpose was not to evaluate teachers' performances but to facilitate reflection and improvement in their practice. It was evident that my practice needed to change: How could I more clearly and efficiently document events that I observed in the classroom? How could the retrieval of observation data and conversations about them be more inclusive and democratic for teachers?

TOOLS FOR FOCUSED OBSERVATION AND REFLECTION

As I settled into a chair at the back of Anna's classroom, I took out my clipboard and oriented it in a different way—horizontally rather than vertically. Today I was going to record my observations of Anna's teaching and Milo's coaching with a visual tool relatively new to me—a Flow Map, used to sequence events. It was evident from the beginning that Anna was not only unsure of the mathematics and the purpose of the lesson, but she lacked assertiveness and control of the class. As I watched her unsuccessfully lead the students through an introductory activity of identifying multiples of 8 on the hundreds chart, I asked myself, What's important to document? What questions, comments, prompts, and actions have the potential to stimulate conversations that can lead to improvement of her teaching? I tentatively lowered my pen to the paper, wondering, How do I document what I see and hear? Where does one event end and another begin? Is an action or dialogue a new event or a substage of the previous event?

Trusting that there are multiple ways to map a lesson, I cast aside my uncertainty and dove in. My pen flew across the paper as my questions guided me to make split-second decisions about what and how to document (Figure 16.1). Curiously, I discovered that the simple act of drawing rectangles around events as they unfolded brought visual clarity to my thinking, which in turn enabled me to focus on the essence of the teaching and learning. As the lesson ended and Milo arranged to meet with Anna later in the day, I looked over my Flow Map. In spite of my "chicken scratch," the representation of my observation was so visually clear that the classroom dialogue and action nearly jumped off the page. At long last I had data that was readily accessible.

Milo's eyes widened as I laid out the Flow Map of the lesson on the table in front of us. He and I sat next to each other as I retold the story, pointing to each event as we went along. At times, it was Milo who deciphered my writing and joined in the storytelling. What amazed both of us was the ease with which we could retrieve events of the lesson and the comfortable, collaborative nature of this process. There was none of the anxiety or defensiveness that can often occur during the postobservation conversation. Instead, our focus was on the map in front of us, with its clear, descriptive evidence of the teaching and learning. In the future, after such a reading of the observation, I would more deliberately include the teacher by asking, "What's missing? What would you like to add to the story?" I have since learned that the simple act of attaching the teacher's observations to the Flow Map and including his or her story in the conversation creates a climate of trust, respect, and growth.

After reading the map of the lesson and discussing how Milo could rephrase some of the questions he posed to students, we looked closely at the Flow Map to determine how he could support Anna in her mathematics teaching. Anna had gotten off to a rocky start, failing to engage her students in the launch of the lesson, so we examined Event 1, "Anna in front of class using pocket hundreds chart to help students find multiples of 8," and Event 2, "Students are inattentive." I asked Milo, "What do you think caused the kids to be inattentive?" and wrote "Students are inattentive" in a rectangle on a clean sheet of paper. Milo proceeded to reflect on the possible reasons: Anna had not given the students a clear sense of the purpose of the lesson; as Anna highlighted multiples of 8 on the hundreds chart, she used a yellow marker, which made the resulting pattern difficult for students to see; it was apparent that many of the students lacked prior experience in exploring patterns of multiples on the hundreds chart— perhaps they should have begun with multiples of a number smaller than 8, such as 2 or 3. As Milo talked, I recorded his responses on a partial Multi-Flow Map (Figure 16.2).

Later in the day, Milo and I met with Anna to talk about the lesson. Knowing how disheartened and overwhelmed she was feeling in her role as a new teacher with no prior training in this mathematics curriculum, we decided to focus only on the beginning of the lesson. Milo opened the conversation by asking, "How do you think things went?"

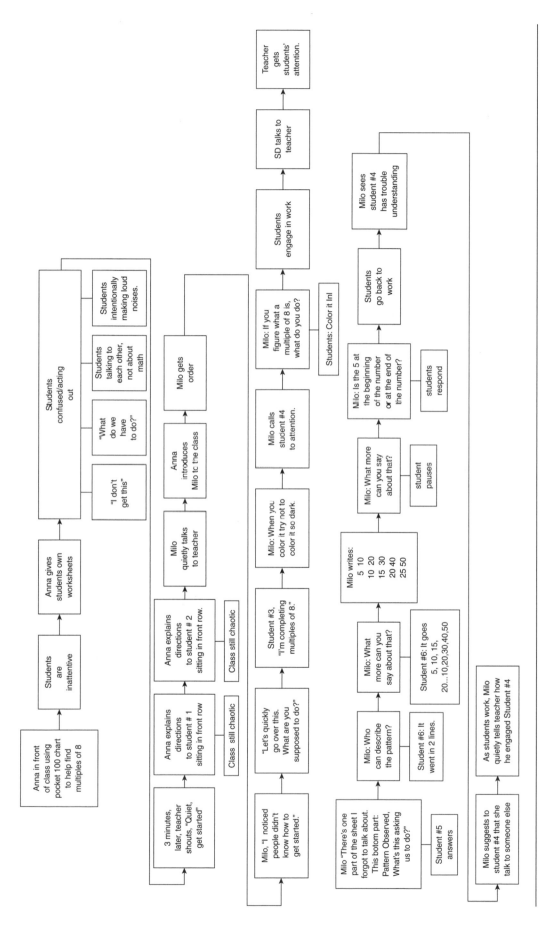

Figure 16.1 Classroom Observation Flow Map

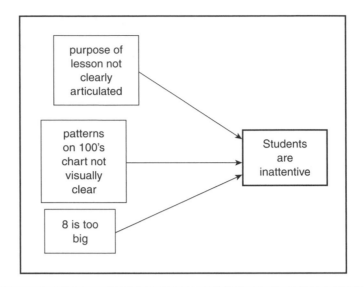

Figure 16.2 Students' Inattentive Multi-Flow Map

Anna responded, "I don't really get the point of this lesson . . . The kids had a hard time getting started, and when I gave them the activity sheet, they were confused. It helped when you stepped in and gave them directions . . ."

Moving his chair next to Anna, Milo said reassuringly, "We noticed some of the same things you did . . ." At this point, he recreated the partial Multi-Flow Map he and I had constructed earlier in the day, starting only with Event #2, "Students are inattentive." He reiterated a cause that Anna herself had just identified, "purpose of the lesson not clearly articulated," and added it to the map. Milo then explained to Anna how an exploration of multiples on the hundreds chart enables students to see visual and numerical patterns that are essential to building a deeper understanding of multiplication and division. He suggested a way to introduce the activity to students. As Anna seemed to grasp the purpose of the lesson, Milo continued. "Something else we noticed was that the kids couldn't really see the highlighting of the multiples of 8, so it was hard for them to find *other* multiples of 8." Milo added another cause of students' inattentiveness to the map: "patterns on the hundreds chart not visually clear."

As he elaborated, Anna nodded in agreement, offering suggestions about how she could use colored acetate squares to more effectively highlight the multiples. Finally, Milo shared his assessment of the students' relative lack of experience with the activity and the ensuing difficulty they had with identifying patterns for such a large number. After adding this third cause ("8 is too big") to the map, Milo engaged Anna in an exploration of multiples of two and three on the hundreds chart, modeling the kinds of questions she could later pose to her students. At the end of our conversation, Anna looked at the partial Multi-Flow Map Milo had constructed and said, "So many people have come into my classroom with vague advice and comments that have just made things worse. This is the first time anyone's given me concrete suggestions about what I can *do*. This has been really helpful—thank you." The map in front of us, elegant in its simplicity, had not only facilitated clear thinking in our process of reflection, dialogue, and inquiry, but it was an immediate document of our conversation and a springboard for further action.

Milo and I walked to the subway station, immersed in our ritual of reflecting on the day, strolling several blocks further than necessary just to continue our conversation. We were energized by the discovery that something significant had happened today—our use of the Thinking Maps had caused a qualitative shift in our work and conversations about teaching and learning. The Flow Map of the lesson had given Milo and me a clear and immediate record of the class dialogue and actions that we accessed and discussed *together*. The Multi-Flow Map had enabled us to question, together and later with Anna, the causes of student inattentiveness, which led to deep conversations about the mathematics, the mathematical thinking of the students, and ways in which Anna could engage her students and support and extend their learning. Most important, the maps had helped us do our best thinking, and as a result, the time we spent together was the most productive it had ever been. Today I had experienced the power of the Thinking Maps as tools for bringing clarity, efficiency, equity, and access to the process of conducting observations and follow-up conversations. As Milo and I parted and I descended the stairs into the subway, I was struck by the realization that I could use the maps to significantly improve another aspect of my work—facilitating schoolwide reform in mathematics teaching.

TOOLS FOR EXPLICIT COACHING IN MODEL LESSONS

Few education initiatives are as complex or as challenging as the implementation of a Standards-based* mathematics curriculum, one whose focus is on teaching and learning for understanding. Such an undertaking often requires teachers to relearn mathematics (what are the big ideas in math and how do they build on each other?) and relearn the ways in which children develop mathematical thinking (how and when do children construct particular understandings and ideas about math . . . and what are their misconceptions?). Perhaps the greatest yet most essential challenge for teachers is to develop pedagogical content knowledge—knowing what interventions (i.e., strategies, models, questions, prompts, and contexts) best support and extend a particular student's understanding of mathematics at any given point in their learning.

Milo's coaching of Anna was a compelling example of how a teacher can develop the requisite knowledge, understanding, and skills for improving student learning. To do so in just a 30-minute conversation, as

---

*This refers to the NCTM (National Council of Teachers of Mathematics, 2000) Standards, upon which reform in mathematics education and NSF-funded mathematics curricula are based.

Milo had with Anna, is even more striking. As I rode the subway that day, I compared Milo's discussion with Anna to those of my own with teachers following my demonstration lessons with their students. Rarely did my conversations with teachers reflect such depth and clarity and get to the heart of mathematics instruction in so short a time.

Since then, I have applied the maps to my design of model lessons in dozens of classrooms, streamlining the process and improving the learning opportunities for teachers. Although teachers in schools where I've worked lacked Thinking Maps training, I discovered that I could lead them through an application of the maps to facilitate clear thinking in all three processes of demonstration lessons: planning and orientation, observation, and reflective conversation.

Part 1: Lesson Planning and Orientation

The structure of the planning phase of my demonstration lessons varies according to the time, money, personnel, and scheduling constraints of a school. Ideally, I spend an hour the first day discussing and planning the lesson with all teachers as a group, and the following day, I model the lesson while the same teachers observe. In most schools, however, where administrators lack the resources to free up all teachers for both planning and observation days, I phone the teacher a few days prior to my visit, as I did with Vera, a special education teacher. Vera asked me to model a lesson in adding and subtracting collections of coins. In the course of our conversation, it became clear that the children lacked the essential prior understanding of how to construct and deconstruct numbers using units of five and ten. Thinking about how I could use a hundreds chart to support the children's development of this idea, I created a Flow Map of a lesson based on a sequence from *Investigations in Number, Data, and Space*.* I shared this map with Vera and other teacher observers in a 30-minute orientation to the lesson plan prior to my modeling of the lesson.

In the days before my use of the maps, my orientation of teachers to the demonstration lesson was an overload of verbal and written information. It included handouts of the learning goals, a lesson overview, and a list of open-ended prompts on what to observe. I could frequently detect a glazed look in teachers' eyes as they attempted to process all I had given them. When I began to introduce the lessons in Flow Map form, however, teachers typically responded to the visually clear sequence of events with comments like, "This is so simple to follow—I can really *see* it!" Furthermore, the questions and prompts embedded in the rectangles of the Flow Map were so visually clear that teachers could readily observe the interventions that served to assess, support, and extend student learning. The process of designing the lesson with the Flow Map not only clarified my own thinking about what's important for children to learn and what I could do and say to support that learning, but it also enabled me to

---

*Investigations in Number, Data and Space, developed at TERC, is an NSF-funded, Standards-based mathematics curriculum for grades K–5.

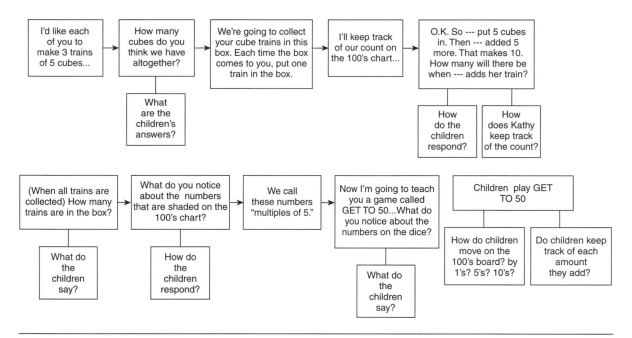

Figure 16.3   Lesson Planning/Orientation Flow Map

think about other specific aspects of the lesson that would be beneficial for teachers to observe.

Part 2: Lesson Observation

Expectations of what teachers should observe and how they can interact with students to support their learning during the model lesson are clarified in the planning and orientation meeting. Teachers often tell me that they don't know what's important to observe while children are at work in math. To support them in developing this knowledge, I embed what I want teachers to observe in the substages of key questions and prompts in the Flow Map of the lesson. In the second stage of the map of the lesson in Vera's class, for example, I directed teachers to note children's answers in response to the question, "How many cubes do you think we have altogether?" (See Figure 16.3) Such prompting invites teachers to be descriptive and accurate in their observations, which they often write directly on the maps next to the corresponding event. In this way, teachers record their observations in the context of the lesson, which makes it easier for them to retrieve and interpret the data at a later time.

Part 3: Reflective Conversation

When we gather after the lesson, I often ask teachers, "How did the lesson change from its original plan?" As teachers examine their maps, they all have an opportunity to share in the retelling of the story, adding clear and descriptive observations of student responses and teacher prompts. I have noticed that the substages of what to observe embedded in the lesson map support teachers in their developing understanding of what and how to observe. A teacher will often point to an event on the map and comment, "I noticed that when you said _____ the child did _____." As we discuss these descriptive observations, questions about the mathematics, development of children's mathematical ideas, and teaching interventions emerge. Why did the lesson change course? What did Alana's counting by ones tell us about her mathematical understanding? How did Kathy know that Juan and Jasmine needed to play "get to 100" instead of "get to 50"? In the context of these discussions, we inevitably examine samples of student work, sorting it into piles representing different strategies and thinking. A Tree Map, with categories of mathematical emphases or strategies and corresponding activities to support the development of those ideas, brings clarity to the process of deciding what next instructional steps are most appropriate for each child. In my conversation with teachers following the model lesson in Vera's class, for example, I used a Tree Map to introduce possible next steps for constructing an understanding of how to add and subtract coin values (see Figure 16.4). During these discussions, teachers frequently share related activities and investigations that have proven successful in their own classrooms. The

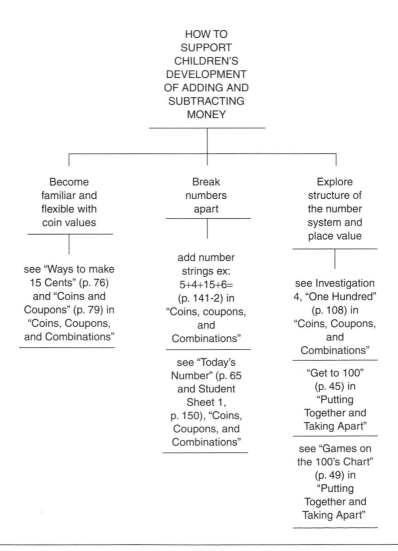

Figure 16.4 Post-Lesson Reflections and Strategies Tree Map

result is a more bountiful tree of instructional possibilities. This inclusion of teachers' ideas on the Tree Map not only validates and honors their prior work and thinking, but it enables them to use their own and each other's experiences as springboards for making new connections and constructing deeper understandings about mathematics, mathematics teaching, and learning.

IMAGINING THE POSSIBILITIES

Thinking Maps have become essential tools for bringing efficiency, clarity, equity, and access to my work in reforming mathematics education in both urban and suburban schools. They not only clarify my thinking about what's important to observe in a lesson, but they provide a readily accessible visual documentation of the lesson observation. This access deflects teacher anxiety by giving the observer and the observed equal entry into the reflective conversation. Further use of the maps enables the teacher and me to engage in a non-threatening inquiry and analysis of events that focuses on the teaching and learning, rather than on the teacher. The maps have also streamlined my approach to conducting model lessons, a key element of ongoing support to schools implementing standards-based mathematics curricula. The Flow Map of the lesson not only directs teachers to focus on the questions and prompts essential to the teaching, but it highlights student and teacher responses that are important for them to observe and document during the lesson itself. Since the reflective conversations are rooted in rich, descriptive, readily accessible observation data, opportunities for teachers to deepen their understanding of mathematics and children's development of mathematical ideas are maximized. Most important, the maps provide teachers with tools for constructing the pedagogical content knowledge necessary for improving student learning.

17

Thinking Maps®: A Language for Leading and Learning

Larry Alper, M.S.

Topics to be discussed:

- facilitating constructivist conversations across a whole school
- a Circle and Tree Map for creating unified understandings and deeper communication within a faculty
- linking leadership and learning using Thinking Maps for school-wide transformation

CREATING THE SPACE

"I want you to tell me the names of the fellows on your baseball team,"
Lou Costello asks his partner, Bud Abbott.

"I'm telling you," says Abbott, "Who's on first, What's on
second, I Don't Know is on third."
"I'm asking you. Who's on first?"
"That's the man's name."
"That's who's name?"

"Yes."
"Well, all I'm trying to find out is what's the guy's name on
first?"
"No, no. What's on second base."
"I'm not asking who's on second."
"Who's on first."

(Abbott & Costello, n.d.)

As a child (and even today as an adult) I roared with laughter at this bit of word play and miscommunication. I took special delight in being in on the joke and thoroughly enjoyed feeling smarter than the hapless Costello. It was so easy to see, even as a nine-year-old, how this problem could be solved. Yet I never once wished to see the routine end differently.

While this routine is entirely appropriate for two comedians on the vaudeville stage, we expect and need more from each other in our conversations in our school settings. To serve the children we teach and to grapple with the complexity and profound implications of our work, we need to have what Maxine Greene (1995) refers to as the "conversations that echo from somewhere else, some deep place." We need conversations that are rich in ideas, alive with uncertainty, and propelled by the anticipation of new learning. When time and deliberate attention are provided to open the space between and among people, these conversations can give full expression to people's thoughts and imaginings.

Yet many of the conversations we have often lack humor and frequently devolve into a competition between ideas, a closing of doors rather than the creation of possibilities. People are quick to adopt and defend positions. They argue, debate, and ultimately defeat or are defeated by the ideas of others in the group. At best, under these conditions, outcomes are negotiated and the results are more like settlements. In the end, there is very little enthusiasm for the results, and the process is simply done and the task completed. Constructivist conversations, however, move people beyond the centrality and certainty of their own ideas and motivations. Multiple ways of knowing and seeing are encouraged and positions give way to possibilities. "Conversation," writes Donald Schon (1987), "is collective improvisation." Like musicians highly attuned to the sound and emotion coming from each other's instruments, people in constructivist conversations create ideas rich in texture, depth, and dimension.

Positional discussions are clearly inadequate in promoting the depth of thinking necessary to address the complex pedagogical, moral, and ethical dimensions of the decisions teachers and administrators must make in their work. Alternatively, propositional conversations invite people to offer their ideas for consideration, to open their thinking up to be scrutinized and even enlarged upon by others. Such conversations demonstrate that ideas can be starting places for inquiry as opposed to endpoints for debate. The sharing and proposing of ideas forms a landscape for learning and possibility, defining the school as a "home for the mind" (Costa, 1991).

Cultivating this landscape so that it inspires our imagination becomes an educational imperative for schools. It is there where we will find the conversations we need if we are to look at things "as if they could be otherwise," (Greene, 1995) and to construct alternative realities in response to new and existing challenges.

Skillful leadership is necessary to create the space for the conversations we need that will define the school as a learning community. Such leadership enables participants to embrace ambiguity and devote themselves fully to collective inquiry. "Leaders as teachers," writes Senge (1990), "help people restructure their views of reality . . . and therefore to see new possibilities for shaping the future." Regardless of whether leadership is being exercised by the principal, teacher leader, or leadership team, the leader's ability to engage participants in meaningful and respectful conversations will significantly influence the learning that occurs for all members of the school community.

All too often our best intentions as leaders are thwarted not by simply employing the wrong strategy but by failing, as Senge says, to foster "strategic thinking." This failure creates frustration, invites cynicism, and promotes a lack of confidence in the efficacy of the organization. If, as Lambert (1995) states, conversation is the "medium" that provides the context for school communities to develop their common understandings, beliefs, and practices about teaching and learning, then what skills or strategies do leaders need to guide members of the organization through this tenuous, yet essential, process?

THINKING MAPS: A LANGUAGE FOR LEADING AND LEARNING

Six years ago, our school decided to commit to the use of a common language for teaching and learning that would extend to all curriculum areas and across all grade levels, having relevance in the multiple contexts that form the school experience. "Learning how to learn together" was stated as one of the central purposes of our school. It wasn't a prescription for teaching and learning we were after, but a way to facilitate the fundamental thinking processes that were inherent to learning and vital to constructing knowledge and deepening understanding. Clearly, then, a common language, a way of talking about, forming, and representing each other's thinking, was essential to the foundation we were building to support us in this common purpose. We knew that words alone would be inadequate and not necessarily the most effective or democratic way to involve all members of the school community in this effort. Facility with language, something that challenged many of the children with whom we worked, might be a worthy educational goal, but it could not be the foundation for our school community. In order to enable every child to fully, authentically, and personally become engaged in the learning process, we needed a new language, a way to empower children as learners where learning is something they do rather than something that is done to them. We didn't state all of this explicitly, but as it turned out, we knew it when we saw it. What we didn't anticipate was how our own interactions as adult members of the community would be affected by the outcome of this search.

The language our school community decided to adopt as part of our foundation for learning was Thinking Maps. This work had immediate appeal, as it facilitated the use of language and the expression of ideas with visual forms and was designed to encourage the individual and collaborative construction of knowledge and understanding. Importantly, Thinking Maps were not prescriptive or task specific but could be applied to all areas of the curriculum and throughout the life of the school. We saw Thinking Maps as an opportunity to provide our students with tools that could help them reveal the full range and depth of their thinking. Disempowered in so many aspects of their lives outside of school and frustrated by the limitations of their language development and internal disorder, many of our students were in great need of concrete tools with which to be active and confident learners. Learning was, for many of them, an uncertain and discouraging journey. Thinking Maps, we believed, could enable them to navigate the unknown with greater excitement for the possibilities that learning represented and more certainty in their ability to succeed. Having read and discussed excerpts from *Visual Tools for Constructing Knowledge* (Hyerle, 1996), regular and special education teachers expressed equal enthusiasm for the work. It was obvious that all our students would benefit from access to these tools and the opportunity to enhance, extend, and apply their fundamental thinking processes to learning.

Our work with Thinking Maps began with a full-day training for the entire faculty. It was evident from the beginning that the impact was not only going to be on the students but on the staff as well (see Chapter 10, A First Language for Thinking in a Multilingual School). Not unlike our students, we also learn by patterning information and linking ideas. We are not always confident when facing ambiguity or comfortable expressing our thoughts or considering the ideas of others. As we worked to develop our facility with Thinking Maps during that first day and in subsequent training opportunities, we became fully engaged with each other's ideas and discoveries. The visual nature of the maps allowed us to externalize our thoughts, making it easier for us to be curious about each other's points of view, identify patterns, and discover and create structures from our thinking that would otherwise not have existed. Assuming the role of learners, we experienced the maps as we hoped our students would. Time was suspended as we were inspired by the activity of generating ideas together. Diane Zimmerman (1995) describes this infusion of energy into group dynamics in this way: "When group members become excited about the emerging relevance of the conversation, the group self-organizes around the emerging concepts." Clearly, Thinking Maps were facilitating this rich communication among us by creating a safe, noncombative way to build meaning together. Our connectedness was strengthened by the thinking we were doing in concert, as insights were made and as we moved beyond the boundaries of our initial ideas. Not surprisingly, we recognized the value of the maps to our work with each other and sought to apply them more deliberately to our own interactive processes.

EXAMINING OUR PRACTICES

The first major task we undertook using the maps as a tool to facilitate our thinking and decision making was the development of our writing program. Our Action Planning Team, which included teachers, parents and an administrator, had determined from state and local assessment data and teacher input that our students' level of performance in writing was not where we believed it could be. We acknowledged, too, that together we had not given enough attention to the area of writing and that our approach to teaching writing, across grades and in content areas, lacked coherence and connectedness. The recent introduction of Thinking Maps into our school reinforced our belief in common experiences upon which our students could construct new knowledge and develop their confidence and independence as learners. How then, we asked, could we apply this to the area of writing? We decided to use Thinking Maps to guide this inquiry and to assist us in establishing a strong foundation upon which to design our program.

At a subsequent staff meeting we used a Circle Map (Figure 17.1), one of the Thinking Maps for defining things in context, to begin our process of responding to the question, "What does a quality writing program look like?" People were asked to write five thoughts on individual pieces of paper that were then placed on a board with the question in the center. The group was invited to look at the collection of ideas before discussing them. Just as the writing down of the ideas before placing them in the Circle Map gave people a chance to formulate their ideas, this silent viewing gave each of them an opportunity to consider the range of thinking before entering into conversation. Having the Circle Map to look at together gave us a common place to direct our attention and a central focus, the question, for our thinking. We followed this activity with an opportunity for people to ask questions of clarification, give fuller expression to their ideas, and share their individual frames of reference. Not only were staff members involved as regular and special educators, but several teachers in the group were writers themselves, adding another dimension to the reasons for their thinking. This aspect of the maps, the surfacing of multiple frames of reference, would continue to evolve for us as an important tool for looking beyond the surface of things to appreciate their full meaning and significance.

The next step in this process was to see the connections between and among the ideas we generated. We used a Tree Map to categorize and

Figure 17.1   Quality Writing Program Circle Map

group the information and did so, again, initially without conversation. People were invited to move the papers on which individual ideas were written into clusters of related content. As they were formed, these clusters could be added to or changed as people made new connections and certain groupings became apparent. The discussion that followed gave us another opportunity to consider the information, this time in categories, in order to identify connections and add what might be missing. The Tree Map included items related to content and pedagogy, desired student performance outcomes, and qualities associated with being a writer. What we had created in this process was an agreed-upon set of criteria that we would use to evaluate various approaches to teaching writing.

Using the maps as a tool for how to think about this task gave us a way to see, understand, and value each other's ideas. From the beginning, the focus was as much on how we *wanted* to think about this topic as it was on what we thought about the topic. Consequently, people could remain comfortable with the formative nature of the conversation, knowing that we were building toward a common understanding and shared set of guiding principles for designing our school's approach to teaching writing.

Our use of the maps began to extend into other aspects of our work together and not always in response to major undertakings. They were useful in grade-level meetings, committee work, and in general, in any context where the facilitation of thinking could lead to richer, more meaningful, and productive interactions between and among the people in our school community. "How do we want to think about this?" became the leading question for many of the conversations we were having. In response, one or several of the maps would be identified as the appropriate tool to assist us in these conversations. Our library-media specialist, Andra Horton, observed that, "Thinking Maps help us to harness ideas and put them together in powerful ways." As a result, we were able to enter these conversations knowing there was a way to get to the final destination without needing to know what that was from the start. "It's the difference," said Ms. Horton, "between seeing a pyramid and knowing how to build it."

Our school's capacity to respond to serious challenges was strengthened by our ability to effectively engage with each other in the face of difficult issues. No community is entirely free of problems or conflict, and this was true for our school as well. The character and, ultimately, the success of a community are often defined not by the issues themselves but by how the people within it, individually and collectively, respond to the challenges. As a group, our staff had always been inclined to confront our issues. We tried to view challenges as opportunities to strengthen our school and do better work with children. We also felt an obligation to model for our students the same personal and collective efficacy we wanted them to develop. "Freedom," writes Maxine Greene (1978), "involves the capacity to assess situations in such a way that lacks can be defined, openings identified, and possibilities revealed." Taking constructive action requires having the tools to do so. We began to see Thinking Maps as an essential tool to draw upon in response to the complex and sometimes confounding issues we typically faced. Not only did we have the desire to respond, but now we had, in the maps, additional resources to help us do so more effectively.

SEEING OPENINGS AND OPPORTUNITIES

School communities are living organisms and exhibit the full range of emotions of the people within them. Stress is not only specific to the individuals within the community but can, in its many manifestations, begin to characterize the entire environment. Our school's Coordinating Committee, a representative group of staff members that meets weekly to guide the overall direction of our school, recognized that this was starting to happen in our school. With input from the staff, the Coordinating Committee determined that this issue needed to be addressed. They realized that this was delicate territory we were entering, with the very real potential for things to get worse before they improved. Conversations about stress can provoke anxiety, exaggerate differences, and lead to finger pointing. The committee knew that we needed a thoughtfully designed process that would enable people to name and give definition to what they were experiencing. The process also needed to be restorative and transforming. We needed more than a group hug and certainly wanted to avoid adding to the existing tension.

Once again, we saw Thinking Maps as an ideal tool for helping us address this challenge. By providing a place for people to express the holism of their thinking, the maps locate ideas in each person's humanness. They provide people with a way of identifying where they are in their thought processes and a compass for navigating the journey ahead. As one staff member expressed, "Thinking Maps enable us to make the transition from the place we started to what we don't yet know." The ability of the maps to give people the confidence to go forward would prove to be especially important as we worked on an issue with such a high level of risk inherent in it.

We began the process with a question, as we try to do before entering any discussion or line of inquiry. "What are the landmines in the landscape of your professional work?" we asked. The imagery was purposely chosen to affirm the powerful component of people's feelings and to acknowledge the seriousness of the issue. After doing an individual Circle Map to define this for themselves and frame it within the context of their own experiences, people then joined small groups to share and combine their thoughts into a common Circle Map as shown in Figure 17.2. As these

Figure 17.2   Landscape of Stress Circle Map

initial conversations unfolded, people became less guarded while giving each other support and recognizing similarities in their experiences. What evolved was a shared reality, a group narrative woven together from the feelings, thoughts, and events from each person's life. We had good reason to be hopeful that we could repair what had been damaged and, in Maxine Greene's (1978) words, "move through the openings, to try to pursue real possibilities." The maps effectively opened space between and among us, allowing us to see what was there and to imagine how it could be different.

With the different Circle Maps displayed on the walls of the room, we talked about what we noticed and the ways in which our assumptions were being challenged. During the process, our thinking about the problem changed and our appreciation for each other deepened. Next, the Coordinating Committee took the Circle Maps and used a Tree Map (Figure 17.3) to group the information into categories. The committee chose titles for the categories that represented the individual items and gave the staff a way to think about the actions people could take, individually and collectively, to strengthen our school community. In preparation for the next meeting, the committee sent a memo to staff members with the Tree Map attached. The memo concluded by saying,

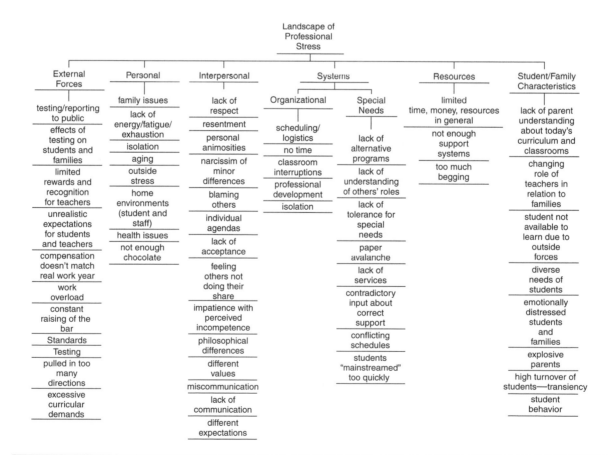

Figure 17.3 Landscape of Professional Stress Tree Map

In preparation for our next combined staff meeting on Thursday, we ask that you give thought to the following two questions: In what way might I act, particularly in the Personal and Interpersonal categories, that can contribute to the strengthening of our school community? What concrete steps can we take to "repair the lacks," particularly in the areas where we have the greatest degree of control—Personal, Interpersonal, and Systems? While we ask that you give equal weight to each of these questions, it is only the second that we will discuss at the meeting. It is our hope and expectation that your consideration of the first will be ongoing and that in doing so, each of us will be mindful of the impact our actions have on our collective ability to make real the possibilities we identify and the vision we have for our school community.

At the next meeting, we asked staff to respond to the Tree Map and tell us whether it accurately reflected the conversation we had had at the previous meeting. We were then able to generate possible action steps and give further direction to the Coordinating Committee to develop a comprehensive plan for the staff to consider and, ultimately, to implement. It seemed that we had successfully taken charge of a difficult situation and could move ahead with a shared sense of purpose and a demonstrated commitment to the well-being of our school.

Having Thinking Maps as a tool to conduct these difficult conversations was reassuring and empowering to people. Deb Abbott, a third-grade teacher in our school, said, "By seeing your thinking, you can examine it, you don't have to stop there." The reassurance comes, in part, from the maps' ability to help us formulate and capture our thinking and pursue the next level of thought beyond the familiar. "You're not going to forget it [your thoughts]," said Ms. Abbott. "You can reflect on it and build on it." When done collaboratively, the use of the maps can enable a group to build and strengthen its connections, even when confronted with issues that could easily pull it apart.

CONSTRUCTIVIST CONVERSATIONS

The ability of people to make meaning together, visualize the unknown, and formulate effective action is vital to the success of any organization. In today's school environment, where change is not an event but an ever-present reality, it is imperative that people develop the individual and collective capacity to process information, transform it into new understandings, and shape their futures. Constructivist conversations awaken people to possibilities and help them give shape to ideas not yet fully formed. The collaborative nature of these conversations helps organizations build an identity around a common purpose. Constructivist conversations provide a way for members of the learning community to share their individual frames of reference and develop trust and confidence in themselves and each other. The construction of knowledge and meaning is not solely an individual activity but is, more powerfully, a social one. In this way, groups of people interact to interpret, reflect upon, and examine each other's ideas and experiences. As people experience uncertainty together in this context, ambiguity is embraced as the realm of possibility. Trust, respect, and colleagueship develop through collective engagement with compelling ideas and the collaborative meaning-making process.

Constructivist conversations, according to Lambert (1995), "serve as the medium for the reciprocal processes that enable participants in a school community to construct meaning toward a common purpose about teaching and learning." As a consequence of such a dynamic, members are more likely to feel proud of their association with the organization, be committed to its work, and become inspired to think beyond the familiar. In this way, the organization is transformed into a generative community, one in which new ways of thinking are encouraged and novel ideas are formed.

During the past year, well over 200 school leaders have participated in a two-day seminar using the text, *Thinking Maps: Leading With a New Language* (Alper & Hyerle, in press). This seminar guides participants in the understanding and application of Thinking Maps as a twenty-first century language for surfacing and communicating the breadth and depth of people's ideas and for building meaningful and sustainable solutions together. The story of one of these school leaders captures the transformational potential of Thinking Maps as she reflects, in an e-mail, on the impact that this work had on her leadership and the implications for the entire school community and, in particular, on the students:

> Well, I did it! Today was the test of using my plan to address issues around Professional Climate in our school! No, to be honest . . . I almost chickened out last night and then again this morning. In the end, though, I stuck with the original plan and I can't begin to tell you how powerful the experience was! My staff approached the tasks with honesty and openness. Using Thinking Maps we were able to get all the issues out on the table in a respectful manner. Some of the stuff was painful. I just kept going. By the end of the morning we had developed ideas and plans, people were sharing and working together, there were even tears! For the remainder of the day I have received positive feedback, praise, and thanks for my work. Even one person who came in unwilling to join our circled tables and sat isolated from the group ultimately pulled her chair in and ate lunch with us, worked with a team to solve a scheduling issue and thanked me!!!! . . . We are approaching our school year in a positive, can-do atmosphere and our students will only benefit.

This experience shows that constructivist conversations require leaders who have the tools to enlist people's participation. "Good leaders," said library-media specialist Andra Horton, "are in control of keeping a constructive focus while keeping people engaged."

David Hawkins (1973) describes the importance of having " . . . some third thing . . . in which they can join in outward projection" to move people beyond self-consciousness and the conventions of their thinking. This third thing can open the space for possibilities to exist and be jointly constructed. Thinking Maps become the third corner of Hawkins' "I-Thou-It" triangle and provide us with the "common engrossment for discussion." The use of Thinking Maps promotes curiosity, thinking in action, and collaboration. They give us the confidence to embrace complexity and deepen our appreciation for each other's ideas and experiences.

On the most fundamental level, Thinking Maps help us to have the conversations that truly make a difference in how we think and in what we are able to do with our ideas. In the context of the profusion of challenges we face as educators, these tools are essential to the pursuit of our collective ideals and aspirations. "All we can do . . ." writes Maxine Greene, "is cultivate multiple ways of seeing and multiple dialogues in a world where nothing stays the same" (1995, p. 16).

References
by Chapter

Foreword

Atkinson, R., & Raugh, M. R. (1975). An application of the mnemonic keyword method to the acquisition of a Russian vocabulary. *Journal of Experimental Psychology: Human Learning and Memory, 104,* 126–133.

Bull, B. L., & Wittrock, M. C. (1973). Imagery in the learning of verbal definitions. *British Journal of Educational Psychology, 43,* 289–293.

Chapter 1: Thinking Maps as a Transformational Language for Learning

Hyerle, D. (1996). *Visual tools for constructing knowledge.* Alexandria, VA: Association for Supervision and Curriculum Development.

Hyerle, D. (2000). *A field guide to using visual tools.* Alexandria, VA: Association for Supervision and Curriculum Development.

Ogle, D. (1988, December/1989/January). *Implementing strategic teaching.* Educational Leadership (46), 47-48, 57-60.

Chapter 2: Linking Brain Research to Best Practices

Gerlic, I, & Jausovec, N. (1999). Multimedia: Differences in cognitive processes observed with EEG. *Educational Technology Research and Development, 47* (3), 5-14.

Hyerle, D. (1996). *Visual tools for constructing knowledge.* Alexandria, VA: Association for Supervision and Curriculum Development.

Hyerle, D., & Yeager, C. (2000). *Thinking maps training of trainers resource manual.* Raleigh, NC: Innovative Sciences.

Jensen, E. (1996). *Brain-based teaching and learning.* Alexandria, VA: Association for Supervision and Curriculum Development.

Marzano, R., Pickering, D., & Pollock, J. (2002). *Classroom instruction that works.* Alexandria, VA: Association for Supervision and Curriculum Development.

Payne, R. (1998). *A framework for understanding poverty.* Highlands, TX: RFT Publishing.

Sousa, D. (1995). *How your brain learns.* Reston, VA: NASSP.

Sylwester, R. (1995). *A celebration of neurons: An educator's guide to the human brain.* Alexandria, VA: Association for Supervision and Curriculum Development.

Wolfe, P. (2002). *Brain matters.* Alexandria, VA: Association for Supervision and Curriculum Development.

Wolfe, P., & Sorgen, M. (1990). *Mind, memory and learning.* Napa, CA: Authors.

Chapter 3: Leveling the Playing Field for All Students

Caine, R. N., & Caine, G. (1994). *Making connections: Teaching and the human brain.* Alexandria, VA: Association for Supervision and Curriculum Development.

Cazden, C. B. (1973). Problems for education: Language as curriculum and learning environment. *Daedalus, 102,* 135–148.

Denckla, M. (1998, November). *Understanding the role of executive functions in language, academics, and daily life.* Paper presented at American International College, Springfield, MA.

Singer, B. D., & Bashir, A. S. (1999). What are executive functions and self-regulation and what do they have to do with language learning disorders? *Language, Speech, and Hearing Services in Schools, 30,* 265–273.

Singer, B. D., & Bashir, A. S. (in press). Developmental variations in writing. In B. Schulman, K. Apel, B. Ehren, & E. Silliman (Eds.), *Handbook of Language and Literacy.* New York: Guilford Press.

Vygotsky, L. (1962). *Thought and language.* Cambridge, MA: MIT Press.

Zimmerman, B. J. (1989). A social cognitive view of self-regulated academic learning. *Journal of Educational Psychology, 81,* 329–339.

Chapter 4: Tools for Integrating Theories and Differentiating Practice

Cohen, J. (Ed.). (1999). *Educating minds and hearts.* Alexandria, VA: Association for Supervision and Curriculum Development.

Costa, A., & Kalick, B. (2000). *Activating and engaging habits of mind.* Alexandria, VA: Association for Supervision and Curriculum Development.

Dunn, R., & Dunn, K. (1992). *Teaching elementary students through their individual learning styles.* Needham Heights, MA: Allyn & Bacon.

Gardner, H. (1993). *Multiple intelligences: The theory in practice.* New York: Basic Books.

Goleman, D. (1995). *Emotional intelligence: Why it matters more than IQ.* New York: Bantam.

Chapter 5: Closing the Gap by Connecting Culture, Language, and Cognition

Boyer, E. (1983). *High school: A report on secondary education in America.* New York: Harper and Row.

Delpit, L. (1995). *Other people's children: Cultural conflict in the classroom.* New York: New Press.

Eisner, E. (1994). *Cognition and curriculum.* New York: Teacher's College Press.

Feuerstein, R. (1980). *Instrumental enrichment.* Baltimore, MD: University Park Press.

Jensen, E. (1998). *Teaching with the brain in mind.* Alexandria, VA: Association for Supervision and Curriculum Development.

Levine, M. (1993). *All kinds of minds.* Cambridge, MA: Educators Publishing Service.

Mahari, J. (1998). *Shooting for excellence.* New York: Teacher's College Press.

Vygotsky, L. (1962). *Thought and language.* Cambridge, MA: MIT Press.

Chapter 6: Maps for the Road to Reading Comprehension: Bridging Reading Text Structures to Writing Prompts

Armbruster, B. (Ed.). (2002). *Put reading first.* Washington, DC: U.S. Department of Education.

DePinto-Piercy, T. (1998). *The effects of multi-strategy instruction upon reading comprehension.* Unpublished doctoral dissertation, University of MD. College Park.

Graves, D. (1997). *Forward: Mosaic of thought*. Portsmouth, NH: Heinemann.

Hyerle, D. (2000). *A field guide to using visual tools*. Alexandria, VA: Association for Supervision and Curriculum Development.

Resnick, L. B. (1983). Toward a cognitive theory of instruction. In S. Paris, G. Olson, & H. Stevenson (Eds.), *Learning and motivation in the classroom*. Hillsdale, NJ: Erlbaum.

Vygotsky, L. (1962). *Thought and language*. Cambridge, MA: MIT Press.

Chapter 7: Empowering Students: From Thinking to Writing

Buckner, J. (2000). *Write . . . from the beginning*. Raleigh, NC: Innovative Sciences.

Buckner, J., & Johnson, M. (2002). *Write . . . for the future*. Raleigh, NC: Innovative Sciences.

Clay, M. (1975). *What did I write? Beginning writing behavior*. Portsmouth, NH: Heinemann.

The College Board. (2003, April). The neglected "R": The need for a writing revolution: The report of the National Commission on Writing in America's Schools and Colleges. Princeton, NJ: College Entrance Examination Board.

Costa, A., & Kallick, B. (2000). Encouraging and engaging habits of mind. Alexandria, VA: Association for Supervision and Curriculum Development.

Chapter 8: Meeting the Challenge of High-Stakes Testing in Middle School Mathematics

Deshler, D. D., Schumaker, J. B., Lenz, B. K., & Ellis, E. E. (1984). Academic and cognitive intervention for learning disabled adolescents, Part II. *Journal of Learning Disabilities, 17*, 170–179.

Goleman, D. (1995). *Emotional intelligence: Why it matters more than IQ*. New York: Bantam.

Mercer, C. (1983). Arithmetic. In *Common learning difficulties of LD students affecting math performance* (p. 345, Table 14.2).

Wallace, G., & McLoughlin, J. A. (1988). *Learning disabilities: Concepts and characteristics*. New York: MacMillan.

Chapter 9: Thinking Technology

Curtis, S. (2004) *Mapping the Standards*. Raleigh, NC: Innovative Sciences, Inc.

Hyerle, D. (2000). *A field guide to using visual tools*. Alexandria, VA: Association for Supervision and Curriculum Development.

Hyerle, D., & Gray Matter Software, Inc. (1998). *Thinking maps software*. (Version 2.0, Innovative Learning Group, 2004). Raleigh, NC: Innovative Sciences.

McKenzie, J. (2003). *FNO: From now on: The educational technology journal*. Retrieved from www.fno.org.

Moersch, C. (2002). *Beyond hardware: Using existing technology to promote higher-level thinking*. Danvers, MA: International Society for Technology in Education.

Chapter 11: Feeder Patterns and Feeding the Flame at Blalack Middle School

Costa, A. & Kallick, B. (2000) *Activating and engaging the habits of mind*. Alexandria, VA: Association for Supervision and Curriculum Development.

Hord, S., Rutherford, W., Huling-Austin, L., & Hall, G. (1987). *Taking charge of change*. Alexandria, VA: Association for Supervision and Curriculum Development.

Hyerle, D., & Gray Matter Software, Inc. (1998). *Thinking maps software.* (Version 2.0, Innovative Learning Group, 2004). Raleigh, NC: Innovative Sciences.

Tomlinson, C., & Allan, S. (2000). *Leadership for differentiating schools and classrooms.* Alexandria, VA: Association for Supervision and Curriculum Development.

Chapter 12: Embracing Change: The Evolution of Thinking in a K–12 School

Costa, A. L. (1991). *The school as a home for the mind.* Palatine, IL: IRI/Skylight.

Hyerle, D., & Gray Matter Software, Inc. (1998, 2004). *Thinking maps software.* Raleigh, NC: Innovative Sciences, Inc.

Perkins, D. N., & Salomon, G. (1989). Teaching for transfer. *Educational leadership.* 46(1), 22–32.

Swartz, R. J., & Perkins, D. N. (1989). *Teaching thinking: Issues and approaches.* Pacific Grove, CA: Midwest.

Chapter 13: The Mississippi Story

Ball, M. K. (1998). *The effects of Thinking Maps on reading scores of traditional and nontraditional college students.* Doctoral dissertation, University of Southern Mississippi, Hattiesburg.

Buckner, J. (2000). *Write . . . from the beginning.* Raleigh, NC: Innovative Sciences.

Chapter 15: Inviting Explicit Thinking

Curtis, S. (2001). *Inviting explicit thinking: Thinking maps professional development: Tools to develop reflection and cognition.* Unpublished masters thesis, Antioch New England Graduate School, Keene, NH.

Schon, D. (1983). *The reflective practitioner: How professionals think in action.* New York: Basic Books.

Sparks, D. (1997). Reforming teaching and reforming staff development: An interview with Susan Loucks-Horsley. *Journal of Staff Development, 18,* 4, 20–23.

Chapter 16: Mentoring Mathematics Teaching and Learning

National Council of Teachers of Mathematics. (2000). *Principles and standards for school mathematics.* Reston, VA: Author.

Chapter 17: Thinking Maps: A Language for Leading and Learning

Abbott, B., & Costello, L. (n.d.). Who's on first? From the film, *The Gay Nineties.*

Alper, L. & Hyerle, D. (In press). *Thinking Maps: Leading with a new language.* Raleigh, NC: Innovative Sciences.

Costa, A.L. (1991). *The school as a home for the mind.* Palatine, IL: IRI/SkyLight.

Greene, M. (1978). *Landscapes of learning.* New York: Teachers College Press.

Greene, M. (1995). *Releasing the imagination: Essays on education, the arts, and social change.* San Francisco: Jossey-Bass.

Hawkins, D. (1973). The triangular relationship of teacher, student, and materials. In C. E. Silberman (Ed.), *The open classroom reader.* New York: Vintage.

Hyerle, D. (1996). *Visual tools for constructing knowledge.* Alexandria, VA: Association for Supervision and Curriculum Development.

Lambert, L. (1995). Toward a theory of constructivist leadership: Constructing school change: Leading the conversations. In L. Lambert, D. Walker, D. P. Zimmerman, J. E. Cooper, M. D. Lambert, M. E. Gardner, et al. (Eds.), *The constructivist leader* (pp. 28–103). New York: Teachers College Press.

Schon, D. A. (1987). *Educating the reflective practioner.* San Francisco: Jossey-Bass.

Senge, P. M. (1990). *The fifth discipline.* New York: Currency Doubleday.

Zimmerman, D. (1995). The linguistics of leadership. In L. Lambert, D. Walker, D. P. Zimmerman, J. E. Cooper, M. D. Lambert, M. E. Gardner, et al. (Eds.), *The constructivist leader* (pp. 104–120). New York: Teachers College Press.

About the Contributors

Chris Yeager, M.Ed. is a former high school English teacher and school administrator who combines her 20 years of classroom experiences with current research in effective instruction and brain research to impact student achievement. She is the lead consultant for Innovative Learning Group and conducts Thinking Maps training nationally.

Bonnie D. Singer, Ph.D. is president of Innovative Learning Partners, which provides language and learning intervention to school-age children in the Boston area and school consultation and teacher training nation-wide. She is also codeveloper of the EmPOWER strategy for teaching expository writing. Her research interests lie in the relationship between cognition, language, and learning.

Alan Cooper, B.A., B.Ed. Dip Tchng. ANZIM is a New Zealand indepen-dent consultant specializing in thinking skills and how learning occurs. As Headmaster of St. George's School for 17 years, he was known for taking responsible risks in educational innovation, including the first implemen-tations of Thinking Maps and the Dunn and Dunn Learning Styles models in New Zealand.

Yvette Jackson, Ed.D. is the Executive Director of the National Urban Alliance for Effective Education. In this capacity, she works with school district administrators and teachers across the country to customize and deliver systemic approaches to accelerate literacy and achievement for urban students. She oversees the design of tailored courses of study in cognitive strategies and instructional practices that focus on literacy in the context of culture, language, and cognition.

Thomasina DePinto Piercy, Ph.D. is a principal with 18 years of K–5 teaching experience. As a collaborative writer about data-driven, whole-school student performance change, she provides support for colleagues looking for similar significant and lasting results as have occurred at Mt. Airy Elementary.

Jane Buckner, Ed.S. is a national educational consultant and author of works focused on developing writing proficiency in students from kindergarten through high school. She is presently a lead consultant with Innovative

Learning Group working with whole-school implementation of *Write . . . From the Beginning®* and *Write . . . for the Future®*.

Janie B. MacIntyre, M.Ed. is a middle school teacher, researcher, and educational consultant who was named as a *USA Today* Teacher Team member and a Christa McAuliffe Scholar. As a trainer with Innovative Learning Group, she has facilitated Thinking Maps training with over 3000 teachers in multiple states.

Daniel Cherry, M.Ed. currently directs the New Hampshire School Administrators Leading with Technology (NHSALT) as part of a Gates grant for the NH State Department of Education. He is a former elementary educator and technology coordinator.

Stefanie R. Holzman, Ed.D. is currently the principal of a large, urban, multiethnic, multilingual elementary school in Long Beach, California. She has also been an internal literacy consultant for K–8 schools, a regular, special education, and Title I teacher, and a lecturer at California State University, Long Beach.

Edward V. Chevallier, M.Ed. has enjoyed serving as a principal, teacher, and education consultant and Thinking Maps trainer. His work in public education began at the elementary school level as a teacher and principal. Since 1996, he has served as Principal at Blalack Middle School in Carrollton, Texas.

Gill Hubble, M.A., LTCL Dip Tchng is an international consultant on teaching thinking strategies, the design of whole-school thinking and learning programs, and organizational change. Associate Principal of St. Cuthbert's College for 16 years, she is now researcher and consultant to the Advanced Learning Center and Centre for Excellence at the college's Collegiate Centre.

Marjann Kalehoff Ball, Ed.D. is a professor of English and Development of Critical Thinking and Study Skills at Jones County Junior College in Mississippi, and serves as a consultant for Innovative Learning Group. Believing that learning is a continuing process that can be fostered across all levels of education, she is convinced that Thinking Maps are an indispensable tool of learning for age or ability differentiations.

Ho Po Chun, M.Ed. is a former teacher and elementary principal in the Singapore schools. Presently she leads the implementation of Thinking Maps for the Innovative Learning Circle in Singapore and is dedicated to developing the thinking abilities of students across Singapore.

Kathy Ernst, M.S. has spent 30 years teaching children and teachers in elementary and middle schools and has served on the faculty of the Leadership in Mathematics Education Program at Bank Street College of Education. She has facilitated the implementation of standards-based mathematics curricula in schools, working with teachers to support children's construction of mathematical ideas.

Index

CORWIN PRESS

The Corwin Press logo—a raven striding across an open book—represents the union of courage and learning. Corwin Press is committed to improving education for all learners by publishing books and other professional development resources for those serving the field of K–12 education. By providing practical, hands-on materials, Corwin Press continues to carry out the promise of its motto: **"Helping Educators Do Their Work Better."**